MW01253017

Buddhism, the Internet, and Digital Media

Buddhism, the Internet and Digital Media: The Pixel in the Lotus explores Buddhist practice and teachings in an increasingly networked and digital era. Contributors consider the ways Buddhism plays a role and is present in digital media through a variety of methods including concrete case studies, ethnographic research, and content analysis, as well as interviews with practitioners and cyber-communities. In addition to considering Buddhism in the context of technologies such as virtual worlds, social media, and mobile devices, authors ask how the Internet affects identity, authority and community, and what effect this might have on the development, proliferation, and perception of Buddhism in an online environment. Together, these essays make the case that studying contemporary online Buddhist practice can provide valuable insights into the shifting role religion plays in our constantly changing, mediated, hurried, and uncertain culture.

Gregory Price Grieve is Associate Professor in Religious Studies at the University of North Carolina, Greensboro, Director of MERGE: a Network for Collaborative Interdisciplinary Scholarship in UNCG's College of Arts and Sciences, and co-chair of the American Academy of Religion's section on Religion and Popular Culture. A leader in the field of digital religion, and a pioneer in the emerging field of religion in digital games, he is the author of *Retheorizing Religion in Nepal* (2007) and co-editor of *Playing with Religion in Digital Games* (2014).

Daniel Veidlinger is Associate Professor in Comparative Religion and Humanities at California State University, Chico and is the author of *Spreading the Dhamma: Writing, Orality and Textual Transmission in Buddhist Northern Thailand* (2006). He is on the editorial board of Oxford Bibliographies Online: Buddhism and his chapter "When Friend Becomes a Verb" was an early study of religion and social media.

Routledge Studies in Religion and Digital Culture

Edited by Heidi Campbell, Mia Lövheim, and Greg Grieve

1 **Buddhism, the Internet, and Digital Media**
The Pixel in the Lotus
Edited by Gregory Price Grieve and Daniel Veidlinger

Buddhism, the Internet, and Digital Media

The Pixel in the Lotus

**Edited by Gregory Price Grieve
and Daniel Veidlinger**

Routledge
Taylor & Francis Group

NEW YORK AND LONDON

GUELPH HUMBER LIBRARY
205 Humber College Blvd
Toronto, ON   M9W 5L7

First published 2015
by Routledge
711 Third Avenue, New York, NY 10017

and by Routledge
2 Park Square, Milton Park, Abingdon, Oxon OX14 4RN

Routledge is an imprint of the Taylor & Francis Group, an informa business

© 2015 Taylor & Francis

The right of the editors to be identified as the author of the editorial material,
and of the authors for their individual chapters, has been asserted in
accordance with sections 77 and 78 of the Copyright, Designs and Patents
Act 1988.

All rights reserved. No part of this book may be reprinted or reproduced or
utilised in any form or by any electronic, mechanical, or other means, now
known or hereafter invented, including photocopying and recording, or in any
information storage or retrieval system, without permission in writing from
the publishers.

Trademark Notice: Product or corporate names may be trademarks or
registered trademarks, and are used only for identification and explanation
without intent to infringe.

Library of Congress Cataloging-in-Publication Data

Buddhism, the internet, and digital media : the pixel in the lotus / edited by
  Gregory Price Grieve and Daniel Veidlinger.
    pages cm. — (Routledge studies in religion and digital culture ; 1)
  Based on presentations at a symposium about Buddhism and digital media
at California State University, Chico in November 2011.
  Includes bibliographical references and index.
  1. Buddhism—Social aspects—Congresses.   2. Internet—
Religious aspects—Buddhism—Congresses.   3. Digital media—
Congresses.   I. Grieve, Gregory P. (Gregory Price), 1964– editor of
compilation.   II. Veidlinger, Daniel M., editor of compilation.
  BQ4570.S6B82 2014
  294.30285—dc23
  2014015795

ISBN: 978-0-415-72166-0 (hbk)
ISBN: 978-1-315-86298-9 (ebk)

Typeset in Sabon
by Apex CoVantage, LLC

Printed and bound in the United States of America by Publishers Graphics,
LLC on sustainably sourced paper.

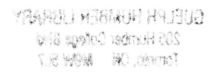

Contents

PART III
Buddhism, Media, and Society

PART IV
Case Studies

Tables and Figures

FIGURES

TABLES

1 Introduction

Daniel Veidlinger

When smartphone apps remind people when to meditate (Wagner and Acca-rdo, Chapter 8, this volume) and Buddhist monks bless temples that are built out of pixels in online virtual reality systems (Falcone, Chapter 10, this volume), there can be little doubt that the Internet, mobile phones, video games, and other incarnations of digital technology are changing the face of religion in the world today (Cowan and Dawson 2004, 1). While shaped by culture, digital media also afford new ways of being human by reconfigur-ing relationships, multiplying actors, and increasing the velocity, frequency, and volatility of our daily transactions (Hassan and Thomas 2006, 42). If we are to understand Buddhism in the twenty-first century, then the many features of these changes must be incorporated into the academic study of religion. Consider, for instance, in 2001, just a few years into the public use of the Internet, the Pew Foundation's (2001) "CyberFaith: How Americans Pursue Religion Online" demonstrated that already more than 25 percent of Americans were searching for information about religion online, and that number has been rapidly increasing. It is clear that all of the world's reli-gions, both great and small, are becoming deeply affected by the growing electronic network that spans the globe.

These considerations prompted the organization of a symposium about Buddhism and digital media at California State University, Chico, in November 2011, out of which the chapters in this volume emerged. We asked a simple, but what proved to be rewarding, question: "What is digital Buddhism?" To answer this query, this volume examines many facets of the relationship between Buddhism and digital media through a variety of methods, including concrete case studies, ethnographic research, cognitive psychology, historical investigation, and content analysis—in an attempt to map out the contours of this new and exciting field.

As is well known, religion and media historically have had a close rela-tionship. The earliest uses of media starting from the oral transmission of myths to the printing of the first Bibles were largely in service of religion, and now the modern study of both religion and media is intersecting as scholars highlight the embodied and participatory nature of each. As the study of religion has shifted from a focus on belief systems to "embodied practices that cultivate relations among people, places, and non-human forces," so the study of media has turned from a focus on message transmission to "embodied forms of participation in extended communities" (Morgan 2013, 347). What this means, as Walter Ong argues (1967), is that different media afford different religiosities. Ong suggests that religion began in an era of orality, was transmitted into visual form through the writing of manuscripts as well as the printing of books, and is now taking shape in the world in a new way via electronic media (Grieve 2012). A host of other thinkers have realized since Ong that along with other physical embodiments of religion such as dress, images, and sacred spaces, media "structure experiences of the transcendental," as anthropologist Birgit Meyer has said (2006, 20), and therefore both religion and media should be studied in concert.

Over the past few years, a number of scholars have begun to study religion and new media (Brasher 2001; Campbell 2010; Cowan and Dawson 2004; Hojsgaard and Warburg 2005; Karaflogka 2006) and have questioned how these affect notions of community, authority, identity, and practice, but how does Buddhism fare in this conversation about digital religion? Not terribly well, for as Kyong Cho (2011) notes in his comprehensive survey of digital religious scholarship, these studies tend to approach the topic from a decidedly Western perspective. In fact, those pioneering the study of digital religion have often overlooked the large digital footprint of Asian religions, even though many forms of Asian spirituality, including Buddhism, yoga, and meditation have had an even bigger impact in the digital environment than in offline society. For example, while the Pew Foundation's "U.S. Religious Landscape Survey" (Pew Foundation 2007) indicates that American Buddhists account for only 0.7 percent of the nation's population, research shows that Buddhist related activities constitute around 5.3 percent of online religious practice in the virtual world of Second Life (Grieve 2010), and other online environments register similarly high rates of Buddhist engagement, as Ostrowski delineates in Chapter 11. We therefore offer these chapters in order to begin to fill in this lacuna and hope that this volume will stimulate further research in the field of Buddhism and digital media.

We focus here on Buddhism and digital media not only because we feel that it has been understudied, but also because Buddhism in particular possesses historical, philosophical, and practical attributes that are salient to the topic at hand. In fact, digital media and Buddhism have shared an intimate but little-known link from the very beginning. Consider, the translation of information into a series of ones and zeros that is the hallmark of digital technology is only possible due to the invention of the idea of zero by Indian mathematicians in the middle of the first millennium who were probably inspired by the Buddhist idea of emptiness. The very word *zero* derives from the Sanskrit Buddhist term *shunya*, meaning "nothing."

As the world's oldest extant missionary religion, and one without a central authority, Buddhism has adapted throughout its history more completely than any other religion to the contours of the societies in which it has found itself, and as such can be used effectively as a prism through which to analyze the features of its host environment, be it China, Thailand, Tibet, America, or the Internet.[1] In fact, it has changed so completely in different environments that whether its various manifestations can even be considered the same religion has been debated at length (Hubbard and Swanson 1997). Besides this history that has primed Buddhism for a rich life in the new digital frontier, Buddhist philosophy has dealt more extensively than any other religion with the question of whether or not the world of experience is real (Newland 2009), and as such is a potent source for thinking about the nature of virtual reality, as Falcone does in Chapter 10. The centrality in Buddhism of desire and its dangers also provides a unique vantage point into the manifold desires generated by current ways of living in our mediated, hurried, and uncertain culture, where the decoupling of production from the physical world and the empowering of imagination to call forth virtual realities has replaced an earlier needs-based society with one powered by desire and consumption.

We also find that the way Buddhism questions the idea of a fixed Self dovetails well with the shifting identities that are a hallmark of life in the World Wide Web, as Veidlinger discusses in his chapter. Because of the importance of meditation to the practice of Buddhism, questions of the nature, extent, and meaning of embodiment in the digital world come to the fore in relation to this religion as well. Buddhism has also, more than other religions, long recognized the importance of *upaya*, or skillful means for disseminating the teachings, which allow for unorthodox practices in the name of strengthening the message of the Buddha, as Wagner and Accardo point out herein. The studies in this volume therefore ask how far the *upaya*-like use of Buddhism can slide before it becomes merely a gimmick. Are many of the incarnations of Buddhist-related themes in digital media actually skillful means for disseminating real Buddhism, or just dharma dilution and commercialization? Given this background, it is perhaps not surprising that, as Prebish points out in Chapter 5, the first scholarly online journal in the field of religious studies was focused on Buddhism. These and many other points of contact between Buddhism and digital media will be discussed in the following chapters.

A BRIEF HISTORY OF BUDDHISM AND MEDIA

There has been a great deal of discussion about how media affect the messages they carry, as summarized most famously in Marshall McLuhan's maxim "the Medium is the Message" (McLuhan 1964). The strong version of this idea is that different communications media transform the very experience we have of space and time in different ways, and can eclipse the actual content of the message being transmitted. With this theory, the psychological effects of television, radio, the Internet, or any other medium are so great that they shape thought in specific ways regardless of the content they are conveying. The architecture of media can be thought of in a way similar to physical architecture, where the design of a building can radically shape the way the people living in it behave, allowing the flow of movement in some directions but not in others. There are forces at work in different media, based on the various ways they impinge the senses, that can override the discursive meaning of the content that they carry. The weak version of this theory, which is more commonly held, is that the medium is one crucial element among many that must be taken into consideration when analyzing the effects of an act of communication, along with the content.

Oral media, according to McLuhan, tend to create a tribal society, with nonlinear thinking, and a more emotional way of living, whereas print tends to detribalize society, because ideas can travel far and wide beyond the boundaries of a small group and unite disparate parties in common ways of thinking through joint readership. As writing and printing developed, people became exposed to more different viewpoints from different quarters, and what was considered strange and foreign gradually became more acceptable and more commonplace. This expands the vision of people in society and allows for social changes to take place with less resistance. It leads also to more linear thought and thus gives rise to the rule of reason over emotion, according to some media theorists (Goody 1977). Electronic mass media such as radio and television, because of their far-reaching, one-way broadcasts, can be used to consolidate power and authority in the hands of those who control the media, who now have the unprecedented ability to shape the thoughts of millions on a daily basis. As mass media develop, there is a clash between the expansive intellectual vistas fostered by easy access to a great many different ideas, and the tendency for those who control the media to use this one-way channel to consolidate their power by controlling what information is allowed to get to the people. Digital media, according to this scheme, have the ability to create virtual tribes of people who have not actually met, and unlike print or radio, these media engage many senses at once and allow for a much greater questioning of authority through two-way channels. The two-way information flow enabled by the Internet can foster greater criticism and lead to challenges from below to those on top who had in the past controlled access to the mass media (Lull 2000, 38). There are also more quotidian examples of how media might affect the development of religion and other cultural features. Consider the life of a young person in a small town in Kansas. Before the Internet, would this person have had easy access to Buddhist teachings? Most likely not. In that sense, the specific communications technology of the Internet affords the possibility that this person would come into contact with Buddhist teachings online, either through podcasts, videos, text, or other media. Here, then, the medium affects whether the message is received at all, regardless of whether it also affects the message itself.

In order to understand how media has influenced the development of Buddhism, its texts and its practices, we should start at the beginning and understand the communicative environment in which it emerged. The peripatetic *shramana*, or wandering philosopher, known as the Buddha knew that communicating his message to as many people as possible would be a key element in the success of his *Dharma*, or teachings. From the beginning, he stressed that monks should go forth and spread the teachings in their own language (*Vinaya* II, 139), and from that time, communication has played a crucial role in Buddhism. Buddhism, as the oldest extant proselytizing religion, has always had a penchant for utilizing the latest developments in communications technology to spread its message. The Buddha lived probably during the fifth century BCE in northeast India before writing was used in that region (von Hinuber 1989), and therefore all of his sermons were retained and passed on through an oral tradition that partook of the astonishingly sophisticated tradition of Vedic memorization (Staal 1986), and added some of its own techniques (Allon 1997). The *Suttas* all begin with the phrase "*evam me sutam*" which in Pali means, "Thus have I heard," and stands as a vestige of their oral origin. Monks would spend many hours of each day memorizing texts, and much of their training and the very organization of the early *sangha* was structured to foster the memorization and transmission of the teachings (Veidlinger 2006a). The texts themselves were usually designed for memorization, and a number of their formal features developed to facilitate memorization (Collins 1992). For example, there is a great deal of repetition and use of stock phrases that could be put together like pieces of a puzzle by the well-trained reciter. There are also many verse passages that are often found embedded within prose passages, often conveying similar content. This use of meter as well as repetition assisted in the memorization and preservation of the texts as they were transmitted through time, and numbered lists such as the Three Jewels, the Four Noble Truths, the Seven Factors of Enlightenment, and the Eightfold Path are ubiquitous. Here, we already see evidence of one of the key elements of media theory, namely that the medium used to transmit a message will often have profound effects on the shape and form of its content. Many early Buddhist texts evolved to be easily memorized as much as to embody the Buddha's teachings.

Once writing came to India in the middle of the third century BCE, it was the great Buddhist king Ashoka who was the first to use it in any appreciable way. He was quick to see the benefits of this new technology and placed inscriptions on rocks and pillars at key points throughout his kingdom that communicated his decrees to the people and helped to promote the Dharma as well. Most of the evidence of early writing in India in the centuries after Ashoka is likewise Buddhist in nature, such as donative inscriptions on *stupas* and other sites of Buddhist import (Salomon 1995). During all this time, there is little evidence that Hindus were using writing for any religious texts—quite the contrary, the great epics that were taking shape in the first few centuries BCE such as the *Mahabharata* show clear signs of oral composition and transmission, both in their internal structure, their use of oral formulas, meter, and the divergent textual traditions that emerged. The Theravada Buddhist tradition holds, on the other hand, that the Pali canon was written down at the Fourth Council held by learned monks in Sri Lanka during the first century BCE (*Mahavamsa* 33.100). If true, this would certainly be the earliest organized project to transmit religious texts in writing in the ancient Indic world. We know further that Mahayana Buddhism employed writing during its earliest stages of development, and indeed many of the oldest texts such as the Lotus Sutra and Perfection of Wisdom Sutras explicitly enjoin the faithful to write out copies of the texts and to honor them as the materialization of the word of the Buddha. The use of the communication technology of writing, then, was far more associated with Buddhism than with any other Indian religion (Veidlinger 2006b).

Moving a few centuries later in history, we find that one of the most important developments in human communication was a product of the Buddhist milieu in medieval China: printing evolved in Buddhist monasteries during the heyday of the religion in the Tang dynasty (618–907 CE) (You 2010, 56–62). It is likely that the admonition to generate merit by copying the Mahayana texts inspired Buddhists during this period to carve the pages of sacred texts such as the Diamond Sutra and the Lotus Sutra onto wooden blocks and print many copies in what were the first printed books anywhere in the world. Buddhism thus played a crucial role in the development of printing technology specifically, and of some of the first mass-produced items more generally, which set the stage for the development of the modern digital technologies that permeate life today.

The above makes clear that Buddhism has long had an affinity for the latest technologies and has used every means at its disposal to transmit the Dharma far and wide. In that sense, the marriage of Buddhism and digital media is nothing new. Buddhist monks and laypeople were well represented among those travelling the Silk Road through Central Asia into China. We can, in fact, think of this trade route as the Internet of its day—an artery along which goods and, perhaps even more importantly, ideas were communicated from people of remarkably different ethnic, linguistic, and cultural backgrounds. The library at Dun Huang along the eastern edge of the Taklamakan Desert boasts a truly astonishing variety of Buddhist texts in such languages as Sogdian, Parthian, Tokharian, Uighur, Chinese and Sanskrit, attesting to the thriving intellectual and cultural life that was taking place along the trade routes that converged at this oasis (Hansen 2012). The idea of transmitting messages to people who are geographically and culturally distant is, therefore, deeply entwined with Buddhist history, although of course the speed with which this process occurs has greatly increased on the Internet of today. We should also note that when radio was introduced in Asia, it was eagerly taken up by Buddhist preachers to communicate sermons and canonical readings to the masses. Tape cassettes were also used for this purpose and helped to allow people in remote villages to gain access to the teachings of the leading preachers and scholars of the day (Engel and Engel 2010, 88).

As we move into the contemporary period, it is perhaps not surprising that many of the pioneers of computing were very interested in Buddhism, such as the well-known cases of Steve Jobs, who for a significant period considered himself a Zen Buddhist and Mitch Kapor, who called the first commercially successful spreadsheet program "Lotus." From the very beginning, Buddhism and Buddhist ideas loomed large in the development of modern computer science. MIT mathematician Norbert Wiener, who pioneered the field of cybernetics in the 1940s, described it as "the study of messages as a means of controlling machinery and society" (quoted in Turner 2006, 22) and emphasized that it was a systems approach to organization rendering the traditional, hierarchical command *chain* into a more effective command *cycle* in which feedback was incorporated into the calculus of the system. Wiener himself quickly began, through his studies of cybernetics, to take on a remarkably Buddhist understanding of human beings, as Grieve explores in this volume, even if he did not recognize it as such.

Douglas Engelbart, another key player in the development of digital technology, was the head of the Augmentation Research Center at the Stanford Research Institute, which was working on ways to use technology to increase human efficiency and performance. His team developed the mouse and hyperlinking technology, and he also became very interested in Erhard Seminars Training (est) in the 1970s, encouraging his entire team to attend est seminars (Vallee 2003, 65). While not formally identified with Buddhism, est did owe a good deal to Buddhism. In particular, the idea at the very core of the training, namely that we must be able to distinguish the mental baggage that we bring to an event from the raw elements of the event itself which we cannot control, is a key insight in Buddhism as well. Werner Erhard, the founder of est, has said, "Of all the disciplines that I studied, practiced, learned, Zen was the essential one" (Bartley 1978, 121).

The founding editor of seminal cyberculture publication *Wired*, Kevin Kelly, was also fascinated by Buddhism, and along with many of the contributors to Wired was a key player in the Buddhist and Beatnik-inspired counterculture of the 1970s (Turner 2006). Kelly himself explicitly connects a lot of his ideas about complex adaptive systems to Buddhism:

> Zen Masters once instructed novice disciples to approach Zen meditation with an unprejudiced "beginner's mind." The master coached students, "Undo all preconceptions." The proper awareness required to appreciate the swarm nature of complicated things might be called hive mind. The swarm master coaches, "Loosen all attachments to the sure and certain." . . . The Atom whirls alone, the epitome of singleness. It is the metaphor for individuality: atomic . . . Another Zen thought: The Atom is the past. The symbol of science for the next century is the

dynamical Net . . . The Net is an emblem of multiples. Out of it comes swarm being—distributed being—spreading the self over the entire web so that no part can say, "I am the I."

(Kelly 1994, 25–26)

Once computers were developed, many more formal Buddhists, like the enterprising faithful of old, were quick to take advantage of these devices to spread the Dharma. In the late 1990s, the Vipassana Research Institute (VRI), founded by wealthy Indo-Burmese businessman S. N. Goenka, produced a CD-Rom containing the entire Pali canon based on the Burmese 1956 edition produced at the sixth council to honor 2,500 years since the Buddha's Nirvana (www.tipitaka.org), and there have been numerous other projects to put the Dharma into a digital form. The VRI edition allows the text to be read in a variety of scripts, including Latin, Devanagari, Sinhalese, Burmese, Thai, and even Mongolian. A Thai edition of the Pali canon from 1928 has been digitized and put on a CD-ROM by Mahidol University, and the website www.AccessToInsight.org has put a great many English versions of the texts online. Currently, there are many searchable databases, including the Chinese canon (http://21dzk.l.u-tokyo.ac.jp/SAT/index_en.html) as well as the Tibetan canon (http://www.tbrc.org). This has radically changed the shape of Buddhism and has greatly affected the authority of the monks who previously were the sole guardians of the sacred texts. Until these relatively recent developments, most common people in Buddhist countries had access to the teachings of the religion only through the sermons given by physical monks. Now, the entire canon in a variety of languages is at the fingertips of anyone with Internet access.

Not only have the texts of Buddhism become available in digital format, but in keeping with the emphasis in Buddhism on using all means available to transmit knowledge about the religion, Buddhists and scholars of Buddhism were also among the first people to establish Internet-based discussion forums, the oldest of which is Buddha-L. Buddha-L came into being in 1991, at which point there were few discussion forums to use as a model. The Buddhist Studies WWW Virtual Library was another early resource from 1992 containing such things as bibliographies, biographies, directories, Buddhist electronic-texts, poetry, and sermons. The *Journal of Buddhist Ethics* founded in 1994 was the first peer-reviewed online journal in Religious Studies, as Charles Prebish relates in Chapter 5 of this volume, and has been a model for many other online journals established since that time.

We are now seeing the development of communities of Buddhist practitioners online, known as cybersanghas, which as Prebish (2004) has pointed out include several types: sites that provide information about events connected to real-world communities, online extensions of existing Buddhist sanghas that allow for the practice itself to occur online—virtual temples—and virtual sanghas that exist online only, with no corresponding physical meeting place.

There are also many groups connected to Buddhism on social networks such as Facebook and in virtual worlds such as Second Life. YouTube videos, podcasts and especially, as Beverley Foulks McGuire discusses here in Chapter 12, blogs about topics related to Buddhism proliferate, and there are e-cards, smartphone apps providing daily doses of Buddhist wisdom, virtual tours of Buddhist sites and temples in Asia, and everything else under the sun, including an online edition of the *Shambhala Sun*. The Internet is also used to mobilize political opinion about Tibet and create a sense of community in face of Chinese oppression, as both Laura Osburn (Chapter 3) and Christopher Helland (Chapter 9) examine in this volume. In the future, there is little doubt that Buddhism's digital presence will expand even more as these technologies pervade every corner of our lives, which will necessitate maps of the Buddhist cyberspace such as that provided by Louise Connelly here in Chapter 4.

WHAT IS BUDDHISM?

Any volume of collected works on Buddhism must deal with the question of what exactly the object of study is. Countering some of the arguments given in Jamie Hubbard and Paul Swanson's *Pruning the Bodhi Tree: The Storm Over Critical Buddhism* (1997), we argue that there is no one authentic form of Buddhism. In fact, it has become fashionable to speak of *Buddhisms* rather than *Buddhism* because the manifold varieties of this religion differ so greatly from one another that it can be misleading to conceive of it as a unitary religion. Helen Tworkov (1991), an editor with the Buddhist publication *Tricycle Magazine*, puts it very well when she observes:

> There is no one way to be a Buddhist. Like other world religions, Buddhism has proved capable of providing something for everyone. The many sects that now exist in the United States reflect the compelling and flexible dimensions inherent in any body of ideas that has been tested by time and has crossed continents. There are a growing number of voices here concerned with the shape of American Buddhism, concerned with arbitrating which interpretations seem appropriate for this society and which may be better left behind in Asia. But whose America? Whose Buddhism?

Yet, while there may not be one essentialized Buddhism, it is important to trace out what adherents are talking about and practicing online. We frequently see people online talking about "Buddhism" without making any distinctions between the various different schools and their divergent doctrines. Even as basic a division as Mahayana and Theravada is not recognized in many of the blogs and forums and mobile applications that are discussed in this volume, which allows us to read into them any number of possible Buddhist ideas.

Broadly speaking, Buddhism in Asia can be divided into two main schools: Theravada and Mahayana. The Theravada school claims to reflect the earliest teachings of the historical Buddha, and its canonical texts are preserved in an Indic language related to Sanskrit called Pali, that was similar to the language that the Buddha would have spoken. These texts highlight a number of ideas as the key teachings of the Buddha, and these have been endorsed by the tradition as containing the core doctrines of Buddhism. The Four Noble Truths were supposedly laid out in the *Dhammacakkappavattana Sutta*, which is viewed as the first sermon of the Buddha shortly after he became enlightened. Here, the First Noble Truth states that all things are characterized by *dukkha*, most commonly translated as "suffering" but also having connotations of unsatisfactoriness. An important part of the ontology of suffering in the Buddhist conception is the idea of impermanence. All things are impermanent, and in a constant state of flux. Whatever comes into being will eventually cease to be, whether it is a person, a mountain, an idea, or even a god. As a corollary, the idea of *anatman* holds that there is no permanent, eternal substrate that forms the core of the human being, such as a soul, but rather we are a conglomeration of five separate and ever-changing aggregate parts that include the physical body, sensations, perceptions, mental formations, and consciousness. The Second Noble Truth says that suffering arises due to a cause, namely desire. It is our desire to possess things that leads to suffering because since all things are impermanent, including the objects of our desire and we ourselves, these desires, even if they are temporarily satisfied, will always remain ultimately unfulfilled. This leads to suffering. The Third Noble Truth explains how to achieve the cessation of this suffering, which is effected through ridding ourselves of desires. If we can fully conquer our desires, then we can escape from that cycle of continual desire and dissatisfaction. The Fourth Noble Truth outlines an Eightfold Path to achieve this blissful state, known as Nirvana, that includes disciplined living, moral behavior, and meditation.

The Buddha outlined a universal law of causality that he termed *pratitya samutpada,* which is often translated as *conditioned origination*. It states that things come into being due to certain conditions, and when those conditions cease, the thing itself ceases to be. The Buddha said that this was at the core of his teachings, and that by understanding this, one could understand the key to the Dharma. This law holds in the moral realm as well, leading to an ethical system based on the idea of *karma*, which says that all morally charged actions have a related effect: good deeds will lead to good results in this life or in a future life, and bad deeds will lead to bad results. As long as one has karma, one will be reborn, and when desire is completely rooted out, the force that binds karma to oneself is destroyed and one can achieve full Nirvana, after which one is reborn no more.[2]

In Mahayana Buddhism, which arose about 500 years later, the idea of *pratitya samutpada* was understood to describe a world that was characterized by emptiness, known as *shunyata*. The mutual conditioning of all things, and the lack of any self-existent substrate, meant that all things are interconnected in a web of causes and conditions, with no one thing truly existing independently. Some took that to mean that nothingness is the fundamental ontological reality and that the world of our senses is a kind of illusion, without substantial reality. The notion of Two Truths was developed to account for the apparent opposition between the conditional reality of the world as we perceive it, replete with real substances that are different from each other, and the ultimate reality of undifferentiated emptiness. Other Mahayana schools, such as Yogacara, focused more on the role of the mind in the creation of the world of experience and have been taken to be a form of idealism by some philosophers. Another development in the Mahayana tradition is the idea of the Bodhisattva as a being who, out of great compassion, vows to help all beings achieve Nirvana, rather than the earlier Arhat, who strives to reach the ultimate state for his or her own benefit. Because the Bodhisattva was viewed as being able to transfer good karma to the devotee, Mahayana Buddhism also became more devotional in tone than was Theravada, although devotion has also been a feature of Theravada from the earliest times for which we have records.

It is easy to see that these different forms of Buddhism can resonate in various ways with different features of digital media. For example, Mahayana insight on virtual reality could be based on its ideas of emptiness that suggest that the world we generally think of as real is in some sense not truly real, or the Mahayana emphasis on compassion could come into play when examining how seeing videos on YouTube of the suffering of others across the globe might elicit compassionate feelings in viewers. Theravada emphasis on *anatman* could have an affinity for the fluid nature of personal identity that is highlighted by the different personas that people use in different Web-based communities, or Theravada analysis of the nature of desire could shed light on the role played by desire in creating and using digital media.

Charles Prebish has developed the notion of two Buddhisms to describe the significant fissures between those traditional Buddhists in America who are of Asian descent, often known as "ethnic" or "heritage" Buddhists, and those who have converted at some point in the recent past, usually but not exclusively of European heritage (Prebish 1993, 187). Besides the Theravada/Mahayana divide, the cultural and practical divisions between Asians with a long Buddhist heritage and Westerners who have converted more recently must also be taken into consideration when analyzing the effects of digital technology on Buddhism, and McGuire touches on this dilemma as it comes out in some Buddhist blogs in Chapter 12. These groups generally worship in different places; for example, one is hard pressed to find an Asian from a traditional Japanese background attending a Dharma Talk at the

San Francisco Zen Center, and likewise there are precious few non-Japanese converts who attend the Soto Zen temple in Japantown in San Francisco. Scholars such as Paul Numrich have written about two congregations that operate in parallel worlds with little mutual interaction, with the Asians engaged in merit-making and the converts practicing meditation and studying Buddhist philosophy (Numrich 1996). It is to be expected, therefore, that these different groups would have a different relationship to technology. If an Asian youth has no great interest in Buddhism but is forced to attend a service with his parents, he might find very different uses for his iPhone—for example, furtively playing a game to prevent boredom during a long sermon—than would a convert to Buddhism who is eager to learn as much about the religion as she can, who might perhaps use a Buddhist app on her iPhone while pretending to work when the boss approaches her cubicle. The more conservative heritage Buddhist communities will in general be somewhat less likely to adopt the new technologies into their Dharma practice, as these may be viewed as possible challenges to established forms of authority or as excessive encroachment of Americanism into their dearly held traditions. On the other hand, since converts are already looking to change something about their lives, they may be more receptive in general to new technologies, whereas heritage Buddhists are more likely to be trying to preserve age-old traditions that are already under threat by the modern Western world. This is certainly not always the case, though, for heritage Buddhists such as Tibetans, who see other factors as more threatening to their way of life than Westernization, might embrace digital technology even more eagerly than converts in order to get the message that they are being oppressed out to as many people around the globe as possible, as Helland and Osburn note in their chapters.

Having said all of this, then, we ask that the reader take the use of the term "Buddhism" in this volume as representing some combination of the above ideas, as all of them are legitimate forms of Buddhism, even though they are all quite different from each other. There is no one authentic form of Buddhism, and therefore it should be kept in mind that the points made in the different chapters herein may be more or less appropriate to different versions of what comes under the rubric of Buddhism, and the term is not intended to account for all possible versions of the religion in any one chapter.

WHAT ARE DIGITAL MEDIA?

Having looked at the meaning of the term *Buddhism* in the title of this volume, it is now appropriate to clarify the nature of *digital media*. The key aspect of digital media is that here information is "digitized," meaning that it is reduced to a series of ones and zeros that can be stored and decoded by machines to render the content visible once again. Smart phones, Mp3 players, dashboard GPS devices, DVDs, personal computers, and video games are all examples of digital media, and, of course, the Internet itself operates based on digital signals flowing at light speed through the vast network of satellites and cables that spans the Earth. These media harness the power of electricity to store, send, and display messages in different ways, and they are an extension of modern developments in both communication and mass production that started in the nineteenth century. Because digital media reduce all images and sounds to numerical codes, this means that they can be described in mathematical terms and can be manipulated algorithmically, regardless of whether they consist of sound, pictures, or text. Another feature of digital media is that the representation of information in terms of binary numerical code means that the content has become completely independent of the medium. Digital information can be stored in virtually any form, as long it can record at least two different pieces of information, binary code, representing a 0 and a 1. A key feature of digital media is that they enable random access to data just as human memory does, which is quite different from older analog forms of electric communication, such as phonograph records or cassette tapes, which have to be played through in a linear manner in order to find the information for which one is searching. Digital media also speak to each other through the universal language of binary codes, and can be connected into complex networks that communicate with each other and can expand and integrate new nodes, giving them the ability to completely transform existing social institutions, communities and practices. In fact, the breathtaking range of affordances of digitization has promoted an ideology of this new technology that itself borders on the religious. Digital media are often seen as "more than a new way of communicating, but as a new vision for society: its practices are often posed as revolutionary, and tied to the triumph of human creativity and freedom over dogma and blind tradition" (Grieve 2012, 109). It is therefore inevitable that any religion that becomes wrapped in these technologies will soak up some of this millennial outlook.

Grieve (2012) identifies three main ways that digital religion differs from analog religion which should be considered here: interactivity, hypertextuality, and dispersal. He defines interactivity as "the technical ability of users to intervene, respond and see the effects of their intervention in real time" (108). For instance, when one goes to a site online where one can click on a prayer wheel and cause it to turn, and then read a message saying, "You have just received good karma"—that is interactivity. Hypertextuality is the use of links that connect one set of content with another. These links can connect text to associated pictures, videos, audio content, or other webpages and create the sense of immersion into an endless sea of connected information. For example, hypertext technology allows one who is reading about the chanting styles of Tibetan monks to click on a link that will take one to a video of monks chanting. Lastly, "dispersal" refers to the decentralization of digital media, and highlights the fact that they are woven into a whole host of everyday items, from one's phone to one's car. As Grieve points out, "these three traits differ from analog media, and hence analog religion, which is typically static in its production and engagement as well as linear in its format, which demands sequential engagement. Thus, digital religion offers higher degrees of flexibility of engagement" (2012, 108).

Finally, Grieve suggests, "digital religion operates as a workaround, or an innovative temporary solution, to our experience of religiosity in contemporary life. Digital religion emerges within what Zygmut Bauman (2005) calls liquid modernity, a period of global capitalism where life is constantly changing, highly mediated, hurried, and uncertain. As a workaround, Digital Religion is a means of overcoming the problems of a 'liquid modern life,' but because it is an impromptu and temporary response, it also implies that a permanent solution is not ready at hand" (Grieve 2012, 105). In that sense, digital religion is ever changing, as the Buddhist notion of constant flux holds. Modern life, in part due to those very digital technologies, is moving and changing at such a pace that no institution, and certainly no religion, can remain in place. There is a constant game of catch-up being played, where the changes in the ways we live, work, and play demand changes in our religious views and practices as well, and the very digital technologies that are altering the one can be used to create "workarounds" that allow the other to keep pace. Digital is not, and according to this theory, could never be, in stasis but is always adapting to the needs of "liquid modern life." For example, as work leaves the confines of the office and takes over one's life at all times in the always-on, cellphone-enabled world of today, so too does digital Buddhism create a workaround with a daily Dharma app that pushes Buddhist teachings to that same cellphone, since the time to actually attend a temple talk has disappeared. Thus, digital media and religion are coming together in a unique way that addresses the concerns, dilemmas, and opportunities of modern life in a wired age.

A WALK THROUGH THE CHAPTERS OF THE VOLUME

In order to best lead the reader through this brave new world, we have divided this volume into four sections. The book begins with a section on methodology that serves to outline different approaches to doing research on digital Buddhism. In Chapter 2, Gregory Grieve sketches an ethnographic research method that emerged from two years of study in the virtual world of Second Life and its Zen Buddhist communities. He explores how to theorize the virtual and its relation to the actual using the Buddhist idea of Two Truths doctrine. He suggests that there is not a strict division between the virtual and the actual worlds, and calls for a classic ethnographic method based on participant observation and thick description to be used for online research. Whereas Grieve is concerned with negotiating the relationship between online and offline worlds, in Chapter 3 Laura Osburn is concerned with negotiating the decentralized and ever-changing networks of the Internet and emphasizes the importance of situating narratives within their specific Internet-based structural and relational contexts. She looks at the hyperlinking and narrative framing strategies used by political, religious, and cultural stakeholders invested in supporting or defying the interests of the Free Tibet Movement, and also gives practical advice for researchers about how to read and store the ever-changing data. In the final chapter of the method section, Chapter 4, Louise Connelly is also concerned with the ever-changing structure of the digital world, and demonstrates that mapping out Buddhism on the Internet requires an approach that can adapt to a medium and culture that is always in flux. She, therefore, presents a flexible typology for mapping different areas of the Buddhist cyberspace in order to better understand how the Internet is being used, for what, and by whom. She creates a typology that captures the integrated and dynamic nature of the different platforms online, which includes online virtual worlds and games, social media, websites, and mobile applications.

The next section of this volume, "Historical Approaches," contains two chapters on different aspects of the history of digital Buddhism. First, in Chapter 5, Charles Prebish discusses the origins of the *Journal of Buddhist Ethics* that was founded in July 1994. Originally planned as a traditional, hardcopy scholarly journal, it ended up becoming the first completely peer-reviewed online journal in the discipline of Religious Studies, and continues to be the prototype for online journals in the discipline. The chapter also covers the creation of a second online journal called the *Journal of Global Buddhism* and concludes that Buddhist Studies has much to benefit from availing itself of the affordances of online publishing. In Chapter 6, Gregory Grieve traces the historical roots of the mindfulness practices that are common in much digital Buddhism, which practitioners describe as a spiritualized awareness of the interwoven relationship of people and their environment. He finds that mindfulness bears only a family resemblance to pre-modern Asian practices, and is actually a form of spiritualized cybernetic thought that emerged in postwar America. The chapter first traces this emergence in California's counterculture, where it functioned as an alternative to an overly technological society. Grieve then outlines how it was co-opted by Silicon Valley, and corporate culture, more generally.

The third section of this volume, "Buddhism, Media and Society," looks at some of the social effects of the integration of Buddhism with digital media. First, in Chapter 7, Daniel Veidlinger focuses on the rapid spread of seminal Buddhist ideas through the Internet and examines the possibility that the impact of the vast network of instantaneously transmitted messages that constitute what is known as the Social Web is itself a prime factor in the upsurge of interest in Buddhism. He argues that the penetration of key Buddhist ideas, such as radical interdependence and decentered selves into the ways that the online population construes the world, can be attributed to the cognitive changes in the human mind that occur with the extensions of human senses offered by the unparalleled power of modern communication technologies, which may lead to significant changes in the acceptance of Buddhist ideas in society as these technologies become more pervasive. Next, in Chapter 8, Rachel Wagner and Christopher Accardo look at personal technologies, such as smartphones, and explore the tension between their socially isolating features and their communicative affordances that connect people. They put this issue into the context of Buddhism by examining how innovative programmers have begun to translate elements of Buddhist belief and practice into forms accessible via these mobile devices, pointing out that as Buddhist teachings are transformed into digitized, structured programs on mobile devices, they are experienced largely individually as a more traditional group context for these practices dissolves in the flow of modern life. On the other hand, these apps do allow us to carve out a space for Buddhist practice that meshes with contemporary times and can facilitate the communication of Buddhist messages to people who would otherwise not be in a position to receive them at all.

The final section of this volume includes four case studies that look at particular examples where Buddhism and digital media come together. Chapters 9 and 10 look at the creation of community, or what has been called the cybersangha. In Chapter 9, Christopher Helland examines the significant impact of new media on the maintenance of Tibetan religious and cultural identity in diaspora. Despite "geographical" Tibet being subsumed under the Chinese state, the Tibetan government in exile has begun to actively engage new media to promote their autonomy and maintain their religious and cultural identity. Moving from an analysis of an actual region that is using the Internet to construct a virtual online community, in Chapter 10, Jessica Falcone engages in a study of a Buddhist community that exists only online. Her chapter looks at Buddhist materiality in the virtual world of Second Life, an online environment in which the content is largely created by its denizens who themselves establish virtual spaces, relationships, and economies. The substance of "things" in Second Life may seem suspect, but she argues that the materiality of holy objects in cyberspace—such as prayer wheels, altars, and Buddhist art—is no immaterial matter for Buddhist practitioners who worship there; in fact, they function in remarkably similar ways to actual world objects.

Chapters 11 and 12 look at how digital media has been used to spread Buddhist teachings, or what could be called the cyber-Dharma. Not only is the Internet a key tool for maintaining a Buddhist community among Tibetans in exile and residents in Second Life, but it is also an important element in the life of communities closer to home (at least the home of most of our authors). In Chapter 11, Allison Ostrowski looks at America's obsession with Buddhism that has blossomed since its introduction in the 1800s and notes that there is a strong presence of American Buddhism on the World Wide Web. Here, she explores the American cybersangha, discovers who these members are, and demonstrates how they use the Internet to learn about or interact with Buddhism and other Buddhists. In Chapter 12, Beverley McGuire focuses closely on one particular form of interaction among Buddhists online, the blogosphere. This space encompasses an incredibly diverse demographic, including monastics, lay teachers, Buddhist practitioners, academics, and scholar–practitioners. The chapter explores the formal characteristics of blogs, considers some of the challenges of identifying an online community in the Buddhist blogosphere, and explores the complexity underlying the social construction of personal identity within Buddhist blogs.

CONCLUSION

In our digital world, there is no doubt that enormous changes are on the march across many aspects of society. Thomas de Zengotita (2005) summarizes the new state of media well when he writes,

> The real world is reconstituting itself on a plane that transcends ancient solidarities of nature and custom, craft and industry. The whole process has been accelerated since the invention of modern communication technologies (telegraph, photograph, telephone), and it crossed a qualitative threshold in the past couple of decades, with the rise of the new media (17–18).

This volume aims to assess how digital media affect Buddhism and to help us understand what new forms of Buddhist practice, belief, and community are emerging within this digital nexus.

Buddhism—a religion that has historically adapted very successfully to new environments, and also holds the idea of constant change as one of its defining ideologies—is thriving in this new world, as the chapters in this volume show. Its ideas are being imbibed by many more people than have ever had access to them before, its rituals are being reconfigured for online virtual worlds and mobile apps, its communities that are spread out across the globe are communicating with each other in new and unprecedented ways, its authority structures are being challenged in some cases and upheld in others, its scholars are publishing important studies online, and the whole process is being recorded and commented on in innumerable blogs.

When one looks at the chapters in this volume, one might be prompted to wonder how profound the role of digital technology is in the changes that are recorded here. Is technology an independent agent able to shape society, moving it in directions that are dictated by the logic of the technologies that are being employed? Or does it mainly respond to other modifications that are taking place in society at the time, and attempt to build the best workaround to deal with them as seamlessly as possible? As David Morgan reminds us, we need to recognize that "technologies mediate the body and the world around us, and that religions, like every other cultural activity, are and always have been mediated in some way. The pay-off of this recognition is that technologies of sensation structure the felt-life of a religion, telling us much about how people build and maintain their worlds, and what roles religions play in the ongoing work of cultural construction" (Morgan 2013, 351). It is impossible to determine at this point with certainty what role technology has in shaping religion, and what role religious practices and attitudes have in developing technologies that will accord with them, but these chapters should leave little doubt that something is definitely going on. We believe that the eclectic approach taken here, involving scholars from a number of different disciplines, some with more of a background in communications and media studies, and others with a background in Buddhology, some in anthropology and others in textual studies, is the best way to capture the manifold and mutual effects of new media and Buddhism. We hope that this first volume will motivate others to help with further research in this direction, so that we can come to a better understanding of the interconnected web of Buddhism, the Internet, and digital media.

NOTES

1. Studies of how Buddhism adapted to the various cultural environments in which it has found itself have focused on such places as China (Park 2012), Thailand (McDaniel 2011), Tibet (Kapstein 2002), and America (Prebish 1999).
2. There are countless resources for learning about the basic ideas of Buddhism. One of the most comprehensive online sites with a very large database of texts, teachings, and explanations is www.buddhanet.net.

REFERENCES

Allon, Mark. 1997. *Style and Function: A Study of the Dominant Stylistic Features of the Prose Portions of Pāli Canonical Sutta Texts and Their Mnemonic Function*. Tokyo: International Institute for Buddhist Studies of the International College for Advanced Buddhist Studies.

Bartley, William. 1978. *Werner Erhard: The Transformation of a Man: The Founding of est*. New York: Clarkson N. Potter.

Bauman, Zygmunt. 2005. *Liquid Modernity*. New York: Polity.

Brasher, Brenda. 2001. *Give Me That Online Religion*. San Francisco: Jossey-Bass.

Campbell, Heidi. 2010. *When Religion Meets New Media*. London: Routledge.

Cho, Kyong. 2011. "New Media and Religion: Observations on Research." *Communication Research Trends* 30(1): 4–22.

Collins, Steven. 1992. "Notes on Some Oral Aspects of Pali Literature." *Indo-Iranian Journal* 35(2–3): 121–135.

Cowan, Douglas, and Lorne Dawson, eds. 2004. *Religion Online: Finding Faith on the Internet*. New York: Routledge.

Engel, David, and Jaruwan Engel. 2010. *Tort, Custom and Karma: Globalization and Legal Consciousness in Thailand.* Stanford, CA: Stanford University Press.
Goody, Jack. 1977. *The Domestication of the Savage Mind.* Cambridge, UK: Cambridge University Press.
Grieve, Gregory. 2010. "Virtually Embodying the Field: Silent Online Meditation, Immersion, and the Cardean Ethnographic Method." *Heidelberg Journal of Religions on the Internet* 4(1). http://www.ub.uni-heidelberg.de/archiv/11296. Accessed October 14, 2013.
———. 2012. "Digital Religion." In *Digital Religion: Understanding Religious Practice in New Media Worlds,* edited by Heidi Campbell, 104–118. New York: Routledge.
Hansen, Valerie. 2012. *The Silk Road: A New History.* Oxford: Oxford University Press.
Hassan, Robert, and Julian Thomas, eds. 2006. *The New Media Theory Reader.* Berkshire, UK: Open University Press.
Hinuber, Oskar von. 1989. *Der Beginn der Schrift und Fruhe Schriftlichkeit in Indien.* Mainz: Akademie der Wissenschaften und der Literatur.
Hojsgaard, Morten, and Margit Warburg, eds. 2005. *Religion and Cyberspace.* London: Routledge.
Hubbard, Jamie, and Paul Swanson, eds. 1997. *Pruning the Bodhi Tree.* Honolulu, HI: University of Hawaii Press.
Kapstein, Matthew. 2002. *The Tibetan Assimilation of Buddhism.* Oxford: Oxford University Press.
Karaflogka, Anastasia. 2006. *e-religion.* London: Equinox Publishing.
Kelly, Kevin. 1994. *Out of Control.* Reading, MA: Addison Wesley.
Lull, James. 2000. *Media Communication, Culture: A Global Approach,* 2nd ed. New York: Columbia University Press.
McDaniel, Justin. 2011. *The Lovelorn Ghost and the Magical Monk.* New York: Columbia University Press.
McLuhan, Marshall. 1964. *Understanding Media: The Extensions of Man.* New York: McGraw Hill.
Meyer, Birgit. 2006. *Religious Sensations: Why Media, Aesthetics, and Power Matter in the Study of Contemporary Religion.* Amsterdam: Vrije Universiteit.
Morgan, David. 2013. "Religion and Media: A Critical Review of Recent Developments." *Critical Research on Religion* 1(3): 347–356.
Newland, Guy. 2009. *Introduction to Emptiness.* Ithaca, NY: Snow Lion.
Numrich, Paul. 1996. *Old Wisdom in the New World: Americanization in Two Immigrant Theravada Buddhist Temples.* Knoxville: University of Tennessee Press.
Ong, Walter. 1967. *The Presence of the Word: Some Prolegomena for Cultural and Religious History.* New Haven, CT: Yale University Press.
Park, Jungnok. 2012. *How Buddhism Acquired a Soul on the Way to China.* Sheffield, UK: Equinox.
Pew Foundation. 2001. *Cyberfaith: How Americans Pursue Religion Online.* http://www.pewinternet.org/2001/12/23/cyberfaith-how-americans-pursue-religion-online/. Accessed February 18, 2014.
———. 2007. *US Religious Landscape Survey.* http://religions.pewforum.org/pdf/report-religious-landscape-study-key-findings.pdf. Accessed August 18, 2012.
Prebish, Charles. 1993. "Two Buddhisms Reconsidered." *Buddhist Studies Review* 10(2): 187–206.
———. 1999. *Luminous Passage: The Practice and Study of Buddhism in America.* Berkeley: University of California Press.
———. 2004. "The Cybersangha: Buddhism on the Internet." In *Religion Online,* edited by Douglas Cowan and Lorne Dawson, 135–147. New York: Routledge.

Salomon, Richard. 1995. "On the Origin of the Early Indian Scripts: A Review Article." *Journal of the American Oriental Society* 115(2): 271–279.

Staal, Frits. 1986. *The Fidelity of Oral Tradition and the Origins of Science.* Amsterdam: North Holland Publishing.

Turner, Fred. 2006. *From Counterculture to Cyberculture: Stewart Brand, the Whole Earth Network, and the Rise of Digital Utopianism.* Chicago, IL: University of Chicago Press.

Tworkov, Helen. 1991. "Many Is More." *Tricycle,* winter edition. http://www.tricy cle.com/editors-view/many-more. Accessed September 7, 2013.

Vallee, Jacques. 2003. *The Heart of the Internet: An Insider's View of the Origin and Promise of the On-line Revolution.* Charlottesville, VA: Hampton Roads.

Veidlinger, Daniel. 2006a. *Spreading the Dhamma: Writing, Orality and Textual Transmission in Buddhist Northern Thailand.* Honolulu: University of Hawaii Press.

———. 2006b. "When a Word Is Worth a Thousand Pictures: Mahayana Influence on Theravada Attitudes Towards Writing." *Numen* 53(4): 405–447.

You, Yong. 2010. *The Diamond Sutra in Chinese Culture.* Hacienda Heights, CA: Buddha's Light Publishers.

Zengotita, Thomas de. 2005. *Mediated: How the Media Shapes Your World and the Way You Live in It.* New York: Bloomsbury.

Part I
Methodological Considerations

2 The Middle Way Method
A Buddhist-Informed Ethnography of the Virtual World of Second Life

Gregory Price Grieve

If it (the world) were not empty,
How could there be another world?
If the world were unlimited,
How could there be another world

The Fundamental Wisdom of the Middle Way, XXVII.21

;-)

Scott Elliott Fahlman (1982)[1]

On a conventional level, virtual worlds are treated as places to which users go. Ultimately, however, they are just pixels on the screen that users manipulate through keystroke and mouse click. Such empty pixels are transformed into lived worlds by the digital media practices that afford sociability. Consider for example, on December 12, 2008, I received an email message reminding me that an online meditation session was starting in five minutes at the Hoben Mountain Zen Retreat (HMZR).[2] The Hoben Buddhist community exists in the virtual world of Second Life, a three-dimensional immersive, interactive digital platform in which millions of Residents employ onscreen representations, called avatars, to explore, communicate, and socialize. By the end of my fieldwork in 2011, tens of millions of people had spent a large percentage of their lives together online in this virtual world. Perhaps unexpectedly, Buddhist meditation played a central role for many of them. By the end of 2008, Second Life's Zen Buddhist cloud consisted of five groups, which included 3,756 members in five regions. During my research, the largest of these groups was Hoben, which had 1,586 members, who participated in approximately seventy-five. Often labeled Western, convert, or Anglo Buddhism, such popular practice centers on several facets of the Buddhist tradition: the therapeutic, the non-hierarchical, the non-violent, the ecological, and, most importantly, the meditative.

As part of my research, I had been trying to go inworld at least once a day, so I opened my Second Life Viewer, much as one would a Web browser,

Figure 2.1   Author's research *avatar*, Clint Clavenham, at the Hoben Mountain Zen Retreat (HMZR), in the Shangrila *region* of Second Life. (Second Life Snapshot by Gregory Grieve)

such as Safari or Firefox.[3] I logged on and, after entering my password, and hitting return, my research avatar, Clint Clavenham, materialized in Shangrila, the region in which HMZR was located.

I was no longer just typing on the keyboard, but was also aware of standing in front of a wooden building, through the glass door of which I could see a long wooden altar with incense, candles, flowers, and a large statue of Shakyamuni Buddha. I pushed through the door and greeted everyone with a _/!_, an emoticon that represents a *gassho*, a gesture of palms together and fingers pointing upward in prayer position. On this day, I was welcomed by name by many of the sixteen practitioners.

Later that night, after the Hoben meditation session had ended, I teleported over to the home of Hope Long, the Resident hosting the Friday night open discussion of the Second Life Agnostic Buddhist Group (ABG). When I entered the room, Hope walked over and said, "Clint. love your robes ;) (an emoticon for winking)." Clint is a stern-looking man with a bald head and glasses, and my avatar was wearing for the first time free monk robes that had been handed out at the Hoben *zendo*. Hope Long is the founding member of ABG, and holds much authority in the group, often directing the flow of conversation with just a few well-chosen words or, in this case, a single emoticon. I looked around and noticed to my chagrin that none of the sixteen other avatars were wearing vestments. Instead, they were dressed in fairly typical everyday Second Life attire—short sparkly skirts, ball gowns, faded jeans, t-shirts, and someone in a Native American costume. I felt out of place.

This chapter asks what the best method is for describing, analyzing, and understanding the sociability afforded by media practices that compose virtual world Buddhist practices such as that found on Second Life. One might assume a quantitative or historical analysis could capture such subtle practices, maybe that it would be enough to interview and survey members, or simply concentrate on written sources and material culture. True, I actually use all these methods to support and contextualize my findings. I argue, however, that ethnography, especially as articulated by the anthropology of Buddhism, proves the most efficient method for recording virtual practices on their own terms, because it does not just record people's narratives, but rather highlights the media practices by which religion is imagined, enacted, embodied, and realized. A conventional ethnographic approach suggests that digital ethnographies should take a middle path between denying the cultural distinctiveness of virtual worlds, and maintaining that they are radically different social spaces. Often, digital ethnography suffers from one of these two extremes. For instance, the anthropologist James Clifford declared, in *Routes: Travel and Translation in the Late Twentieth Century*, that such online ethnographic studies were at best "awkward" (Clifford 1997, 61).[4] On the other hand are researchers such as Tom Boellstorff, who writes in *Coming of Age in Second Life: An Anthropologist Explores the Virtually Human* that virtual worlds ought to be studied "on their own terms" (2008, 62).

What emerges from a conventional method is a virtual ethnography that focuses on the implicit level of lived experience reflected in data collected inworld through the use of avatars. With this is mind, during the study's fieldwork my research team explored temples, prostrated before Buddha images, went to Dharma talks, and argued in open discussions about the nature of Buddhism.

The chapter outlines a virtual ethnography by first describing the two truths of social worlds. The chapter goes on to describe our use of participant observation, which was recorded in shared fieldnotes, snapshots, written documents, and material culture, and used to write thick descriptions, which recorded both the media practices as well as their context. The chapter maintains that the ethnography of virtual worlds is made possible because of virtual embodiment, and a social field constituted by the Second Life categories of people, places, groups, and events. Lastly, it reiterates that the conventional social worlds generated by computer-mediated communication dictate the same ethical guidelines as do those of face-to-face studies.

Figure 2.2   Virtual Research Team. Principle investigator and five assistants Sabrina Epps, Rebecca Davis, Kevin Heston, Michelle Lampley, and Jayme Mallindine. (Second Life Snapshot by Gregory Grieve)

THE TWO TRUTHS OF SOCIAL WORLDS: COLLECTING IMPLICIT INWORLD DATA

Emoticons are communicative acts that do not represent spoken speech but whose significance emerges embedded in digital contexts. Still, while a digital media convention, such emoticons exist only in relationship to face-to-face communication that mimics the bodily practices of winking and praying. To understand the use of emoticons, which can stand in for virtual media practices more generally, this chapter turns to the Mahayana Buddhist school of Madhyamaka's theory of realities (Garfield 2001). To be clear, my goal is not to give a precise philosophic definition, but rather to use the concept of two realities to articulate the relationship between the virtual and actual world. At the center is the concept of emptiness, the Buddhist term for the ultimate lack of an independent existence, or essence of phenomena. As Tibetan Buddhism puts it, nothing exists "from its own side"(Garfield 2001, 89). Ultimately, things are empty—however, on a conventional level of everyday interaction, people experience them as real. In fact, in Madhyamaka—a Mahayana Buddhist school of philosophy founded by one of the most important Buddhist philosophers, Nagarjuna—because neither ultimate nor conventional reality can exist on their own but rather emerge only in relation to each other, conventional reality ends up being as true as ultimate reality. In a similar fashion, on a social level, the actual and virtual worlds cannot exist on their own, and emerge dependent on each other. You cannot have one without the other. Ultimately, virtual worlds do not exist, but on the level of social conventions they are a reality as real as the actual world.

Accordingly, to understand the use of media practices such as ;) and _/!_, one must collect data by analyzing their contextualized use in virtual worlds, but one must realize that this reality is only a convention and holds no ultimate existence independent of the actual world. At the most elementary level, data is simply "a difference that makes a difference" (Bateson 1972, 448–466). Yet, what kind of difference does a wink emoticon make? For any phenomenon, there are an infinite number of possible differences arising from their relation with other phenomena. The central task of any methodology is to articulate how and why a researcher has chosen to record a particular difference. This chapter maintains that to study Second Life Buddhist practices on their own terms, one must focus on the often-implicit level of everyday practice by collecting data almost entirely inworld, that is to say from within the virtual world. Some have argued that there is really no difference between on- and offline knowledge formation (Golub 2010). Obviously, because the virtual is dependent on the actual, Second Life boundaries are porous and not hermetically sealed behind the computer screen. Yet, this chapter maintains that it is this very interdependence that generates the conventions of the virtual and actual. Still, while there is ultimately no difference between on- and offline practices, there is nevertheless a conventional difference, and this conventional difference is as real as other social practices that take place in the actual world. What this means is, rather than arguing for an ultimate essential difference between actual and virtual, I argue that virtual worlds are a distinct conventional social space, because they offer new social fields with differing social positions, lifestyles, values, and dispositions (Garfield 2001, 24–46). In fact, one could suggest that the concepts of the virtual and actual do not exist independently of each other, but only exist in relation to each other. In such a case, although virtual worlds lack inherent existence (*svabhava*), they are real on the conventional level of social reality (Garfield 2001, 88–89). Such conventional reality is real because what counts as real depends on our conventions. In fact, it is impossible to speak of reality independent of our conventions.

Treating virtual worlds as conventional social reality generates two methodological practices: focusing on the implicit level, and collecting data inworld. First, to conduct virtual ethnography on its own terms, one must focus on the often-implicit level of everyday practice. In fact, the ethnographer has as her job to articulate a model of lived reality, the purpose of which is to understand culture by making its implicit nature explicit (Grieve 2005; Kosuth 1991). Implicit data indicates what the anthropologist Clifford Geertz refers to as the "local frames of awareness," "a to-know-a-city-is-to-know-its-streets approach to things" (Geertz 1983, 6, 167). Rather than generalizations, universals, or laws, an ethnographic method must collect the data so that one can analyze (if only in hindsight) who winks, and why people wink, and the historic and cultural context of what such winking does. As Geertz writes, in "'Local Knowledge,' and Its Limits: Some *Obiter Dicta*," this means "to clarify what on Earth is going on among various people at various times and draw some conclusions about constraints, causes, hopes and possibilities—the practicalities of [a second] life" (1992, 133).

Second, a two-social-world model necessitates collection of data almost entirely from within the virtual world, as Second Life Residents (Boellstorff, 2008, 60–68). Obviously, reliance on computer-mediated communication raises problems of authenticity. How do you know that the person with whom you are talking is who they claim to be? One could—as Sherry Turkle, the scholar of technology, does—solve this dilemma by only reporting on those interactions where she also met the person face-to-face (1995, 324). We, however, treat Second Life's social field as valid in itself. We took the events, practices, groups, and relationships that occurred in the virtual world, *not* as derivatives of something else, but as legitimate in themselves (Boellstorff 2008). Our point here was *not* to deny the permeability between the virtual and actual. We did not, as Lori Kendel warns in *Hanging Out in the Virtual Pub: Masculinities and Relationships Online*, attempt to treat Second Life as "a completely separate, isolated social world" (2002, 9). In other words, to understand media practices such as Hope's ;) as a conventional reality, it is not enough to simply translate them from the virtual to the actual. It is not enough to say that the emoticon is virtually like an actual wink. Rather, like the two emoticons, data was meaningful because it was generated in that environment.

HOW TO STUDY CONVENTIONAL REALITY: PARTICIPANT OBSERVATION AND THICK DESCRIPTION

Ethnography proves the best method for studying the conventional reality of virtual worlds that involves an embedded sociability. As Nancy Baym writes, "Too often, Internet researchers take the stance that since the Internet is new, old theory and methods . . . have nothing to offer in its exploration" (2009, 180; see Markham and Baym 2009, xv). Following Baym, we argue that Second Life should be studied with a classic ethnography. Ethnography is an open-ended, non-linear method of data collection that is grounded in a field site, where researchers embark on participatory exercises in order to collect materials for which analytical protocols are often devised after the fact (Strathern 2004, 4–6). "Classic" refers to the fact that our method was centered on the two main conceptual instruments in an ethnographer's toolbox—participant observation and thick description.

Participant observation indicates a qualitative method in which, for an extended period of time, researchers live with participants in their own environment while documenting their everyday practices. Participant observation goes beyond a "deep hanging-out," because it documents the implicit level of everyday life (Geertz 1998). Pioneered in the first half of the twentieth century by anthropologists such as Bronisław Malinowski,

E. E. Evans-Pritchard, and Margaret Mead, participant observation is a qualitative method in which researchers take part in the daily activities of the group under study, and record what they observe (Evans-Pritchard 1940; Malinowski 1929; Mead 1928). What makes participant observation an objective research method is that one also needs to stand back and observe by watching and listening, while taking both physical and mental notes. Observation means logging concrete documentation of social structures, examples of everyday life, and everyday utterances. Our observations were recorded in shared fieldnotes, snapshots, material culture, and spooled chat. We took "scratch notes" during our time inworld, and then after logging off would spend almost as much time writing more-detailed descriptions in our fieldnotes—incorporating and describing snapshots, objects, and conversations.

Inworld, participant observation is a way of understanding how ritual and popular religious practices structure the lived reality of virtual worlds (Gellner 1992; Holmberg, 1989; Jordan 1983; Reynolds and Carbine 2000). The goal of all such ethnographic ritual is to create thick description. As Clifford Geertz defines the term, a thick description describes both a social practice and also the context in order for that practice to become meaningful to an outsider. Geertz uses the example of a wink (1973, 5–7). If someone winks, it could mean that they are expressing sexual desire, trying to communicate a secret, or they might "actually have been fake-winking, say, to mislead outsiders into imagining there was a conspiracy afoot" (Geertz 1973, 7). Without knowing the context, we reduce the wink to the thin description that the person is merely "rapidly contracting his right eyelid" (1973, 7). In a similar fashion, in the context of Second Life, one could accurately describe the emoticon ;) as a semi-colon and a bracket, and one could note that it can be found at the end of approximately 0.78 percent of Second Life chat and IM utterances. Yet, such a "thin description" does not explain what this sign means to an insider. In Geertz's words, it does "not uncover the conceptual structures that inform our subject's acts," and allow us to "construct a system of analysis" (1973, 27). One could give a translation, that in online postings, ;) signifies "happily winking," has a family resemblance to simulating a real life wink, and is often used at the end of utterance to emote irony. One could also differentiate it from other emoticons such as :-P (sticking out tongue), and : ((unhappy face). One could reference the first digital media smiley used in 1982, an article on their humorous use in the March 30, 1881, issue of *Puck*; *The National Telegraphic Review Guide* from April 1957; and the use of the number 73 in Morse Code to signify "love and kisses." One could even give a possible genealogy of ;) back to a speech by Abraham Lincoln.[5] The historic, quantitative, and (possibly) genealogical definitions of the winking emoticon, however, cannot replace the rich depth of ethnographically contextualized thick description that generates an understanding that analyzes, synthesizes, and evaluates the imponderabilia of a virtual emoticon.

VIRTUALLY BEING THERE: AN EMBODIED FIELD

An ethnographic field consists of people, conventions, and practices (Bourdieu 1993). In such a case, people are not abstract rational agents, but are embedded bodies (Carrithers, Collins, and Lukes 1985). In the most general sense, embodiment signifies the experience of being in our bodies, and challenges the assumption that subjectivity can be reduced to mind. In the *Phenomenology of Perception,* Merleau-Ponty writes, "In so far as I have hands, feet, a body, I sustain around me intentions which are not dependent upon my decisions and which affect my surroundings in a way which I do not choose" (1962 [1945], 440). Virtual embodiment might seem a contradiction. John Edward Campbell argues, however, we need to challenge the "supposition conflating online interaction with bodily transcendence" (2004, 5). To assume embodiment ends with physical reality imputes a naturalist and romantic notion of an unmediated encounter with the world. I am not arguing the untenable position that somehow, as in the 1982 movie *Tron,* one drags one's physical body into cyberspace. Instead, using Judith Butler's understanding of the body as practice, I maintain that a theory of virtual nondualist embodiment differentiates immersion as performance from immersion as a proprioceptive sensation. In such a case, virtual embodiment can be defined as an immersed bodily performance that occurs in cyberspace.

Second Life is a valid ethnographic field site because it allows embodiment, which as Thomas J. Csordas argues in "Embodiment as a Paradigm for Anthropology," is "a productive starting point for analyzing culture and self" (1990, 5). We maintain that how we experience living in a body is not simply given by nature, but ideological: "we are also bodies in a social and cultural sense, and we experience that, too" (Ihde 2002, xi). Second Life, then, does not lack bodies. What it lacks is the physicality of the actual world. Who or what, then, is the virtual body? In the simplest sense, a virtual body is one that inhabits virtual reality (Balsamo 1996). Explicitly, virtual bodies are a set of mediated practices. For the American post-structuralist philosopher and queer theorist Judith Butler, there is no such thing as a "real" body, which is free of an imaginary construction. The body is a material reality that has already been located and defined within a social context. The body is not a stable platform on which one inscribes an identity, rather bodies are a condensation of performances, feelings, and desires grounded in lived practices.

In Second Life, Residents literally build bodies. One never is one's body, but rather is only the condition of doing it. In fact, the body is not a "being" but a "set of boundaries" (Butler 1990, 177, 44). Understanding the body as a set of boundaries corresponds to Buddhist theories of perception, both contemporary and ancient (Koller 1993, 55–57; Nagatomo 1993, 321–346). Just as one does actual bodies, one does virtual bodies. They are just more obvious, because virtual worlds make explicit the notion that bodies are not born but are constituted through performance (Butler 1986). As Butler (1988) writes, the body should be conceived not as "natural fact but as an historical idea" (254). As she maintains in "Sex and Gender in Simone de Beauvoir's *Second Sex*," bodying is "a modality of taking on or realizing possibilities," which involves "a purposive and appropriate set of acts, the acquisition of a skill" (1986: 36). A theory of virtual embodiment is significant to the study of online religion in three ways. First, virtual embodiment shows why ethnography is possible in cyberspace, and allows for the construction of models to explain online identity and community. Second, virtual embodiment illuminates why virtual worlds, either 3D graphic or textual platforms, are distinct areas of research compared to other online environments, such as Web pages and blogs. I am not arguing that virtual worlds are radically different from other online media, but rather that they are distinct because they have a higher degree of virtual embodiment and, thus, deserve a different method of study. Third, virtual embodiment illustrates that religion—even virtual religion—does not just happen in people's minds but requires bodies, and thus exposes these bodies as "a cultural sign"(Butler 1990: 90). This understanding is supported by recent ethnographic studies of Buddhism in contemporary contexts, which reveals the role of cultural identity in religious practice (Janes 2002; LeVine and Gellner 2005; Makley 2007; Scott 2007).

THE CONVENTIONS OF AN ETHNOGRAPHIC FIELD: PEOPLE, PLACES, GROUPS, AND EVENTS

Bodies make fieldwork in Second Life possible. The field refers to the natural non-laboratory location where the activities in which researchers are interested take place. While ultimately just pixels on a screen, Second Life is a field because it affords social conventions. Our research extends the classic notions of the field from the observation of actual co-located, face-to-face physicality, to digitally mediated real-time embodied interactions in a virtual world. While a contested category, the field as an embodied practice is still critical in defining ethnography as a method (Clifford 1997, 89). Determining what constitutes the core unit of a field is historically one of the main challenges that face ethnographers. Yet, the myth of the ethnographic field as a discreet, bounded geographic locale is proving to be increasingly outdated and untenable as globalization blurs the boundary between "here" and "there" (Fox 1991; Gupta and Ferguson, 1997, 5; Kohn 1995). Still, while the "tent-in-the-village" research model may be under pressure, many ethnographers are surprised (if not appalled) at the thought of an online field site such as Second Life (Amit 2000; Clifford 1997; Delamont, Atkinson, and Parry, 2000). Yet, as is becoming clearer in recent ethnography, a field site can no longer be defined merely as a geographic place. In a Bourdieuian sense, a field locates people and their social positions, which are the result of the interaction between specific rules and a person's *habitus*, the lifestyle, values, dispositions, and expectation of particular social groups that are acquired through the activities and experiences of everyday life (Bourdieu 1984, 1993). As such, a "field site" can no longer be seen merely as a physical location, but rather must be viewed as the intersection between people, practices, and shifting terrains, both physical and virtual. As such, as Christine Hine (2000) writes in *Virtual Ethnography*, "the Internet and similar networks provide a naturally occurring field site for studying what people do when they are online unconstrained by experimental design" (18).

If one does not rely on physical places to demarcate the boundaries, how can one then demarcate a field? As I was "winked" at by Hope, some 75,434 other Residents were online, and millions of others had accounts. If I so desired, I could communicate with other Residents anywhere on the Second Life Grid through group and private instant messages. As an avatar, I could meet these other Residents; socialize; explore; build; and buy, sell, rent, or trade land or goods using the Linden Dollar (L$). Sitting in front of my computer screen, I could also post on the "SLogosphere" that surrounds the virtual world, or even Skype or telephone other Residents. How ought the study demarcate a field? What emerged through trial and error was a field composed of a network of the emic categories for people, places, groups, and events—to use Second Life's own search categories.

"People" is a Second Life search category for *Residents*. Employed throughout the platform and the surrounding *SLogosphere*, instead of the term "user," *Resident* is "meant to give users a feeling of 'belonging' and ownership of the virtual world."[6] Resident was used almost from the beginning of the virtual world, and can be seen as far back as 2003 in the beta testing website, which states, "residents of Second Life will face a host of choices daily . . . [in this] multi-layered boundless universe that is constantly changed by—and constantly changes—its inhabitants."[7] Resident is meant to capture how the Second Life experience differs from "flat" technology like email, and describes someone who "dwells" in a 3D virtual environment.[8] As Robin Linden, the *inworld* name of a Linden Lab's employee, who coined the term, wrote in a Second Life Forum from July 2006,

> the word "users" doesn't do a very good job of describing the two-way nature of Second Life . . . We also thought about "members" (boring!), "citizens" (too political!), and "players" (too game-y). "*Residents,*" however, seems most descriptive of people who have a stake in the world and how it grows.[9]

Places are the virtual environments built by *Residents* in which avatars dwell, and consist of an almost unimaginable variety of venues. As one *builder* said to me, "If you *rez* it, they will come." Places consist of the simulations (*sim*) or *regions*, which are the parcels of virtual land that makes up Second Life's Grid. Using building tools that are part of Second Life viewer software, Residents can create almost any environment they imagine. The backbone of Second Life is the *Grid*, a collection of networked computer servers that implement the presentation of land and *inworld* physics. Second Life's Grids are named after Hindu gods; the primary Grid to which users connect is named after Agni, the Vedic god of fire. The Grid supports *regions*—65,536 m² areas hosted by a single simulator, which can be divided into parcels as small as 16 m². When we first started fieldwork, my team attempted to catalogue all the religious *regions* by *landmarking* them, but after finding more than 500, stopped (cf. Radde-Antweiler 2008). The problem was not just with the sheer number, but that like ice in a quickly flowing stream, the places were forming and dissolving at such a rate that it was difficult to give an accurate count. Unlike the actual world where abandoned buildings leave ruins, in Second Life all that remains is a flat green field. Places that we *landmarked* included: Christian, such as DokimosCafe and the NoahArt Museum; Islamic, such as IslamOnline; Jewish, such as the Second Life Synagogue; and neo-pagan, such as the Sacred Cauldron.

Groups are the most basic and stable Second Life social unit. While people and places come and go, groups remain stable, like ripples in a stream. A group is an organization that contains at least two Residents, and which any Resident can create for L$100 (about US$ 0.60).[10] After January 13, 2011, a Resident could join up to forty-two groups. During the time of our fieldwork, however, a Resident could belong to only twenty-five. Groups have *groupchat* that can be moderated, up to ten different *roles* that give varying amounts of authority and control, and they can own land, as can individual Residents. Groups can be open, in which any one can join, or closed, which are joinable by invitation only. Because landownership was relatively expensive, and necessitated monthly fees, regions tended to be short lived. Groups, on the other hand, are very inexpensive and actually hard to disband. Because of this, they tend to be quite stable, and are the backbone of social clusters. Also, *groupchat* was by far the most popular and effective way of reaching and organizing social units of like-minded Residents. Consider the following examples. On July 18, 2013, when I searched for religious groups, a representative sample included: "Second Life Christians," with 1,383 members, described as "For all those who follow Jesus. Purpose: to strengthen, encourage, and build up one another; to learn and grow; to have life in great abundance"; "Bayt al-Hikmah," with 115 members, who describe themselves as "spiritual-minded people who are seeking better understand of Islam in general and Sufism in particular"; "Jewish Torah Learning," with seventy members. "This group is for Jewish studies in Second Life. We hope to have classes in Jewish philosophy, ethics and law, for interested members of the Jewish faith here in SL"; and "Pagan," with 598 members, which is, "For the Second Life Pagan and Pagan-friendly community. We are the oldest Pagan community in SL. Founded in 2003."

The final category, *events*, indicates performances and other types of religious practice, such as the silent meditation and the open discussion mentioned at the beginning of the chapter. Theoretically, events could include up to 100 Residents at a time. In practice, the largest events tended to attract at the most thirty. Events are important because, beyond intellectual assessments, events make researchers aware of the bodily aspect of virtual religion, and also move analysis beyond scripture into other aspects of religion. Religious practice, like play, has a performative power that goes beyond narrative. As Markku Eskelinen writes in the "The Gaming Situation": "If I throw a ball at you, I don't expect you to drop it and wait until it starts telling stories" (2001). The dynamics of religious performance make researchers aware that Residents are active builders of virtual religion both as they invent new forms and adopt and modify actual world practices. Through events, Residents create culture, authority, and the symbols of ultimate reality by which people order their world.

CONCLUSION: THE CONVENTIONAL TRUTH OF A VIRTUAL WINK

How can one document the significance of a virtual wink? Because it blurs the distinction between the objective language of the scientist and the narrative language of the novelist, ethnographic writing—not to mention virtual ethnographic writing—can challenge modes of objectivity in scholarly writing. This goes even more so for virtual worlds, which hover in that liminal social space between the imagined and the actual. Still, while ethnographies can properly be called fictions in the sense of "something manufactured," because they are grounded in an embodied field, ethnography remains a proven scientific method for understanding religious worldviews (Clifford and Marcus 1986, 6; Gupta and Ferguson, 1997, 1). For many, however, virtual ethnography proves troubling. As Malinowski cautions, researchers should not sit in their armchairs theorizing from a distance, but must spend time learning about, and from, groups of people in their natural surroundings (1961, 7). I maintain that both Buddhist philosophical concepts, as well as the practice of the anthropology of Buddhism, indicate a middle path between those skeptical of virtual worlds as valid social spaces, and those who argue for their ontological distinction.

Framed by the emoticons, _/!_ and ;), this chapter has outlined the formation of a Buddhist-informed virtual ethnographic method that between November 2007 and October 2011 and focused on collecting data *inworld* through a classic ethnography composed of participant observation and thick description. More specifically, my research team's virtual ethnography of Second Life's Buddhist community can help us understand why Hope was winking. On the surface, the Hoben Mountain Zen Retreat and the Agnostic Buddhist Group might seem to reflect the same Western Buddhist worldview. In fact, they held different worldviews whose boundaries were created and policed by practices such as the wearing of virtual robes and the typing of emoticons. For most in Second Life, robes do not have a great significance. For example, often when I was in a non-Buddhist region, people would enquire—as I was asked by a child avatar one time—"why are you wearing a dress?" However, for Second Life's Buddhist community, the wearing of robes is a very important choice that displays much about how they understand their Buddhist practice. For Hoben, the robes marked authentic Buddhist practice, and were a strategy by which they differentiated themselves from other Residents. The *gassho* emoticon played a similar function, and was used to mark speech that was seen as particularly Buddhist, such as at the start and end of a meditation session. As I was later to realize, the Agnostic Buddhist Group saw itself as different from other *inworld* Buddhists, and tended not to wear robes. ABC maintains that the essential core of Buddhism is, "if you see the world clearly, and live honestly within it, you will lead a more joyful life with less strife." Not wearing robes fit into their basic belief that agnostic "Buddhism" adopts the most important basic tenets of Buddhism, and leaves behind centuries of additions from other religions. In the differing conceptions of Second Life Buddhist practice and virtual robes, one finds that the ;), while virtual, was a real and effective way to police community standards, and let me as a researcher know when I had stepped outside the field of the more "traditional" Zen Buddhist cloud.

NOTES

1. Scott Elliott Fahlman, a computer scientist at Carnegie Mellon University, is credited with the first use of an emoticon in computer-mediated communication. This was in a message sent September 19, 1982.
2. Unless stated otherwise, the names of Second Life Residents and regions in the chapter are pseudonyms. This choice was difficult because I desired to give credit to the individuals who became not just subjects, but friends, and without which the study would have been impossible. However, to err on the side of protecting individuals, when information was collected through participant observation, interviews, or surveys, or if there was the possibility that public sources could be tied to a conversant, we use pseudonyms. If the sources are publicly available, we use actual names to give the individual credit.
3. See "Second Life Viewer," http://secondlife.com/support/downloads/ accessed August 24, 2012; "Safari," http://www.apple.com/safari/ accessed August 24, 2012; "Firefox," http://www.mozilla.org/en-US/firefox/new/ accessed August 24, 2012.
4. When I began the study in 2007, this was a hotly contested area, but by 2013 when I finished writing, the consensus was that virtual ethnography was a valid methodology (see Bartle 2004; Baym 2000, 2006, 2010; Boellstorff 2008; Campbell 2005; Chen and Hinton 1999; Curtis and Nichols 1993; Hine 2000; Jones 1999; Markham 1998; Marcus 1995; Dicks, Mason, Coffey, and Atkinson 2005; Miller and Slater 2000; O'Conner and Madge 2001; Witmer, Colman, and Katzman 1999).

5. "Is That an Emoticon in 1862?" *New York Times*, January 19, 2009, http://city room.blogs.nytimes.com/2009/01/19/hfo-emoticon/?_r=0 accessed August 22, 2013.
6. "Resident," http://wiki.secondlife.com/wiki/Resident accessed August 23, 2013.
7. "Press Room," *Linden Lab*, http://lindenlab.com/press_2.php accessed February 15, 2013.
8. Second Life Culture, *UC Second Life Training Guide*, http://ucsltraining.wiki spaces.com/Second+Life+Culture accessed March 22, 2012.
9. "Who Coined the Term 'Resident,'" *Second Life Forums Archive*, http://forums-archive.secondlife.com/139/e9/125712/1.html accessed March 22, 2012.
10. "Video Tutorial/How to Create and Join a Group," *Second Life Wiki*, http://wiki.secondlife.com/wiki/Video_Tutorial/How_to_create_and_join_a_group accessed March 22, 2012.

RESOURCES

"Firefox," http://www.mozilla.org/en-US/firefox/new/ Accessed August 22, 2013.
"Original Bboard Thread in which :-) Was Proposed," http://www-2.cs.cmu.edu/-sef/Orig-Smiley.htm Accessed September 19, 2009.
"Press Room," *Linden Lab*, <http://lindenlab.com/press_2.php> Accessed February 15, 2003.
"Resident," <http://wiki.secondlife.com/wiki/Resident> Accessed August 23, 2013.
"Safari," http://www.apple.com/safari/ Accessed August 22, 2013.
"Second Life Culture," *UC Second Life Training Guide*, http://ucsltraining.wikis paces.com/Second+Life+Culture, Accessed March 22, 2012.
"Second Life Viewer," http://secondlife.com/support/downloads/ Accessed August 22, 2013.
"Video Tutorial/How to create and join a group," *Second Life Wiki*, http://wiki.sec ondlife.com/wiki/Video_Tutorial/How_to_create_and_join_a_group Accessed March 22, 2012.
"What Defines Someone as a Noob," *General Discussion Forum*, http://commu nity.secondlife.com/t5/General-Discussion-Forum/What-Defines-Someone-as-a-Noob/td-p/1717911 Accessed August 22, 2013.
"Who Coined the Term 'Resident'," Second Life Forums Archive, http://forums-archive.secondlife.com/139/e9/125712/1.html Accessed March 22, 2012.

REFERENCES

Amit, Vered. 2000. *Constructing the Field*. London: Routledge.
Balsamo, Anne. 1996. *Technologies of the Gendered Body*. Durham, NC: Duke University Press.
Bartle, Richard. 2004. *Designing Virtual Worlds*. Berkeley, CA: New Riders.
Bateson, Gregory. 1972. *Steps to an Ecology of Mind: Collected Essays in Anthropology, Psychiatry, Evolution, and Epistemology*. Chicago, IL: University of Chicago Press.
Baym. Nancy. 2000. *Tune In, Log On: Soaps, Fandom, and Online Community*. Thousand Oaks, CA: Sage.
———. 2006. "The Emergence of On-line Community." In *Cybersociety: Communication and Community*, edited by S. Jones, 35–68. Newbury Park, CA: Sage.

————. 2009. "What Constitutes Quality in Qualitative Research?" In *Internet Inquiry: Conversations about Methods*, edited by A. N. Markham and N. K. Baym, 173–189. Thousand Oaks, CA: Sage.

————. 2010. *Personal Connections in the Digital Age*. New York: Polity.

Boellstorff, Tom. 2008. *Coming of Age in Second Life: An Anthropologist Explores the Virtually Human*. Woodstock, NJ: Princeton University Press.

Bourdieu, Pierre. 1984. *Distinction: A Social Critique of the Judgment of Taste*. London: Routledge.

————. 1993. *The Field of Cultural Production*. Cambridge, MA: Polity Press.

Butler, Judith. 1986. "Sex and Gender in Simone de Beauvoir's Second Sex." *Yale French Studies* 72(Winter): 35–49.

————. 1988. "Performative Acts and Gender Constitution: An Essay in Phenomenology and Feminist Theory." *Theatre Journal* 40(4): 519–531.

————. 1990. *Gender Trouble: Feminism and the Subversion of Identity*. New York: Routledge.

Campbell, Heidi. 2005. *Exploring Religious Community Online: We Are One in the Network*. Oxford: Peter Lang.

Campbell, John Edward. 2004. *Getting it on Online: Cyberspace, Gay Male Sexuality, and Embodied Identity*. New York: Harrington Park Press.

Carrithers, Michael, Steven Collins, and Steven Lukes. 1985. *The Category of the Person: Anthropology, Philosophy, History*. Cambridge, UK: Cambridge University Press.

Chen, Peter, and S. M. Hinton. 1999. "Realtime Interviewing Using the World Wide Web." *Sociological Research Online* 4. http://www.socresonline.org.uk/4/3/chen.html. Accessed August 27, 2013.

Clifford, James. 1997. *Routes: Travel and Translation in the Late Twentieth Century*. Cambridge, MA: Harvard University Press.

Clifford, James, and George E. Marcus. 1986. *Writing Culture: The Poetics and Politics of Ethnography*. Berkeley: University of California Press.

Csordas, Thomas J. 1990. "Embodiment as a Paradigm for Anthropology." *Ethos* 18(1): 5–47.

Curtis, Pavel, and David Nichols. 1993. "MUDs Grow Up: Social Virtual Reality in the Real World." Paper presented at Xerox PARC, Palo Alto, CA, May 5. http://w2.eff.org/Net_culture/MOO_MUD_IRC/muds_grow_up.paper. Accessed June 23, 2014.

Delamont, S., P. A. Atkinson, and O. Parry. 2000. *The Doctoral Experience: Success and Failure in Graduate School*. London: Falmer.

Dicks, Bella, Bruce Mason, Amanda Coffey, and Paul Atkinson. 2005. *Qualitative Research and Hypermedia: Ethnography for the Digital Age*. London: Sage.

Eskelinen, Markku. 2001. "The Gaming Situation." *Game Studies* 1. http://www.gamestudies.org/0101/eskelinen/. Accessed August 22, 2013.

Evans-Pritchard, E. E. 1940. *The Nuer, A Description of the Modes Livelihood and Political Institutions of a Nilotic People*. Oxford: Clarendon Press.

Fahlman, Scott Elliott. 1982. "Original Board Thread in Which :-) Was Proposed." http://www-2.cs.cmu.edu/~sef/Orig-Smiley.htm. Accessed September 19, 2009.

Fox, Richard. 1991. "Introduction: Working in the Present." In *Recapturing Anthropology: Working in the Present*, edited by Richard Fox, 1–16. Santa Fe, NM: School of American Research/University of Washington Press.

Garfield, Jay. 2001. *Empty Words: Buddhist Philosophy and Cross-Cultural Interpretation*. Oxford: Oxford University Press.

Geertz, Clifford. 1973. "Thick Description: Toward an Interpretive Theory of Culture." In *The Interpretation of Cultures: Selected Essays*, edited by Clifford Geertz, 3–30. New York: Basic Books.

————. 1983. *Local Knowledge: Further Essays in Interpretive Anthropology*. New York: Basic Books.

————. 1992. "'Local Knowledge' and Its Limits: Some *Obiter Dicta.*" *The Yale Journal of Criticism* 5(2): 129–134.

————. 1998. "Deep Hanging Out." *The New York Review of Books* 45(16): 69–72.

Gellner, David N. 1992. *Monk, Householder, and Tantric Priest: Newar Buddhism and Its Hierarchy of Ritual.* Cambridge: Cambridge University Press.

Golub, Alex. 2010. "Being in the World (of Warcraft): Raiding, Realism, and Knowledge Production in a Massively Multiplayer Online Game." *Anthropological Quarterly* 83(1): 17–46.

Grieve, Gregory. 2005. "One and Three Bhairavas: The Hypocrisy of Iconographic Mediation." *Revista de Estudos da Religião* 4. http://www.pucsp.br/rever/rv4_2005/p_grieve.pdf. Accessed August 27, 2013.

Gupta, Akhil, and James Ferguson. 1997. "Discipline and Practice: 'The Field' as Site, Method, and Location in Anthropology." In *Anthropological Locations: Boundaries and Grounds of a Field Science,* edited by A. Gupta and J. Ferguson, 1–46. Berkeley: University of California Press.

Hine, Christine. 2000. *Virtual Ethnography.* London: Sage.

Holmberg, David. 1989. *Order in Paradox: Myth, Ritual and Exchange among Nepal's Tamang.* Ithaca, NY: Cornell University Press.

Ihde, Don. 2002. *Bodies in Technology.* Minneapolis: University of Minnesota Press.

Janes, Craig R. 2002. "Buddhism, Science, and Market: The Globalization of Tibetan Medicine." *Anthropology and Medicine* 9(3): 267–289.

Jordan, David. 1983. "The Anthropology of Taiwanese Society." *American Ethnologist* 10(2): 394–395.

Kendel, Lori. 2002. *Hanging Out in the Virtual Pub: Masculinities and Relationships Online.* Berkeley: University of California Press.

Kohn, T. 1995. "She Came Out of the Field and into My Home." In *Questions of Consciousness,* edited by A. P. Cohen and N. Rappaport, 41–59. London: Routledge.

Koller, John. 1993. "Human Embodiment: Indian Perspectives." In *Self as Body in Asian Theory and Practice,* edited by Thomas Kasulis, Roger Ames, and Wimal Dissanayake, 45–58. Albany, NY: SUNY Press.

Kosuth, Joseph. 1991. *Art After Philosophy and After, Collected Writings, 1966–1990.* Cambridge, MA: MIT Press.

LeVine, Sarah, and David N. Gellner. 2005. *Rebuilding Buddhism: The Theravada Movement in Twentieth-Century Nepal.* Cambridge, MA: Harvard University Press.

————. 2007. *The Violence of Liberation: Gender and Tibetan Buddhist Revival in Post-Mao China.* Berkeley: University of California Press.

Malinowski, Bronislaw. 1929. *The Sexual Life of Savages in North-Western Melanesia: An Ethnographic Account of Courtship, Marriage and Family Life among the Natives of the Trobriand Islands, British New Guinea.* New York: Halcyon House.

————. 1961. *Argonauts of the Western Pacific.* New York: E. P. Dutton.

Merleau-Ponty, Maurice. 1962. *Phenomenology of Perception.* New York: Routledge and Kegan Paul.

Miller, Daniel, and Don Slater. 2000. *The Internet: An Ethnographic Approach.* Oxford: Berg.

Nagatomo, Shigenori. 1993. "Two Contemporary Japanese Views of the Body." In *Self as Body in Asian Theory and Practice,* edited by Thomas Kasulis, Roger Ames, and Wimal Dissanayake, 321–346. Albany, NY: SUNY Press.

Radde-Antweiler, Kerstin. 2008. "Virtual Religion: An Approach to a Religious and Ritual Topography of Second Life." *Heidelberg Journal of Religions on the Internet* 3. http://archiv.ub.uni-heidelberg.de/volltextserver/8294/. Accessed August 22, 2013.

Reynolds, Frank E., and Jason A. Carbine, eds. 2000. *The Life of Buddhism*. Berkeley: University of California Press.

Scott, Rachelle M. 2007. *Nirvana for Sale: Buddhism, Wealth, and the Dhammakaya Temple in Contemporary Thailand*. Albany, NY: SUNY Press.

Strathern, Marilyn. 2004. *Commons and Borderlands: Working Papers on Interdisciplinarity, Accountability, and the Flow of Knowledge*. Wantage, UK: Sean Kingston Publishing.

Turkle, Sherry. 1995. *Life on the Screen: Identity in the Age of Internet*. New York: Simon and Schuster.

Witmer, D. F., R. W. Colman, and S. L. Katzman. 1999. "From Paper and-Pencil to Screen-and-Keyboard: Toward a Methodology for Survey Research on the Internet." In *Doing Internet Research: Critical Issues and Methods for Examining the Net*, edited by S. Jones, 145–161. Thousand Oaks, CA: Sage.

3   Between Network and Story
Analyzing Hyperlinks and Narratives on Websites about Tibet

Laura Osburn

STUDYING BUDDHIST NARRATIVES ONLINE

Let's imagine that you are online and searching for information about the Tibetan Buddhist reincarnation system and religious freedom in the People's Republic of China (PRC). After conducting a Google search, you visit a website from China called Tibet Human Rights (en.tibet328.cn/index.html). The site posts information about Tibet from government-run sources, such as *Xinhua News* and government white papers, all of which view China as having a legally valid historical claim to Tibet as a part of the Chinese nation, and state that there is religious freedom in Tibet. Here you read an article about how the government approves all reincarnations of important Tibetan Buddhist lamas. The article states that this system is a historical continuation of government control established in the *29-Article Ordinance for the More Efficient Governing of Tibet*, written in 1793 during the Qing dynasty (1644–1911) (Xinhua 2009a). You read that this ordinance helped to maintain the purity of Tibetan Buddhism from the pollution of greed and political interests, "won the hearts of all Tibetans," and has now become an integral part of the Tibetan Buddhist faith (Xinhua 2009a).

   You then conduct another Google search and visit the Canada Tibet Committee website, an activist site that supports Tibet's independence from China. You visit the site's "Dharma Resource Centre" (tibet.ca/en/news-room/library/dharma.html), which informs you that Tibetans do not enjoy freedom of religion in the PRC and pleads for you to become involved in the organization to bring authentic religious freedom to Tibet. At the bottom of this page, you open a link to a U.S. State Department report that frames Chinese government control of the reincarnation system as one of the methods that the PRC uses to repress religious activities in Tibet (Bureau of Democracy, Human Rights, and Labor 2009). While both sites discuss Tibetan religious freedoms and state that the PRC's government must approve Tibetan Buddhist reincarnations, these two websites frame these stories in different ways for different purposes.

   How can we study these kinds of oppositional stories about Buddhism and inquire into the function of these stories? First, we have to consider not just what is being said, but also the context in which it is being said. Whereas texts found on websites are not disconnected from the offline social and cultural lives of the producers who create content for these sites, website communication does occur in a technical context that has specific capacities and constraints distinct from offline forms of communication. Specifically, websites afford a hierarchically structured communication space that features hypertextual links that can transmit a Web user to other online communication spaces, such as other websites or social media sites. A website's content exists within this technical context, which is created through the use of code, such as hypertext markup language (HTML) and cascading style sheets (CSS). These forms of code provide the means for a website's producers to make strategic choices about how their website will look, and where, when, and why their site will transmit hyperlinks to another website on the Internet. Therefore, in order to best understand the meaning and function of website narratives about Buddhism, we should include web design and hyperlink connections with the historical, cultural, social, and political context of the stories and storytellers.

In order to properly contextualize narratives within a hyperlink network, we must contend with three methodological challenges: how to analyze the technical and narrative choices made in the online spaces in which we find texts, how to set boundaries to texts, and how to collect and store data. First, we must use a method, or set of methods, that will allow us to analyze the technical and narrative choices made on websites. How we choose these methods depends on the scale of our study and the types of content that we choose to study (such as printed text or images). For example, interpretive analysis on its own may be suitable for a single case study of a webpage, but perhaps less suited for studying an expansive network of hundreds of websites. Second, if we choose to analyze narratives located on multiple websites, it can be difficult to set boundaries to a set of texts, especially when these texts are found among never-ending networks of websites connected via hyperlinks. How do we, as researchers, decide when (and where) a text begins or ends? How do we know when to stop following hyperlinks to other sites when seeking specific types of Buddhist-related stories?

Third, a researcher is also faced with the logistical challenge of how to collect, store, and analyze the immense amount of data that he or she finds online. This challenge can have grave consequences if not attended to, for if there is one thing researchers can count on when it comes to collecting online data, it is that they can't count on their data to always be there in the morning. It is a never-ending life lesson in Buddhist impermanence, rife with frustration and regret. Websites are never truly "finished" and that important page of links to Buddhist resources or articles about Buddhism that you found may no longer exist twenty-four hours later.

This chapter will focus on a study of narratives about Tibet to illustrate why it is important to consider the technical context of online narratives and how one can overcome the methodological challenges discussed above.[1] The narratives under investigation were found on two different—and oppositional—networks of websites: one network of sites that support the Tibet Movement (whose goals may include Tibetan independence from the PRC, greater Tibetan autonomy within the PRC, and/or improved human rights in Tibet), and a network of websites from the PRC that promotes the Chinese Communist Party's (CCP) government propaganda about Tibet and Tibetan refugees. The two methods used to place these narratives in their technical contexts are hyperlink network analysis (HNA) and narrative analysis. HNA is a quantitative method that consists of mapping hyperlink connections between sites, thinking of hyperlinks as social connections, and making sense of these relationships. Narrative analysis is an interpretive method of textual analysis that takes into consideration both the story and the storyteller. I will emphasize how these two methods work in conjunction to situate these narratives among a complex web of social relations between different activist, humanitarian, cultural, and religious organizations. Studying networks of websites makes such a deep analysis of relations possible because they are structurally represented through hyperlinks. I will then address the last two methodological challenges through providing details about the process of sample selection and data collection that utilized the Web crawler and hyperlink mapping program, Issuecrawler[2] and the Web archival software program, HTTrack.[3]

The chapter concludes with some preliminary findings. First, narrative and hyperlink data from these sites suggest that PRC propaganda narratives about religious freedom are a part of a larger narrative framework about improving human rights conditions in Tibet. This framework also encourages the reader to witness these improvements for themselves as a tourist to Tibet. Second, the two Tibet Movement organizations, Canada Tibet Committee and the Australia Tibet Council, use stories that explicitly attempt to appeal to the religious values of their Buddhist readers for the purpose of motivating the reader to donate to the organization and support its goals of bringing about greater religious freedom in Tibet. Of these two organizations, the Canada Tibet Committee appears to have more influence than does Australia Tibet Council in the network. These findings highlight the benefits of using HNA, narrative analysis, and these specific data collection techniques when studying narratives in a network context.

ANALYZING TIBET MOVEMENT NARRATIVES IN AN ISSUE NETWORK

The narratives analyzed in this study concerned the history, politics, and actors involved in supporting or opposing the Tibet Movement. While not all of the narratives were religious narratives, religious themes have played an important role in these stories when activists, governments, Tibetan refugee communities, and other invested stakeholders have told the story of Tibet's history, people, culture, claims to nationhood, current political status, and ongoing human rights concerns. Therefore, narratives about Tibetan monks, the role of Buddhism in Tibetan history and Tibetan society, Buddhist imagery and iconography are important events, actors, and sites within these narratives. The narratives selected for this study were found on thirty-eight separate websites situated within one of two issue networks: an interlinked network of websites that are working on a specific political, social, or cultural issue.[4] Narratives from thirty websites were analyzed from an issue network consisting of approximately two hundred websites supporting the Tibet Movement and eight websites were analyzed from an issue network consisting of approximately twenty websites representing CCP propaganda.

This study conceptually approached the topic of narratives and networks through the theory of sociologist Manuel Castells. Castells's book *Communication Power* (2009) views power as the capacity for a social actor to influence the decisions of another, such as an activist persuading a stranger to support their political cause. For Castells, power is a process of interactions that occur between the various nodes of macro-level social networks, such as news organizations, corporations, and governments, and micro-neurological networks found in the human mind. These neurological networks are what produce different types of human emotions that respond to narratives that attach certain values to a political issue (Castells 2009). Nodes, such as governments or media organizations, that wish to maintain power over these large-scale networks must be able to produce messages that resonate, or elicit a sympathetic emotional response, with the local narratives found in the populace as well as manage and define the types of narratives that are adapted in local contexts (Castells 2009).[5]

To help clarify Castells's understanding of how power is a process between networks and narratives, let's imagine that a local government wants to have a successful advertising campaign to encourage greater use of their new public transit system. Part of the campaign's success in convincing locals to use the transit system relies on it being promoted by a network of organizations and individuals already in power. These may include government representatives that give glowing speeches about the new transit system, media organizations that produce positive news stories about the new transit system, and local businesses that choose to provide their employees with incentives to use public transportation. However, the campaign's success is also strongly reliant on not just the medium of communication (who and what is sending the message), but also on the message itself. If the campaign presents a narrative that embodies the imagined values of the local community—values that are emotionally charged for community members—then the campaign is more likely to succeed than one that does not. If a community prides itself on embodying values of environmental sustainability and feels excited and hopeful about these values, then the campaign message must align greater use of the new transit system with these values in order to succeed in making people change their behavior. In this way, the power to make people change relies on making the message available, having the message encouraged by a network of important social actors (in this example, media organizations, government representatives and local businesses), and making a message that appeals to the public and resonates with their own personal values.

While the example above demonstrates how those already in power (governments, established media, and businesses) can maintain control and change public behavior, activists desiring political change must "reprogram" these same communication networks through creating new value messages that make the public think and feel differently about an issue and motivate them to take action to achieve a specific political goal (Castells 2009). To continue with the example of public transit, if it is a local government that is resistant to building a new transit system, perhaps stating that it would be too costly to construct (a message that may align with community values desiring government thriftiness), activists will need to broadcast a counter-message that aligns with other values already present in the community. In this example, activists could emphasize values of environmental sustainability and deemphasize or refute the narrative of costliness.

However, as those in positions of power already control communication networks in print and television, activists must spread these new messages to the public via alternate methods. Castells (2009) views the Internet as having inherent properties that can provide marginalized communities (and social movements) greater autonomy and power in spreading these messages outside of print and television networks. However, even though these new communication opportunities exist, the new narrative *must* resonate with their intended public's set of values in order for any social change to occur; the Internet, in and of itself, does not create social change (Castells 2009).

In this way, the narrative and hyperlinking strategies of organizations, governments, and other actors that constitute nodes in the two issue networks about Tibet can be analyzed as interrelated variables in the processes of power and social change. Studying website stories about Tibet is important, but so is studying the hyperlinks found on these sites in order to know how accessible these stories may be, and to what other actors and actions a storyteller would like to direct us. In order to pursue this kind of analysis, I had to adopt methods that would illuminate the detailed richness of website content, while also illuminating the broader structural context of hyperlink relations. To this end, I adopted HNA and narrative analysis, which worked in conjunction to analyze the content of each site as well as the structures of each network and hyperlinking strategies of each site.

METHODOLOGICAL CHALLENGES IN ANALYZING NETWORKED NARRATIVES

At the heart of HNA, which developed out of methods of social network analysis,[6] is the researcher's assumption that linking is an inherently social and strategic act (Jackson 1997). These acts are embedded within a Web producer's own culture, history, and personal agenda (Park 2003; Park and Thewall 2003). Examining networks of hyperlinks can provide information about the strategic connections made between organizations, individuals, and groups that each site represents (Garrido and Halavais 2003; Rogers and Marres 2000; Smith 2012; Tremayne, Zheng, Lee, and Jong, 2006), as well as how a user may navigate through the network (Jackson 1997).

This research project on Tibet narratives used a specific type of HNA that maps an issue network. These maps are useful, not only because they provide a macro-level visualization depicting the actors involved in a particular issue, but also because they illustrate who these actors are affiliated with and the strength of ties between actors, or the number of times two websites link to one another. From this type of data, we can infer who has the most influence and authority as an actor of high prestige: that is, who receives the most inlinks from the largest number of sites in the network. We can also learn whether any of the websites act as a bridge, or broker, between sites. This means that a website sits along a path between two unconnected sites (meaning it outlinks to two websites that are not otherwise connected to one another via hyperlinks) and can help a Web visitor move from one site to another.

In conjunction with HNA, I adopted narrative analysis to study the narrative themes and frames of the thirty-eight sites. While there are many interpretive methods for reading website content, I specifically chose narrative analysis, because it has been used in past research to answer questions that focus on complex, subjective meaning-making processes, such as constructing one's national identity as a Tibetan, or constructing the nature of a political or social obstacle in one's path, such as the hardships of becoming a refugee in a foreign country. In particular, narrative analysis can help us to understand how people deal with disruptions to their identity (Riessman 1993) and "critical events" (Webster and Mertova 2007) in order to make sense of their experiences and provide these experiences with meaning within the totality of a person's life story. In the case of Tibet, one example of an identity disruption or critical event would be the Dalai Lama's experience fleeing Tibet and going into exile in India in 1959. Narrative analysis can also uncover how people interpret social reality in ways that empower, or disempower, certain individuals or groups (Moisander and Eriksson 2006), such as social movements or marginalized communities, such as Tibetan refugees. In this way, narrative analysis can help us learn how Tibetans may interpret their experiences and political impact as activists, while also demonstrating how CCP propaganda may narrate the story of the Tibet Movement in a way that attempts to disempower Tibetan refugee influence in Tibet.

Furthermore, narrative analysis places importance not only on the content of these stories, but also on the context in which storytelling takes place. For example, when studying the function and characteristics of website memorials after 9/11, communications scholars Kirsten Foot and Barbara

Warnick and political science scholar Steven Schneider found that narrative practices of memorialization sometimes changed depending on whether they occurred in an offline or online context (Foot, Warnick, and Schneider 2005). They point out that large institutions often create public memorials, such as the Korean War Veterans Memorial in Washington, DC, for the purpose of establishing a uniform narrative about an event (Foot et al. 2005). However, in the case of 9/11 Web memorializing, some large institutions, such as the firm Cantor Fitzgerald, used their website to construct memorials that actively collected individual expressions of mourning from remaining family and friends, such as intimate messages to deceased loved ones (Foot et al. 2005). These individual expressions of mourning created multiple narratives about the tragedy, rather than a uniform institutional narrative (Foot et al. 2005). This suggests that the Web provides a different social context in which narrative types and functions may work in a different way from their offline counterparts.

Since narrative analysis requires knowledge of the context in which storytelling takes place, then a study of narratives found within a network of websites can use HNA to map and measure this context. Furthermore, because HNA alone does not provide any means of interpreting exactly why a website outlinks to another (the textual context in which these links are made), narrative analysis can provide a context for better understanding the HNA data. In this way, narrative analysis and HNA can make up for each other's weaknesses and provide a richer set of findings in terms of understanding what stories about Tibet occur in these networks, the function of these stories, and the relationships between actors telling these stories.

DATA IN FLUX: THINKING THROUGH METHODS OF DATA COLLECTION

As one of the primary goals of this project was to contextualize narratives as they occurred in an issue network during a specific period of time, the data collection plan needed to accomplish the following goals: 1) to choose a sample of sites to undergo narrative analysis and to attempt to ensure that the sample is representative of the different types of actors in the network; and 2) to ensure that the content of sites, information about their hyperlink connections, and data on the overall structure of each issue network was collected at approximately the same time. To accomplish these goals, I utilized the Issuecrawler tool, developed by Internet studies scholar Richard Rogers, to collect preliminary network data for the purpose of choosing a sample. I then used Issuecrawler and HTTrack in conjunction during a one-week period in 2011 to collect a complete network and narrative dataset.

To choose the narrative sample, I selected a series of URLs for conducting a preliminary run of Issuecrawler and set the crawler settings to conduct a co-link analysis within the networks of Tibet Movement and Chinese Communist Party's propaganda sites. A co-link analysis means that the crawler will represent a site as a node in the network if it receives two inlinks from other sites in the network. URLs for the Tibet Movement network were selected from Tibet Online's links page entitled "Major Tibet Sites" (www.tibet.org/siteseeing.html). The URLs to develop the PRC propaganda issue network derived from URL lists from two websites: China Tibet Online (originally the China Tibet Information Center) (eng.tibet.cn) and People's Daily's China Tibet Online (chinatibet.people. com.cn). These two sites were selected because they were listed as the first two English-language sites when searching for the term "Tibet" on China's Google search engine.[7]

After analyzing the results of the two crawls, thirty-eight sites were selected for archiving based on their fulfillment of the following criteria: (1) the rank of a site in the data output produced by the initial crawl, which was based on the number of nodes (other websites) that linked to the site; and (2) whether a site reflected the diversity of sites found within an issue network. For example, in the Tibet Movement issue network, many humanitarian aid sites hold middle to low ranking in the network, however the organizations have very different goals from more prolific, and centralized, activist sites, such as the International Campaign for Tibet (savetibet.org), while also using similar narratives. The small number of sites selected from the propaganda network reflected the few number of sites generated from the initial Issuecrawler results.

The next step was to run the Issuecrawler on the same day as the HTTrack archive software and set HTTrack not only to archive each specific website, but also the pages of any websites that received an outlink from the archived website. This meant that the final dataset would contain the thirty-eight sites as well as any web pages that had received inlinks from one of the thirty-eight sites. This helped to enrich the dataset and provided greater context for why a site created a hyperlink.[8]

After archiving the sample, I conducted a deep reading of the selected sites and generated detailed descriptions of each site's narratives and the contexts in which these narratives were found, in the form of lengthy memos, or short descriptive essays. After completing the memos, I then created categories and subcategories of the types of narratives found on the websites in order to develop cross-site comparisons within and between each issue network. I then placed the raw data output from Issuecrawler into Netminer (Cyram 2013), a social network analysis software application that can measure the influence and authority of each site in terms of its level of centrality in the network. High levels of centrality indicate that a site is well connected to others in the network either through receiving inlinks from a large number of external websites (in-degree centrality) or transmitting outlinks to a large number of external websites (out-degree centrality) (see Table 3.1 and Table 3.2).[9]

Table 3.1 Propaganda Network Websites with Number of Separate Nodes Linking in to Site and In-Degree Centrality Values

Website Name and URL	# of Nodes linking to site	In-Degree Centrality Value
China Tibet Online—English (People's Daily)	5	0.333
China Tibet News—Chinese	5	0.333
Xinhua News	5	0.333
Tibet Culture—English	4	0.267
China Tibet Online—English	4	0.267
China Radio International	4	0.267
Tibet Culture—Chinese	3	0.200
Tibet Travel Magazine	3	0.200
China Tibet News—English	2	0.133
China Tibet Online—Chinese (People's Daily)	2	0.133
China Tibet Online—Chinese	2	0.133
CCTV	2	0.133
Travel China Guide	2	0.133
China Daily	2	0.133
Tibet Human Rights	0	0.000
China's Tibet Magazine	0	0.000

Created by Laura Osburn.

Table 3.2 Top-Ranking Websites with Number of Separate Nodes Linking in to Site and In-Degree Centrality Values

Website Name	# of Nodes linking to site	In-Degree Centrality Value
International Campaign for Tibet	51	0.255
Central Tibetan Administration	48	0.24
Office of HH Dalai Lama	41	0.205
Phayul	35	0.175
Central Tibetan Administration mirror site	32	0.16
Students for a Free Tibet	32	0.16
Tibetan Centre for Human Rights and Democracy	30	0.15
Tibet Online	25	0.125
Free Tibet	24	0.12
Canada Tibet Committee	23	0.115
Voice of Tibet	22	0.11
Tibetan Youth Congress	21	0.105

Created by Laura Osburn.

For example, the Central Tibetan Administration's website (tibet.net) ranks high in in-degree centrality, receiving 980 links from forty-eight websites in the network, but does not transmit links to other sites in the network, leaving the site with zero out-degree centrality. This means that the Central Tibetan Administration appears to hold a position of high prestige in the network (in-degree centrality), since it receives hyperlinks from twenty-four percent of the sites in the network, but is not influential in terms of managing how it directs a user to other sites in the network (out-degree centrality). With zero out-degree centrality, a visitor to the Central Tibetan Administration website may leave the issue network altogether and attempt to find more information about Tibet through a Web search engine, making it possible that their next visit may be to a Tibet Movement website that is not strategically aligned with the Central Tibetan Administration's values and goals, or perhaps even visit one of the PRC propaganda sites.

After using Netminer, I returned to the Web archive to further investigate the locations of specific hyperlinks and their function on the site, such as whether a link was located in a list of link resources, or used to cite a news article. I also returned to the narrative categories developed from the narrative analysis data and reviewed the relationships between a site's narratives and their relationship to other sites in the network. The ability to go back and forth between the website archive, narrative analysis data, and the hyperlink data allowed for investigation into any new insights or questions that arose during data analysis without concern that the content and hyperlinks had changed on the website over time.

PRELIMINARY FINDINGS AND THE IMPORTANCE OF CONTEXT

Several preliminary findings demonstrate the utility of conducting a combination of HNA and narrative analysis when studying narratives on the Web. First, the results of the narrative analysis indicated that CCP propaganda narratives frame government policies as beneficial to Tibetan religious freedom (as well as promoting other forms of human rights for Tibetans). As seen in the example at the beginning of this chapter, CCP's propaganda sites consistently used narratives that framed the government's religious reforms as a method of purifying Tibetan Buddhism from the mire of politics and worldly desires. The sites also provided a historical precedent for control of the Tibetan Buddhist reincarnation system: the Qing dynasty's ritualized use of a golden urn to determine the incarnations of Tibetan Buddhist religious leaders. These websites explained that China adopted the golden urn for this purpose in order to prevent Tibetan political leaders from tarnishing the incarnation system with political interests and "secret deals" (Xinhua 2009b).

This theme of a politics-free Buddhism as a spiritually pure Buddhism is also evident in articles posted on the history of monastic-led riots and protests. In an article found on the Tibet Human Rights website, Tibetologist Liu Wei states, "Those who chant and cultivate themselves in accordance with Buddhist doctrines are real lamas . . . However, those who break the law and do things that have nothing to do with Buddhism should not be considered monks at all" (Xinhuanet 2009). China Tibet Online's article "Religions in Tibet" also reiterates this narrative theme that frames government reforms as mechanisms that liberate Tibetan Buddhism from the impurities of secular concerns and purifies the tradition for authentic religious practice. The website states, "Nowadays, there are no conflicts among religions or among the different sects of Buddhism in Tibet. Modern civilization has not only brought great changes to Tibet, but also make [*sic*] the divine light shine forth from the region's monasteries even more brightly" (China Tibet Online 2005).

While these narratives are in direct response to Tibet Movement narratives about the religious oppression and human rights and are there to persuade the reader to consider the CCP point of view, there is also a secondary goal in providing narratives about improvements in religious freedom: encouraging tourism. Propaganda websites often provided tourism sections on their sites and hosted photographs of tourists and tourism sites (which included many religious sites), tourist-authored travel stories, and news articles that encouraged foreign tourism to Tibet. One of the most explicit invitations to tourists was in the article "Foreigners Asked to Visit Tibet to Experience Traditional Culture" (People's Daily Online 2009). In this article, Syroeskin, the chief researcher of the Presidential Strategy Institute of Kazakhstan, described to the people of Kazakhstan about the cultural activities that he experienced during his 2007 trip to Tibet. After praising the communication and transportation infrastructures in modern Tibet, he states that he found traditional culture still active and supported by Tibetans and Han (People's Daily Online 2009).

This narrative was also embedded in the creation of outlinks transmitted from several propaganda sites (see Figure 3.1). These links were often listed as one of several "related links" or "website links" often showcased at the bottom of a site's front page. For example, Tibet Human Rights listed hyperlinks to other PRC human rights websites, such as Women of China (www.womenofchina.cn), and China Human Rights (www.chinahuman rights.org), along with a link to Travel China Guide (www.travelchinaguide. com), which provides tourism packages to Tibet. Likewise, People's Daily's China Tibet Online website hosted links to other official PRC media organizations, such as China Tibet News (the online version of *Tibet Daily*), while also linking to the government's China Tibet Tourism Bureau website (http://www.xzta.gov.cn/yww/index.shtml) and Travel China Guide. In this way, Web visitors are not only able to read about the CCP's policies of religious freedom, but are also informed that many foreigners misunderstand the reality of Tibet's human rights situation and are encouraged to connect to tourism opportunities and make a visit.

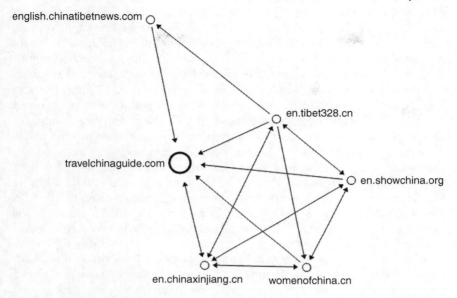

english.chinatibetnews.com

en.tibet328.cn

travelchinaguide.com

en.showchina.org

en.chinaxinjiang.cn   womenofchina.cn

Figure 3.1   Network map of sites linking to Travel China Guide (www.travelchina guide.com). (Created by Laura Osburn)

Another finding was that two Tibet Movement organizations used narratives about religious oppression and religious freedom to specifically resonate with non-Tibetan Buddhist practitioners. On Canada Tibet Committee and Australia Tibet Council, the websites hosted images and texts to emotionally appeal to Buddhist readers by aligning their identification with Buddhism to a personal connection with the Tibetan cause (namely, freedom of religion for other Buddhists). For example, Australia Tibet Council's webpage, "Be a Voice for Tibet" (www.atc.org.au/about-atc-mainmenu-103/be-a-voice-for-tibet-mainmenu-188.html), first asks for a small contribution to the organization, which is followed by a series of images representing Tibet, with the following question posed in large, bold print: "How do you connect to Tibet?" (Australia Tibet Council 2011). The four options of connection presented are "Buddhism," "the environment," "culture," and "human rights." By asking, "How do you connect to Tibet," the site is asking users what issue resonates most with them and their own values? For a practicing Buddhist, the issue that may resonate most powerfully is Buddhism.

As seen in the example at the beginning of this chapter, the Canada Tibet Committee website uses a "Dharma Resource Centre" (tibet.ca/en/newsroom/library/dharma.html) to frame the Tibet Movement cause in a way that aligns Canadian Buddhist identity and values with the need to take action for Tibetans and Tibetan Buddhism. The page opens with a series of quotes, beginning with a quote in large font from the Dalai Lama that states,

"Unless freedom comes to Tibet, then Tibetan Buddhism in Tibet is impossible" (Canada Tibet Committee 2011). This is followed by other quotes, including the 1985 Canadian Chief Justice's definition of religious freedom in Canada, and two statements from the Canada Tibet Committee about working on causes that allow Tibetans to share the same kinds of religious freedoms that Canadian Buddhists enjoy. This is followed by another Dalai Lama quote stating, "To be interested in religion, you have to be involved in politics" (Canada Tibet Committee 2011). The Canada Tibet Committee then makes a plea to Canadian Buddhists to volunteer or contribute donations to their organization (Canada Tibet Committee 2011). As a whole, this space within the Canada Tibet Committee website asserts that China does not support authentic Tibetan Buddhism and that Canadian Buddhists should take action to support efforts for true religious freedom in Tibet. In this way, religious repression is framed as an issue of specific importance for Canadian Buddhists, and that their beliefs and dedication to their religion requires that they join the cause.

With this narrative strategy that appeals to those identifying as Buddhist, we can review whether the sites that carry these messages hold a position of importance in the issue network, which may make it more likely for a Web user to encounter these narratives. As a whole, Canada Tibet Committee holds a relatively high degree of in-degree centrality (see Table 3.2). This suggests that Canada Tibet Committee is a site of relatively high prestige and raises the possibility that someone may visit the "Dharma Resource Centre" page. Australia Tibet Council, however, ranks twenty-first in in-degree centrality (receiving links from only ten nodes), which suggests that Australia Tibet Council does not hold as much prestige in the network, making it less likely that a user will encounter their site or their framing of religious repression as an issue someone can connect to if they have an interest in Buddhism.

If one looks at the local connections between the two sites, one can also see that Canada Tibet Committee appears to be a site of greater prestige and is more likely to be encountered by a Web user wanting to learn more about Tibet (see Figure 3.2). Australia Tibet Council and Canada Tibet Committee both provide outlinks to the Tibet Justice Center (tibetjustice.org) and Tibet Center for Human Rights and Democracy (tchrd.org), however, the Tibet Justice Center and Tibet Center for Human Rights and Democracy only return links to Canada Tibet Committee. As Tibet Center for Human Rights and Democracy is a site with a high level of in-degree centrality (see Table 3.2), the lack of a link to the Australia Tibet Council indicates that the Canada Tibet Committee is more likely to have a visitor encounter these messages about Buddhism. Furthermore, Australia Tibet Council links to Canada Tibet Committee, but Canada Tibet Committee does not return the favor, which places the two in an unequal social relationship. With this information, we can see that, structurally, a Buddhist-information-seeking Web visitor is more likely to encounter Canada Tibet Committee's messages for Buddhist practitioners than the messages found on Australia Tibet Council.

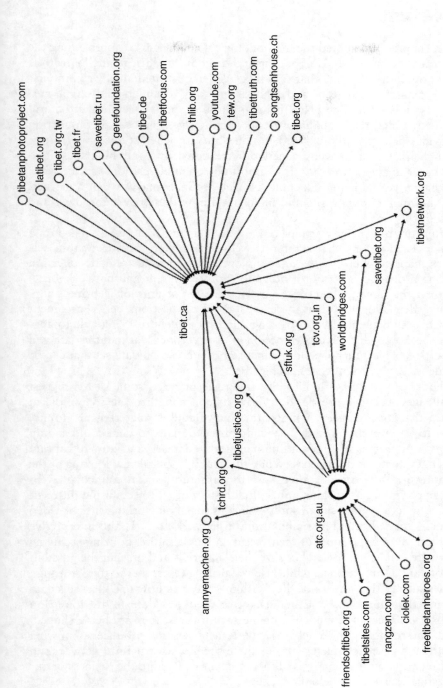

Figure 3.2 Australia Tibet Council (left) and Canada Tibet Committee (right) with inlink connections from direct ties. (Created by Laura Osburn)

CONCLUSION

This chapter highlighted the methodological challenges of approaching the Internet as a site of study about the authority of Buddhist-related narratives and how to handle data that is in flux. As demonstrated above, a combination of narrative analysis and HNA is one way to understand online narratives on websites and place them within their specific technical structural context. Using these qualitative and quantitative methods in conjunction provides data that allows for depth and breadth when studying narratives and their associated website network relations. By combining these two forms of analysis, we can also draw out potential relationships between the narrative and hyperlink choices a Web producer makes when constructing and maintaining a site and understand how these relate to power and authority.

In order to achieve this type of analysis, this research project relied on a data collection plan that combined website archiving software with a network mapping Web crawler and employed both methods of data collection during a one-week period in order to capture content and network structures at the same moment in time. This created a series of website "snapshots" that allows us to make claims about connections between content and hyperlinks while also providing a logistic benefit of being able to analyze the data over an extended period of time without fear that the data will disappear. This data collection plan also provides a rich data set that can be made accessible to other researchers.

For those studying Buddhist texts on the Internet, some of the biggest challenges we have are deciding how to conceptualize the technological space that makes up the context in which Buddhist materials are found, how to set boundaries to that space in order to manage what could end up being a monstrously large and unmanageable dataset, and how to capture this data before it disappears. While this study is specifically looking at the relationship between narratives and the structural–social context of website hyperlink relationships, other Buddhist studies projects using different online spaces as their site of study—such as social networking sites or video games—may also find a combination of network analysis and interpretive methods a useful avenue for their research. Furthermore, utilizing archiving software can help a researcher save their materials and prevent the possibility of data disappearance, while also requiring a researcher to think through issues such as the time frame they wish to study and how to collect this data during that duration. Whether narratives about Buddhism are found on websites, Facebook comments, or message forums, they are being shaped, told, and retold among a network of Internet users and producers; knowing a little about the characteristics of these social and structural networks in combination with an analysis of their content will add to the richness of our investigations into these online texts.

NOTES

1. This chapter is derived from the author's doctoral dissertation (Osburn, forthcoming).
2. Issuecrawler maps networks of websites based on outlinks that are selected by the user. These maps help a user visually locate which websites are concerned on a specific political, social, or cultural issue. The data generated from the crawler can be used in social network analysis software programs to measure relationships between networked sites. For more information, visit govcom. org.
3. HTTrack is a free Web archival software program that copies websites to a local directory, such as your computer or an external hard drive. These "mirrored" sites contain the original site's link structures, as well as the site's HTML, images, and other content. For more information, visit www.httrack. com.
4. For more information on issue networks, see Richard Rogers's (2004) *Information Politics on the Web*.
5. There is a large amount of social movement literature pre-dating *Communication Power*, which provides greater theoretical depth about social activism and framing. For more information please read Snow and Benford's (1998) "Ideology, Frame Resonance, and Participant Mobilization."
6. Social network analysis (SNA) is a quantitative method used to map networks of social relationships, or ties, between nodes that represent individuals or organizations. SNA measures the strength of ties to learn about social influence in a network, as well as the social, economic, and/or cultural benefits of different types of ties. For example, a person who knows many friends or friends of friends, who are active employers in different industries, would have greater social influence (in terms of access to employment opportunities and resources about the job market) than would a person who only has a single friend in human resources.
7. At the time of URL collection, Google.cn was active filtering Tibet Movement sites from the results list, so that PRC-supported sites dominated the first page of results. The search was conducted on March 15, 2010.
8. For example, a site with a page of links listed as "important websites" is different from a context where a link is made to cite an external website's news article on Tibet. The difference is that the creation of an "important websites" page suggests that an organization is actively establishing strategic organizational alliances within the network, not acting as a citation.
9. For more information about basic concepts and measures when conducting SNA or HNA, please read Hanneman and Riddle's (2011) "Concepts and Measurements for Basic Network Analysis."

REFERENCES

Australia Tibet Council. 2011. "Become a Voice for Tibet." Australia Tibet Council. http://www.atc.org.au/about-atc-mainmenu-103/be-a-voice-for-tibet-mainmenu-188.html. Accessed February 8, 2011.
Bureau of Democracy, Human Rights, and Labor. 2009. "China (Includes Tibet, Hong Kong, and Macau)." In *International Religious Freedom Report 2009*. Washington, DC: U.S. Department of State. http://www.state.gov/j/drl/rls/irf/2009/127268.htm. Accessed Febuary 8, 2011.

Canada Tibet Committee. 2011. "Dharma Resource Centre." Canada Tibet Committee. http://www.tibet.ca/en/newsroom/library/dharma.html. Accessed February 8, 2011.

Castells, Manuel. 2009. *Communication Power*. Oxford: Oxford University Press.

China Tibet Online. 2005. "Religions in Tibet." Last modified February 24, 2005. China Tibet Online. http://eng.tibet.cn/2010zj/xzzjgs/201009/t20100917_713546.html. Accessed February 8, 2011.

Cyram. 2013. Netminer 4.1.0. Seoul, South Korea: Cyram Inc.

Foot, Kirsten, Barbara Warnick, and Steven M. Schneider. 2005. "Web-Based Memorializing After September 11: Toward a Conceptual Framework." *Journal of Computer-Mediated Communication* 11(1): article 4. http://jcmc.indiana.edu/vol11/issue1/foot.html. Accessed June 23, 2004.

Garrido, Maria, and Alexander Halavais. 2003. "Mapping Networks of Support for the Zapatista Movement: Applying Social Network Analysis to Understand Contemporary Social Movements." In *Cyberactivism: Online Activism in Theory and Practice*, edited by Martha McAughey and Michael Ayers, 1–23. New York: Routledge.

Hanneman, Robert A., and Mark Riddle. 2011. "Concepts and Measurements for Basic Network Analysis." In *The Sage Handbook of Social Network Analysis*, edited by John Scott and Peter J. Carrington, 340–369. London: Sage.

Jackson, Michele. 1997. "Assessing the Structure of the Communication on the World Wide Web." *Journal of Computer-Mediated Communication* 3(1). http://jcmc.indiana.edu/vol3/issue1/jackson.html. Accessed June 23, 2014.

Moisander, Johanna, and Päivi Eriksson. 2006. "Corporate Narratives of Information Society: Making Up the Mobile Consumer Subject." *Consumption, Markets and Culture* 9(4): 257–275.

Osburn, Laura. Forthcoming. "Networks of Storytellers, Networks of Stories: Relationships between Online Narratives Concerning Tibet and the Tibetan Refugee Community." PhD diss., University of Washington, Seattle.

Park, Han Woo. 2003. "Hyperlink Network Analysis: A New Method for the Study of Social Structure on the Web." *Connections* 25(1): 49–61.

Park, Han Woo, and Mike Thelwall. 2003. "Hyperlink Analyses of the World Wide Web: A Review." *Journal of Computer-Mediated Communication* 8(4). http://jcmc.indiana.edu/vol8/issue4/park.html. Acessed June 23, 2014.

People's Daily Online. 2009. "Foreigners Asked to Visit Tibet to Experience Traditional Culture." China Tibet News. Last modified March 17, 2009. http://english.chinatibetnews.com/voices/2009-03/17/content_216161.htm. Accessed February 8, 2011.

Riessman, Catherine K. 1993. *Narrative Analysis, Qualitative Research Methods*. London: Sage.

Rogers, Richard. 2004. *Information Politics on the Web*. Cambridge, MA: MIT Press.

Rogers, Richard, and Noortje Marres. 2000. "Landscaping Climate Change: A Mapping Technique for Understanding Science and Technology Debates on the World Wide Web." *Public Understanding of Science* 9(2): 141–163.

Smith, Buster G. 2012. "The Tangled Web of Buddhism: An Internet Analysis of Religious Doctrinal Differences." *Contemporary Buddhism* 13(2): 301–319.

Snow, David A., and Robert D. Benford. 1988. "Ideology, Frame Resonance and Participant Mobilization." *International Social Movement Research* 1: 197–217.

Tremayne, Mark, Nan Zheng, Jae Kook Lee, and Jaekwan Jong. 2006. "Issue Publics on the Web: Applying Network Theory to the War Blogosphere." *Journal of Computer-Mediated Communication* 12(1): article 15. http://jcmc.indiana.edu/vol12/issue1/tremayne.html. Accessed June 24, 2014.

Webster, Leonard, and Patricia Mertova. 2007. *Using Narrative Inquiry as a Research Method: An Introduction to Using Critical Event Narrative Analysis in Research on Learning and Teaching.* London: Routledge.

Xinhua. 2009a. "Religious Ritual of Living Buddha Reincarnation." Tibet Human Rights. Last modified March 26, 2009. http://en.tibet328.cn/04/200903/t287021. htm. Accessed February 8, 2011.

———. 2009b. "Tibet's History During Qing Dynasty." China Tibet News. Last modified May 13, 2009. http://english.chinatibetnews.com/Culture/2009–05/13/ content_242871.htm. Accessed February 8, 2011.

Xinhuanet. 2009. "Why Lamas Keep Taking the Lead in Each Riot in Tibet?" Tibet Human Rights. Last modified March 29, 2009. http://en.tibet328. cn/03/1/1/200903/t288230.htm. Accessed February 8, 2011.

4   Toward a Typology and Mapping of the Buddhist Cyberspace

Louise Connelly

Digital technology is developing at an increasingly fast pace and is now accessible through a number of devices. As a result, religion on the Internet is rapidly growing and changing, as well as consisting of many types of overlapping and constantly evolving media and formats, for example: virtual worlds and games such as the Buddha Center in Second Life, mobile applications such as iShrine, websites such as Kagyu Samye Ling monastery and Tibetan Centre, and social media such as The Buddhist Blog.[1] These examples illustrate how Buddhism is emerging online and that this complex environment should be examined in more detail. Heidi Campbell, a pioneer in the field of digital religion, maintains in *When Religion Meets New Media* that there are still "substantive insights" to be gained in a number of areas which future scholars should consider, including Asian religions online and "Buddhist communities' use of new media" (2010, 190–191). Therefore, although there is consensus that Buddhism is a developing area on the Internet, as of yet, there has not been an attempt to categorize the Buddhist cyberspace and to illustrate the complexity and interconnected nature of this specific online environment. This chapter is intended as a first step toward such an exploration.

Due to the vastness and ephemerality of the Internet, it is necessary to identify an approach that will enable us to understand Buddhism in the digital context. Consequently, a categorization of different types of sites and the production of a typology enables such an undertaking. This has been attempted by scholars of religion and digital media, such as Bunt, Helland, and Karaflogka, who have previously presented a number of typologies. Their typologies include an exploration and mapping of the Islamic cyberspace (Bunt 2009), the online religion/religion online classification (Helland 2002), and a categorization of different types of religious websites (Karaflogka 2002, 2006). However, as will be demonstrated, there have been a number of limitations to these typologies, and they do not adequately support the mapping of the Buddhist cyberspace.

Therefore, I propose a "cluster mapping" typology that draws from Bunt, Helland, and Karaflogka, and which proposes four primary categories: virtual worlds and games (VWG), mobile applications (MA), websites (W), and social media (SM). Within the following discussion, it will become apparent that this framework is beneficial where discussions focus on whether the medium is having an impact on traditional Buddhism and, consequently, the emergence of what I refer to as "virtual Buddhism." What I mean by this is whether online Buddhism could engender changes to Buddhist authority, ritual, identity, and communities. While there is not scope to explore these four themes in detail, it is valuable to highlight their importance in relation to the wider conversation pertaining to digital religion (Campbell 2013).

Arguably, mapping the Buddhist cyberspace provides a greater awareness of the construction of this specific environment and also the potential for identifying the possible impact on individuals and Buddhist groups, as well as how religion is being negotiated both online and offline. This is increasingly important in an age when online communication is part of everyday life, as technology can be used to "express and execute . . . beliefs and practices in a wide variety of different forms" (Karaflogka 2006, 150). Potentially, this could result in the emergence of a new type of Buddhism— a type of "virtual Buddhism." That is not to say that up to this point Buddhism has been static. On the contrary, Buddhism has been influenced by and has adapted as a result of politics, geography, and other factors. Therefore, the need to examine Buddhism within the cybercultural context is a natural and necessary undertaking if we are to understand Buddhism in today's world.

Within the past fifteen years, there has been an increasing interest in the academic study of religion and the media, and scholars from different disciplines, including psychology, religious studies, anthropology, and other fields, have raised a number of important questions as well as creating and refining existing methodologies. Among these, three scholars have created specific typologies of religion and the Internet: Gary Bunt (2009), Christopher Helland (2000, 2005), and Anastasia Karaflogka (2002, 2006). Drawing from their approach, it is possible to provide a basis from which to develop a more complete understanding of the shape of religion online, and to consider the challenges and restrictions that exist in relation to examining the religious cyberspace. However, since the creation of these typologies, there have been significant developments and changes in the online environment, such that they do not currently provide a suitable approach for categorizing today's Buddhist cyberspace. Therefore, I have extracted the key elements and I am restructuring them to propose a new typology that includes four categories, namely virtual worlds and games; mobile applications; websites; and social media. The proposed typology will be applied in order to map a section of the Buddhist cyberspace and illustrate the dynamic and interconnected structure of the online environment. In doing so, it raises potential questions as to how Buddhism is represented online and how technology is negotiated by religious organizations and individuals, for example what challenges emerge as a result of Buddhism manifesting online or what is the impact on authority, ritual, community, or identity.

BUDDHIST CYBERSPACE

To begin the discussion, it is important to provide a definition of cyberspace, as often the term is used synonymously with "Internet" or "World Wide Web." The term "cyberspace" was first coined by William Gibson in his novel *Neuromancer* (1993 [1984]), and he likened cyberspace to an online Utopia, a place where anything would be possible. Cyberspace is usually rendered as a notional space or location in which online activities take place. This differs from the term "Internet," which could be said to refer to the actual technology and the platform on which information is shared, and it differs as well from the physical computers through which we participate in this space. It is for this reason that the term "cyberspace" is more appropriate for this discussion, as I will be referring to an online culture and environment that enables users to access information from different devices and be part of the networked society (Campbell 2013, 66).

"Buddhist cyberspace," therefore, can be defined as an online space where individuals and organizations engage with or represent Buddhism and Buddhist communities, identity, ritual, or authority. By addressing each of these themes, a greater understanding of what constitutes the Buddhist cyberspace can emerge. While community and ritual have been addressed to some extent already, the themes of identity and authority as of yet have had little academic attention (Grieve 2010; Lee 2009). Scholars who have examined Buddhist communities include a leading scholar of Buddhism in contemporary society, Charles Prebish, who provided one of the earliest introductions to the study of Buddhism online with *Luminous Passage: The Practice and Study of Buddhism in America* (1999) and later developed the subject in *The Cybersangha: Buddhism on the Internet* (in Dawson and Cowan 2004). Here, Prebish describes the origins of the cybersangha[2] and provides a chronological assessment of some of the different Buddhist communities online, including forums, journals, and real-life communities. Allison Ostrowski, in Chapter 11 of this volume, focuses on communities and their use of the Internet in America, whereas Kim (2005) and Lee (2009) both undertake research into the Korean Buddhist community online. Noticeably, in comparison to the analysis of Islam or Christianity online (see Bunt 2009; Campbell 2010) there is still much to be examined. Ostrowski maintains that there is not enough theory about online Buddhist communities, a view also acknowledged by Hojsgaard and Warburg (2005, 9) and Campbell (2010, 190–193).

Research is also beginning to emerge that focuses on Buddhist ritual online, specifically within the online virtual world of Second Life (Connelly

2010, 2013; both Falcone and Grieve in this volume, Chapter 10 and Chapter 2, respectively). Recently, I explored how Buddhists and non-Buddhists are transporting religious practice online (meditation, spinning virtual prayer wheels, and participating in chanting sessions). For some, meditating online enables them to simultaneously meditate offline and so, in this example, there is no longer a distinct demarcation between the online and offline world (Connelly 2013). The media therefore provides a means by which to engage with religious ritual and potentially change what it means to practice religion. The ramifications of religious practice online could be so extensive that there is a need to explore how individuals and organizations are using online spaces to represent the sacred and practice religion. It is also important to understand how different communication platforms are integrated and how information is disseminated, as these aspects provide further evidence of how Buddhism manifests online.

THREE EXISTING TYPOLOGIES OF RELIGION AND CYBERSPACE

The following section outlines three existing typologies presented by Bunt (2009), Helland (2000, 2005), and Karaflogka (2002, 2006). While all three typologies have useful attributes, I suggest that they do not provide suitable categories to support the current online culture, specifically in relation to how users can access information via newer technologies and engage with Buddhism online.

Gary Bunt

Gary Bunt, a reader in Islamic Studies at the University of Wales, Trinity Saint David, examines the Muslim/Islamic cyberspace which he defines as Cyber Islamic Environments, or CIEs (2009, 46–47). The different platforms (including blogs, social networks, videos, etc.) and aspects (such as, Islamic sects, languages, and relationships) of the CIEs demonstrate how the networks are developing through the Web. This is illustrated as a diagram that "maps the dynamic and evolving series of connections across time and space, itself interlocking with other frameworks and interpretative approaches towards Islam and the Internet" (2009, 45). There are three points which can be extrapolated from this statement: (1) that this is an evolving map, (2) that it needs to be considered alongside other frameworks, and (3) that the boundaries of space and time can be dissipated. By highlighting the importance of interconnectivity, a number of factors require consideration, including how CIEs and Muslims engage online, that the "spiritual is intertwined with the political" (2009, 53), and that it is "no longer a text-only medium" but is multimodal (2009, 286). Moreover, Muslims are responding to changes brought about by the networked society, and, as a result, they are challenging traditional expectations; however, "there is concern within the Muslim community both offline and online about the authority of individuals and websites presenting an 'authentic' Islam" (Campbell and Connelly 2012, 439). Therefore, Bunt's approach to mapping CIEs is an important starting point for mapping the religious cyberspace and provides a number of areas for consideration when mapping the Buddhist cyberspace, specifically the need to highlight the interconnectivity and complexity of the environment.

Christopher Helland

The second typology is presented by Helland, a scholar of sociology of religion at Dalhousie University, Canada, who carried out a survey of websites in 1999. From his analysis, he asserts that there is a demarcation of websites as religion online (informational) and online religion (participatory). Examples of Buddhist websites that could be said to be religion online are university departments or some Buddhist portals or organizations, for example the Network of Buddhist Organisations (http://www.nbo.org.uk/), whereas an example of online religion (participatory) websites would be virtual worlds, such as the Buddha Center in Second Life. Helland also highlights that "it is essential to recognise that the Internet is different things to different people" and the intention of both the site creator and visitor to the site affects how religion is "done" online (2002, 294). Helland (2005) has reconsidered the proposal of the online religion/religion online dichotomy, stating that "at that time there was a clear distinction between religious websites where people could act with unrestricted freedom and a high level of interactivity (online religion) versus the majority of religious websites, which seemed to provide only religious information and not interaction (religion online)" (1).

Helland now argues that there is a merging of religion online and online religion, and no longer can the content of the Internet be clearly categorized as one or the other, as the website will often include both interactive and informative elements. He stresses that the definitions are still "applicable, but it too needs to develop to keep pace with the alterations that have occurred on the Internet medium" (Helland 2005, 2). Dawson and Cowan (2004) present a similar view to that of Helland and conclude, "an increasing number of Web sites fall somewhere between these extremes, offering their visitors some combination of the two" (7). This has become ever more prominent with the introduction of social media sites, as often there will be participatory elements integrated into the informational type of website. For example, a comments feature may be present, or you have the ability to easily share content via the "share" button to your own Twitter, Facebook, or blog followers; or to engage with a synchronous ritual or sermon. The collaborative, participatory, and integrative aspect of cyberspace is more noticeable than ever and, although Helland's categorization of websites is useful, there is no longer a clear demarcation between online religion/religion online, making it necessary to consider how to categorize the current online environment.

Anastasia Karaflogka

The third typology is that presented by Karaflogka, who completed her PhD at the School of Oriental and African Studies, London, in 2006 (2002, 2006). She provides a different approach to Helland and has attempted to categorize various types of websites within a "cyber religious discourse" (Karaflogka 2002, 280). She argues that "a typology [is needed] in order to identify and classify the different approaches, attitudes, applications and functions of religion on and in cyberspace" (Karaflogka 2002, 279). In doing so, she presents the development of a number of typologies—each of which needed refining only a short time after creation—primarily due to the changing nature of the Internet (Karaflogka 2002, 280).

The first typology has four main categories: objective, official webpages, personal, and subjective. The first category, "objective," includes three subcategories: universities, institutions, and academic journals. The second category, "official webpages," includes websites related to religious and non-religious institutions, as well as new religious movements (NRMs). The last two categories are "personal" and "subjective," and include those websites created or owned by individuals or groups, where there may be a critique of other religions or an expression of personal belief (Helland 2002, 280–282).

The second typology was created only a few months after the first one above. This typology has three main areas and many more subcategories than the first typology (Helland 2002, 283). The three main categories are "academic" (originally "objective"); "subjective," which now includes the category of "personal"; and "confessional." Further subcategories were added to enhance each of the main categories. The category "academic" includes subcategories of (1) universities, organizations, institutions, and academic journals; (2) research groups, academic forums, online courses; and (3) online academic books and academic personal publications. The subcategory of "confessional" includes subcategories institutional religions, non-institutional religions, new religious movements, and journals. The third category of "subjective" includes the following subcategories: (1) personal religious groups, discussion forums, and non-religious groups; (2) personalized cyber-rituals and cyber-memorials; and (3) personal publications and magazines (Helland 2002, 283–284).

Karaflogka's list of categories is extensive and includes a wide range of areas. Her typology could be used for mapping Buddhism on the Internet, as these categories are broadly generic; however, it is questionable whether they would be suitable for mapping a cyberspace that has changed dramatically since 2002 (when this typology was first proposed). Moreover, this would be particularly challenging when categorizing sites that are both participatory and informational, and which include integrated platforms—for example a website that encourages participation via comments (e.g., a blog) or collaboration (e.g., a wiki, photo, or video-sharing sites).

Karaflogka's typology also raises an issue in relation to the use of language, as the 2002 typology includes the term "confessional" and contains a subcategory "virtual churches," both of which are not commonly used when examining Buddhism or some other religions on the Internet. While it may never be possible to have a typology that would be suitable for mapping all religions in cyberspace, it is, nevertheless, important to be as inclusive as possible and attempt to avoid normative terminology.

Since Karaflogka's typology in 2002, there have been significant changes not only in the technology but also in how people and organizations are using the Internet (see Campbell 2010, 2013; Wagner 2012). Expectations have shifted from an Internet that was quite static to a mobile culture that is always "switched on." This has resulted in a change in behavior and expectations of how individuals and organizations access information and communicate with each other. Since Karaflogka's categorization, cyberculture within the religious context has changed and is fluid, expanding, and constantly evolving (Karaflogka 2002, 287). This is particularly noticeable with new digital media and the use of mobile devices. Karaflogka's typology does not include a category for mobile applications, which would capture sites such as iShrine: Virtual Buddhist Shrine (http://download. cnet.com/iShrine-Virtual-Buddhist-Shrine/3000–2135_4–10972367.html) or Daily Buddhist Prayers v2 (https://itunes.apple.com/us/app/daily-bud dhist-prayers/id328219107?mt=8). Adding this category to the proposed typology for mapping the Buddhist cyberspace provides an opportunity for researchers to examine how users engage with Buddhism from mobile devices, such as smartphones or tablet devices. Furthermore, it provides opportunities for exploring a more individualistic type of religious engagement that could potentially challenge the traditional concept of religious community (Wagner 2012).

Therefore, similar to Helland's categorization, Karaflogka's typology is not entirely suitable for mapping the current religious cyberspace. This is confirmed by Karaflogka (2006) in her book *e-religion*, where she discusses the 2002 typologies and maintains that they are no longer fit for the purpose and she considers how cyberspace should be examined in light of the constantly changing medium. She states that there are features that need to be considered "such as ephemerality, hypertext links and hypermedia that form distinct and exclusive characteristics, and the important role they play in the construction, formation and dissemination of e-religion" (Karaflogka 2006, 148). Karaflogka (2006, 151) also argues that the online religious landscape provides new opportunities for research into traditional and new religious presences. It is evident that the existing typologies and methodologies for examining an ephemeral environment require continual reflection and adaptation.

TOWARD A NEW TYPOLOGY

A number of approaches could be taken in order to map the Buddhist cyberspace, including a map comprising the Internet Service Providers (ISP) or Internet Protocols (IP) of the websites and visitors. This would focus on the infrastructure rather than the content of the sites and would certainly help to identify owners of the sites and perhaps where they are physically located within the world. However, this would not help facilitate mapping the content, categories of sites, or how they are interconnected. Therefore, I propose a typology that draws from the typologies presented by Bunt, Helland, and Karaflogka and lays out four primary categories, namely, virtual worlds and games (VWG), mobile applications (MA), websites (W), and social media (SM). In addition, each category has been allocated an indicator key (as shown in brackets and in Figure 4.1), as this will be used in the mapping, as discussed in the next section.

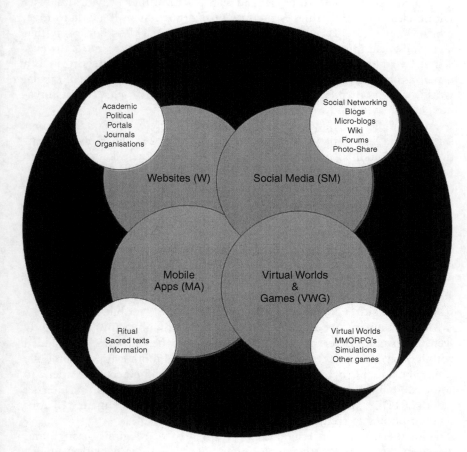

Figure 4.1 Proposed typology—main category and associated sites (cluster). (Created by Louise Connelly)

The rationale for identifying an independent category that solely relates to virtual worlds and games (VWG) can be qualified by the current scholarly work in the area of Buddhism in Second Life (Connelly 2010, 2013; Grieve 2010; Radde-Antweiler 2008; and Falcone, Chapter 10 in this volume). The category of "virtual worlds and games" is probably the simplest type of platform to identify, as it is often clearly branded as a virtual world or game by the creator/owner of the site. With that said, the definition of "games" and "virtual worlds" is often contested (Wagner 2012, 5), and so it is important to present a definition of both games and virtual worlds to ensure clarity. A virtual world can be defined as an online community where users can interact, feel immersed, and have a sense of presence. A virtual world will often require the user to create an avatar (persona or identity) through which they will interact with other avatars. Virtual worlds can include massive multiplayer online role-playing games (MMORPG), or social worlds or simulation platforms.

In contrast, a game can be defined as a platform that provides the user with a clear objective, rules, structure, or end goal, as well as a narrative, which Wagner (2012) refers to as "storytelling" (5). This is not to say that a virtual world cannot also be a game, such as *World of Warcraft*. However a social virtual world such as Second Life is generally not categorized as a game, as there is no goal or reward structure, rather it is a social virtual world, with its own currency (Linden dollars), in which participants (avatars) engage with one another (Connelly 2013, 128).

An example of a Buddhist location in Second Life is the Buddha Center (http://secondlife.com/, in-world address, 137, 130, 21), where avatars participate in Buddhist meditation, spin virtual prayer wheels, and listen to Buddhist sermons (Connelly 2010, 2013). In relation to Buddhist games on the Internet, an example is the Dharma Games website (http://www.dharmagames.org/), which states that the games will help users to learn Buddhist principles. The games include collecting lotuses while avoiding monsters that represent bad deeds. Another game on the site is to deliver prayer flags for a festival while avoiding Mara's demons (Mara is often depicted as luring the Buddha or individuals from the spiritual path). These examples illustrate the different type of sites within this category where visitors engage with Buddhist practice or concepts.

The second category within this typology is that of "mobile applications" (MA), which merits its own category, as the use of mobile apps has recently seen a substantial increase and could be said to be, for some, embedded within everyday life. Trends indicate that the use of mobile apps and mobile technology are likely to increase in the future, with 35 percent of American adults owning a smartphone, 87 percent using this to access the Internet (Smith 2011, 1), and a typical smartphone user having approximately 18 apps on their phone (Purcell, Entner, and Henderson 2010, 4).

With the increase in religious apps, this area of religious activity and development requires further exploration, potentially aligning with Wagner's six categories, which are religious apps relating to (1) prayer, (2) ritual, (3) sacred texts, (4) social media, (5) self-expression, and (6) meditation (Wagner 2012, 102–105). The rationale for assigning a specific category for the Buddhist mobile app (MA) rather than including it within the category for websites (W) is twofold. First, the website is purely a hosting platform from which users can download the app, rather than actually engaging with the app. For example, iShrine enables users to light virtual incense and this is done via the app on the mobile device, not the website that simply hosts the download of the app. Second, the religious app is an area that is likely to see considerable development in the future and so having a specific category for this will target an area of Buddhism online that has had little attention up to this point.

Notably, Wagner claims that the smartphone app could be changing the concept of religion and providing us with a more individualistic style of religion, as opposed to a communal religion, as technology provides "us with the ability to collect 'apps' that support our beliefs, habits, and current preferences" (2012, 102). If this is true, then it challenges us to negotiate the use of media in relation to our personal belief structures and our understanding of religious identity. The ability to personalize and customize religious space via the app potentially provides users with greater opportunities to explore different religions and re-form existing ones.

The third category is "social media" (SM), which can be defined as platforms that provide users with the ability to share, interact, or create information with other users. For example, a Facebook page provides users with the option to write comments/upload images or "like" posts made by others. Examples of social media within this category include social networking sites, such as Facebook; blogging and micro-blogging platforms, such as Blogger, Wordpress, or Twitter; photo or video sharing sites, such as Flickr or YouTube; and collaborative information tools, such as wikis. A good illustration of a Buddhist social media site is the Facebook page for the Kannonji Zen Retreat, which relates to a Zen Buddhist community (sangha) in Second Life. The plethora of social media platforms is vast and continues to expand, making it important to capture this aspect of the Internet.

Moreover, this category encapsulates the participatory element that Jenkins (2009) defines as "a culture with . . . strong support for creating and sharing creations, and some type of informal mentorship whereby experienced participants pass along knowledge to novices" (xi). Some other definitions are proposed by Cheong, Poon, Huang, and Casas (2009), who refer to the "interactivity between users" (293), and Rettberg (2008), who defines blogs as "digitally mediated social networks" (64). Furthermore, the participatory aspect of popular culture where individuals present themselves to others can enable a person to make meaning out of everyday life (Lynch 2002, 65). Even the mundane intricacies of everyday life can have significance as it results in unique experiences for the person who is participating with the site (Goffman 1969, 28–82).

One of the features of social media is the deep integration between and among different platforms. For example, a user can tweet and this will immediately show on their Facebook page, or they may have their Twitter feed integrated into their blog or website. The ability to use social media to engage with different audiences simultaneously can be a powerful tool for religious organizations (and individuals). Erica Baffelli (2013) discusses an example of this in relation to Japanese New Religious Movements and their use of video sharing sites to legitimate their organization and belief structure.

The final category is "websites" (W), which includes organizations, institutions, journals, and academic sites. These are similar to the categories presented in Karaflogka's typology and also align with Helland's "informational" category. With the integration of different media and accessibility of the Internet through other devices (iPad, smartphone, etc.), a website can no longer be easily categorized into the religion online/online religion framework. It is for this reason that this category is intended to cover websites that cannot be defined solely as one of the other three categories; namely, (1) games and virtual worlds, (2) social media, or (3) a mobile application. They may, however, be host to other categories, such as a social media feed or a link to download a mobile app. In many instances, the website will be presented as the hub or main platform in relation to these other integrated platforms.

One of the challenges with presenting a typology, such as the one above, is how to visually illustrate the main categories as well as the integration between categories. It is for this reason that a hierarchical depiction has not been used, and instead I propose a cluster diagram (see Figure 4.1). The diagram illustrates the potential for integration between the four main categories, as well as examples of the type of sites associated with each of the four categories.

THE MAPPING OF THE BUDDHIST CYBERSPACE

As has been outlined earlier in this chapter, cyberspace can be considered as a space without geographic boundaries. Maps of the Internet are not necessarily objective or complete, as "space–time laws of physics have little meaning online. This is because space on the Internet is purely relational. Cyberspace consists of many different media, all of which are constructions; that is, they are not natural but solely the production of their designers and, in many cases, users" (Dodge and Kitchin 2001, 3). Any attempt to map a fluid environment is therefore challenging and would benefit from an interdisciplinary approach (Hojsgaard and Warburg 2005, 9), in order to examine the culture and content of cyberspace (Campbell 2013; Cheong et al. 2009, 293).

The process of mapping the Buddhist cyberspace involves two stages. The first is the sourcing of the website and identifying whether it is the main/primary website or an integrated site and then assigning the associated categorization. This will provide a basis from which to commence building the cluster map. For example, a university website (W) may include a blog or Twitter feed (SM), but ultimately the website is the primary website/platform. To some extent, this may be subjective but generally the intention and purpose of the site will be clearly identified by the owner/creator.

The second stage is the identification of the integrated platform/category associated with the main category and then assigning one of the four categories (virtual worlds and games; social media; mobile app; website). This is where the cluster mapping begins to emerge, as there may be a number of interconnected categories. By taking this approach, there is no longer a clear demarcation of religious sites/platforms; rather, there is a depiction of an integrated online environment. For example, when considering a Buddhist group, community, or individual presented on the Internet, there may be multiple categories represented, as befits the integrated nature of digital technology. Therefore, it is important that the approach taken here incorporates the interconnected nature of the different platforms. By capturing this, we begin to understand how the Internet is being used, by whom and for what, and this provides an opportunity to address some of the six research concerns presented by Dawson and Cowan (2004, 10–11): (1) improved studies on how the Internet is being used and by whom, (2) a study of "the nature and quality of people's experiences," (3) understanding the negotiation of religious practice offline and online, (4) comparative studies, (5) identifying the implications of technology on religion, and (6) whether one type of religion is more suited to the Internet than others. In addition, mapping the Buddhist cyberspace could help to determine whether the increase in religious practice online is challenging "the assumption of access, spatial reach, and responsibilities of religious organizations" (Cheong et al. 2009, 291). By mapping this specific cyberspace, as well as others, it could indicate where there are trends, similarities, or notable differences between different religious cyberspaces, thus providing a detailed depiction of religion on the Internet.

To further explain how the Buddhist cyberspace can be mapped, the following provides a snapshot of eight different Buddhist platforms/websites in the Buddhist cyberspace using the typology, as shown in Figure 4.2. The example includes two Buddhist blogs, two Buddhist communities in Second Life, a website for an offline organization, a journal, a Buddhist Studies department at a university, and a mobile application. The two-stage process is applied and the primary category is identified and subsequently the integrated categories are sourced and categorized. The second stage may not always be necessary, as exemplified with the Journal of Global Buddhism website (W), which does not connect with any other sites/categories and so stands alone in the diagram.

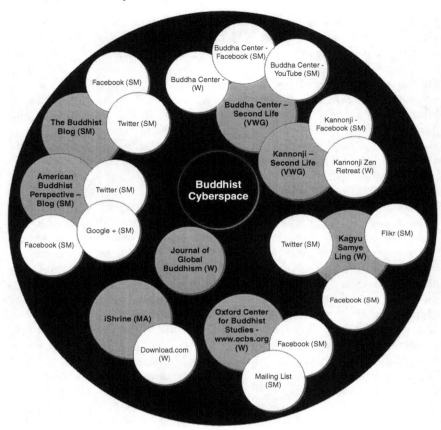

Figure 4.2 An extract of the Buddhist Cyberspace mapped using the proposed typology. (Created by Louise Connelly)

Exploring this in more detail, the Virtual Worlds and Games (VWG) category includes two Second Life locations (the Buddha Center and Kannonji), which are shown to overlap in the diagram, as they both belong to the same virtual world (Second Life). They each have a number of integrated categories, associated with the Buddhist community in Second Life, including a Facebook profile (SM) and a website (W). For the purpose of this exercise, two websites (Oxford Centre for Buddhist Studies and Kagyu Samye Ling) have been chosen to illustrate how the website (W) category could be mapped within the Buddhist cyberspace. However, if further websites were to be included, they may overlap if they contain hyperlinks to each other.

Further examples of integration are illustrated in relation to the two blogs: The Buddhist blog, (http://www.thebuddhistblog.blogspot.co.uk/)

and The American Buddhist Perspective, (http://www.patheos.com/blogs/americanbuddhist/) which link to each other through their blogroll (a list of links to blogs recommended by the blogger). This is typical of the blog community, as two in five (41 percent) bloggers have a blogroll (Lenhart and Fox 2006, 38).

What begins to emerge is a complex interconnected diagram of a very small section of the Buddhist cyberspace. If this were to be expanded further, there would be further connections and mini cluster maps created in relation to a much bigger and more complex map of the Buddhist cyberspace.

What can be concluded from this snapshot and cluster map (Figure 4.2) is that the Buddhist cyberspace is both large and complex and will require further examination and mapping in order to assess what impact, if any, the Internet is having in relation to individuals and organizations, as well as implications for the four areas identified earlier in the chapter, namely authority, community, identity, and ritual. Moreover, the typology will require constant refinement in order to meet the needs of this constantly changing environment.

CONCLUSION

In this chapter, I have introduced the concept of "virtual Buddhism," established why a typology is needed, examined existing typologies and proposed a new typology. Finally, I have illustrated how a small section of the Buddhist cyberspace would look if this typology were to be used. In addition, the relationship between technology and religion and the potential impact technology may have in relation to the four themes of authority, community, identity, and ritual has been introduced, however further examination of these areas is needed.

It is important to acknowledge the valuable contribution that Bunt (2009), Helland (2002, 2005), and Karaflogka (2002, 2006) provide for categorizing the religious cyberspace, even if, by their own admission, these typologies no longer fit the purpose. Nevertheless, they provide a starting point and an approach that can be considered, developed, and redefined to enable the mapping of the Buddhist cyberspace. Consequently, the proposed typology includes four distinct categories and by applying this typology, it is possible to create a representation of the Buddhist cyberspace. This has been visually depicted as a cluster diagram rather than a hierarchical model, and in doing so it captures the integration between the main category and the integrated categories. Significantly, this illustrates the construction and complexity of the Internet, thus demonstrating how the Internet is being used and for what.

Understanding how Buddhism online is being expressed, explored, and potentially repurposed by individuals and organizations enables a greater awareness of what it means to be Buddhist and to engage with Buddhism

in the online context. To some extent, technology "may encourage the creation and development of new religious structures" (Karaflogka 2006, 148),
and, if this is occurring, then it could impact on traditional constructs of
Buddhism, resulting in the emergence of a new type of Buddhism—virtual
Buddhism. The emergence of virtual Buddhism could potentially result in
changes to Buddhist authority, community, identity, and ritual. For example,
Buddhist ritual might be led by individuals online, who claim to be a voice
of authority but would not be accepted as such offline. As a result, possible
tensions are created between traditional and online religions. On the other
hand, many traditional Buddhist organizations are using the Internet to
engage with a wider audience. Therefore, the Internet can both "empower
and challenge" traditional religion (Campbell 2013, 15).

By exploring the Buddhist cyberspace, we see that there are a number of
specific changes arising in relation to the online and offline paradigm. For
some, there is a negotiation and blurring between the offline and online
space. This is clearly illustrated at the Buddha Center in Second Life, where
many of the participants will meditate offline at the same time as their avatar is sitting on a virtual meditation cushion in the Buddhist temple in Second Life. Many participants meditate in this way because they may not
have offline access to a Buddhist teacher or facilitator. In this way, Second
Life provides an opportunity to meditate with other like-minded individuals and be a member of a Buddhist community (Connelly 2013; Ostrowski,
Chapter 11, this volume). In addition, the use of virtual artifacts in online
rituals, such as a meditation cushion, incense, and a singing bowl, provides
the ritual with perceived authenticity and equates it to rituals found offline
(Connelly 2013, 134).

Another example where the online/offline boundary is blurred is the use
of blogging as a means of religious practice in the Korean Won Buddhist
community (Lee 2009). Lee (2009, 99) examines the use of blogging as a
tool for Buddhist monks to "cultivate the self" by maintaining an online
diary. The blog provides a means by which monastic monks and nuns
can record their spiritual journey and share this with the public if they so
choose. In doing so, a dialogue can take place with potential followers. Lee's
research illustrates that blogs are a prominent platform within the online
religious landscape, which Schneider and Braunstein (2010) maintain is due
to "their ease of publication and use" (8). They go on to say:

blogs have changed the shape of public discourse in society as a whole
and around religious questions in particular . . . blogging is a powerful
and flexible medium, one uniquely suited to providing the space for
vibrant, diverse, and productive discussions about religion.

(Schneider and Braunstein 2010, 8)

Therefore, if we use the proposed typology to map the Buddhist cyberspace, it will enable a greater understanding of Buddhism in the twenty-first

century. In addition, it will allow conclusions to be drawn and align with the scholarly consensus that religion and media "are meeting on common turf: the everyday world of lived experience" (Hoover and Clark 2002, 2), and that "the study of lived, popular cultures can inform our broader concepts of religion and the sacred" (Lynch 2007, 158). This analysis, then, can help us to understand religion within modern cultures, through examining how media is being used to develop religious identities and communities.

Initial findings indicate that this approach will work, however further analysis and refinement will be required in order to address the challenges and questions that arise when dealing with the constantly changing landscape, as "cyberspace is more than a simple map" (Karaflogka 2002, 287). Importantly, any mapping exercise will only provide a snapshot at a specific time, as the ephemerality of the Internet cannot be overcome. This is just the beginning but it could provide a basis from which further detailed mapping takes place, and thus provide a valuable contribution to research within media, religion, and culture studies as well as other disciplines. Ultimately, by exploring the changing religious landscape through different approaches, including mapping the Buddhist cyberspace, we can come to a greater understanding of the relationship between technology and Buddhism.

NOTES

1. For example, Second Life, http://secondlife.com/; Virtual Buddhist Shrine, http://download.cnet.com/iShrine-Virtual-Buddhist-Shrine/3000–2135_4–10972367; Samye Ling, http://www.samyeling.org/; and The Buddhist Blog, http://thebuddhistblog.blogspot.co.uk/.
2. According to Prebish (1999, 203), Gary Ray first coined this phrase in 1991.

REFERENCES

Baffelli, Erica. 2013. "Japanese New Religions Online: Hikari no Wa and "Net Religion." In *Digital Religion: Understanding Religious Practice in New Media Worlds*, edited by Heidi Campbell, 207–214. London: Routledge.

Bunt, G. R. 2009. *iMuslims: Rewiring the House of Islam*. London: Hurst.

Campbell, H. 2010. *When Religion Meets New Media*. London: Routledge.

———. 2013. *Digital Religion: Understanding Religious Practice in New Media Worlds*. London: Routledge.

Campbell, H. A., and L. Connelly. 2012. "Cyber Behavior and Religious Practice on the Internet." In *Encyclopedia of Cyber Behavior*, edited by Z. Yan, 434–446. Hershey, PA: IGI Global.

Cheong, P. H., J. H. Poon, S. Huang, and I. Casas. 2009. "The Internet Highway and Religious Communities: Mapping and Contesting Spaces in Religion-Online." *The Information Society* 25(5): 291–302.

Connelly, L. 2010. "Virtual Buddhism: An Analysis of Aesthetics in Relation to Religious Practice within Second Life." *Heidelberg Journal of Religions on the Internet* 4(1). doi: http://dx.doi.org/10.11588/rel.2010.1.9383.

————. 2013. "Virtual Buddhism: Buddhist ritual in Second Life." In *Digital Religion: Understanding Religious Practice in New Media Worlds,* edited by H. Campbell, 128–135. London: Routledge.

Dawson, L. L., and D. Cowan, eds. 2004. *Religion Online: Finding Faith on the Internet.* London: Routledge.

Dodge, M., and R. Kitchin. 2001. *Atlas of Cyberspace.* London: Pearson Education.

Gibson, W. 1993 [1984]. *Neuromancer.* London: Harper Collins.

Goffman, E. 1969. *The Presentation of Self in Everyday Life.* London: Allen Lane.

Grieve, G. 2010. "Virtually Embodying the Field: Silent Online Meditation, Immersion, and the Cardean Ethnographic Method." *Heidelberg Journal of Religions on the Internet* 4(1). doi: http://dx.doi.org/10.11588/rel.2010.1.9384.

Helland, C. 2000. "Online Religion/Religion Online and Virtual Communitas." In *Religion on the Internet: Research Prospects and Promises, Religion and the Social Order,* edited by D. E. Cowan and J. K. Hadden, 205–223. New York: JAI Press.

————. 2002. "Surfing for Salvation." *Religion* 32(1): 292–302.

————. 2005. "Online Religion as Lived Religion: Methodological Issues in the Study of Religious Participation on the Internet." *Heidelberg Journal of Religions on the Internet* 1(1). doi: http://dx.doi.org/10.11588/rel.2005.1.380.

Hojsgaard, M. T., and M. Warburg, eds. 2005. *Religion and Cyberspace.* London: Routledge.

Hoover, S. M., and L. S. Clark. 2002. *Practicing Religion in the Age of the Media: Explorations in Media, Religion, and Culture.* New York: Columbia University Press.

Jenkins, H. 2009. *Confronting the Challenges of Participatory Culture: Media Education for the 21st Century.* Cambridge, MA: MIT Press.

Karaflogka, A. 2002. "Religious Discourse in Cyberspace." *Religion* 32(4): 279–291.

————. 2006. *e-religion.* London: Equinox Publishing.

Kim, M. C. 2005. "Online Buddhist Community: An Alternative Religious Organization in the Information Age." In *Religion and Cyberspace,* edited by M. Hojsgaard and M. Warburg, 138–148. London: Routledge.

Lee, J. 2009. "Cultivating the Self in Cyberspace: The Use of Personal Blogs among Buddhist Priests." *Journal of Media and Religion* 8(2): 97–114.

Lenhart, A., and Fox, S. 2006. *Bloggers.* PEW Internet & American Life Project. http://www.pewinternet.org/2006/07/19/bloggers/.

Lynch, G. 2002. *After Religion: "Generation X" and the Search for Meaning.* London: Darton, Longman and Todd.

————. 2007. *Between Sacred and Profane: Researching Religion and Popular Culture.* London: I.B. Tauris.

Ostrowski, A. 2006. "Buddha Browsing: American Buddhism and the Internet." *Contemporary Buddhism* 7(1): 91–103.

Prebish, C. S. 1999. *Luminous Passage: The Practice and Study of Buddhism in America.* Berkeley: University of California Press.

————. 2004. "The Cybersangha: Buddhism on the Internet." In *Religion Online: Finding Faith on the Internet,* edited by D. Cowan and L. L. Dawson, 135–150. New York: Routledge.

Purcell, K., R. Entner, and N. Henderson. 2010. "The Rise of Apps Culture." Pew American Life Project. http://www.pewinternet.org/2010/09/14/the-rise-of-apps-culture/.

Radde-Antweiler, K. 2008. "An Approach to Religious and Ritual Typography of Second Life." *Heidelberg Journal of Religions on the Internet* 3(1). doi: http://dx.doi.org/10.11588/rel.2008.1.393.

Rettberg, J. W. 2008. *Blogging.* Cambridge, UK: Polity Press.

Schneider, N., and R. Braunstein. 2010. *The New Landscape of the Religious Blogosphere.* Social Science Research Council. http://blogs.ssrc.org/tif/religion-blogosphere/.

Smith, A. 2011. "35% of American Adults Own a Smartphone." Pew American Life Project. http://www.pewinternet.org/2011/07/11/smartphone-adoption-and-usage/.

Wagner, R. 2012. *Godwired: Religion, Ritual and Virtual Reality.* New York: Routledge.

Part II

Historical Approaches

5 Online Peer-Reviewed Journals in Buddhism

The Birth of the Journals of Buddhist Ethics and Global Buddhism

Charles S. Prebish

In my book *Luminous Passage: The Practice and Study of Buddhism in America* (Prebish 1999), I related a fanciful story about a lunchtime conversation that took place at the founding meeting of the International Association of Buddhist Studies (IABS) in Madison, Wisconsin, in 1976. The gist of the conversation revolved around the presumably wishful thinking of a group of young scholars imagining a future time when computers could be programmed with the entire grammar and lexicon of the Sanskrit, Pali, Chinese, Tibetan, and Japanese languages, and then instantly deliver impeccably accurate, totally spontaneous, and completely cross-referenced translations of Buddhist texts. Nobody even thought of suggesting that it would be helpful to have all of those computers networked, because none of those lunchtime discussants had ever actually touched a computer. Now, little more than a quarter-century later, every one of those members present at the discussion spends a major portion of their day sitting in front of a computer screen, cell phone, or tablet—sometimes in an airport, hotel room, or park—reading and composing electronic mail, engaging in social networking, and tweeting in a worldwide Buddha-field that is only a mouse-click or even voice-command away, and creating sophisticated scholarship that includes characters from all of the languages mentioned above.

It took nearly a decade for any seeds of that 1976 discussion to bear fruit. At its 1983 meeting in Tokyo, the IABS formed a "Committee on Buddhist Studies and Computers." And it was more than another decade until Jamie Hubbard's amusing and engaging article, "Upping the Ante: budstud@millenium.end.edu," appeared in the Winter 1995 issue of the *Journal of the International Association of Buddhist Studies*, outlining his early experiences and frustrations with computers in Buddhist studies. In his article, Hubbard noted, "The three major aspects of computer technology that most visibly have taken over older technologies are word processing, electronic communication, and the development of large-scale archives of both text and visual materials" (Hubbard 1995, 309). By the end of the century, computer technology had become sufficiently important to the discipline of Buddhist studies that the Twelfth Conference of the IABS, held in Lausanne, Switzerland, on August 23–28, 1999, devoted two entire panels to the topic. This paper addresses the second of Hubbard's concerns—electronic communication—and focuses on the creation of the first scholarly online journals in Buddhist studies (and the entire field of religious studies, as well).

THE FORMATIVE PROCESS

In the January 1979 issue of *Religious Studies Review*, Frank Reynolds of the University of Chicago wrote an important and useful article entitled "Buddhist Ethics: A Bibliographical Essay." Curiously, though, he began his piece with the somewhat discomforting note, "Unfortunately, modern scholars have devoted relatively little attention to the study of Buddhist ethics" (Reynolds 1979, 40). Considering the importance of ethical conduct in the lives of hundreds of millions of practicing Buddhists, Reynolds's assessment, although accurate, was lamentable. By October 1992, when Charles Hallisey published "Recent Work on Buddhist Ethics" as the follow-up to the *Religious Studies Review*'s first effort in this area, things had changed dramatically, both in terms of the volume of publications on Buddhist ethics and their scope (Hallisey 1992, 276–285).

Shortly thereafter, as a testament to the burgeoning interest in Buddhist ethics as a worthy scholarly field of inquiry, I approached a number of university presses about the possibility of beginning a traditional, hardcopy journal devoted solely to research in Buddhist ethics. The disconcerting reality, explained in careful detail by each press, was that small, specialized, scholarly journals were expensive to produce, maintain, and distribute, thus resulting in a major financial loss for the sponsoring press.

The project was immediately shelved . . . until May 1994. In early May, as a result of a review article written by me on Damien Keown's *The Nature of Buddhist Ethics* (Prebish 1993, 95–108), Keown and I began to communicate via email about our shared interest in Buddhist ethics. It didn't take the trans-Atlantic discussion very long before the issue of a journal devoted to Buddhist ethics came up. Previously unknown to me, Keown had lots of computer experience and technical knowledge, so quite literally within a few days and somewhat unexpectedly, Keown popped up with the electronic question: "Why don't we create an electronic journal?" I responded in the affirmative, but because I considered my own computer skills less than adequate for the anticipated task, I immediately consulted Wayne Husted, a Penn State religious studies colleague who had helped me set up my computer, complete with electronic mail. Husted felt it was a great idea and suggested that the journal could be made available through FTP, Gopher, and the World Wide Web. This would allow individuals with minimal facilities and systems to access the journal via anonymous FTP, and those with full Internet access and higher-end equipment to read the journal online via the World Wide Web. Both individuals and university libraries could utilize Gopher. At that point, I was embarrassed to admit that I didn't know what

FTP, Gopher, and the World Wide Web were, much less how they applied, but Husted and Keown supplied an intensive, albeit speedy, course on computer literacy, and soon the three of us were engaged in a month-long plan to launch the aptly named *Journal of Buddhist Ethics (JBE)*.

We decided that an academic, peer-reviewed journal should have a proper editorial board of outstanding scholars in the subject area of the journal, so we began identifying and contacting potential editorial board members, hoping to reinforce our own initial notion about the efficacy of the proposed journal as well as solicit the participation of these renowned scholars. Within a month, we had lined up twelve highly respected members of the Buddhist studies establishment to serve on the editorial board. However, since nobody was certain if a Buddhist ethics journal would be attractive to denizens of the Internet, the newly identified editors conferred, and decided that when announced, it would also be useful to solicit subscriptions from potential readers, asking them to send their names and email addresses. While the *JBE* would be free, and indeed not distributed, but instead offered on a "self-serve" basis, this list of subscribers could be used to distribute information regarding materials as they would be added to the continuously published journal. Beyond this, a list of subscribers would be a means of determining how many people were sufficiently interested in the *JBE* to make the effort to "subscribe." Now all we had to do was implement our vision!

Keown and I began to define the parameters of the scholarly extent of our effort. Over several weeks of intensive discussion, careful thought was given to the production of a brochure that would describe the aims, policies, topics, subscription methods, submission procedures, and other matters. The two most critical features involved defining why one should create such a journal in the first place, and what topics should be included. Regarding the former, we discovered that while other disciplines had utilized the electronic format for peer-reviewed journals for some time, Buddhist studies and religious studies had not. Investigation of the Internet revealed not one comprehensive peer-reviewed journal in either of those entire fields. The closest efforts were a book review journal known as *Ioudaios*, published in Canada, and a partly refereed journal known as *Gassho*, published almost single-handedly by Barry Kapke (under the auspices of "DharmaNet International," an electronic network based in Berkeley, California). For the latter issue, Keown and I delineated a list of ten topic areas: (1) Vinaya and jurisprudence; (2) medical ethics; (3) philosophical ethics; (4) human rights; (5) ethics and psychology; (6) ecology, animals, and the environment; (7) social and political philosophy; (8) cross-cultural ethics; (9) ethics and anthropology; and (10) interfaith dialogue on ethics. As a final touch, in hopes of providing a useful service to potential subscribers, we decided to include a "Global Resource Center" in the journal's World Wide Web site, providing links to every other electronic Buddhist resource we could locate in the world, and a section called "Bulletins," in which various announcements of importance for Buddhist studies scholars could be posted.

Husted, Keown, and I recognized the potential that an online journal would have for the quick and efficient publication of material. In this spirit, it was decided to have individuals submit manuscripts for consideration via email or on a computer disk in any popular word-processing format (e.g., WordPerfect or Microsoft Word), with a second copy in human-readable ASCII format. At that stage, there would be no requirement to conform to any one standard layout or style sheet, or to show foreign language diacritics. A copy of the manuscript would then be distributed to the appropriate members of the editorial board for blind peer review. If the manuscript was accepted for publication, the author would be notified and asked to revise and/or reformat the manuscript following conventions given by the editors (and forwarded to authors in a "Guide for Preparing Electronic Manuscripts"). The final version would then be returned to the editors.

While Keown and I were formulating the academic boundaries of the *JBE*, Husted was working on the journal's structure. Contacting a very cooperative staff at the Pennsylvania State University's Center for Academic Computing, he established an anonymous FTP site on their FTP server and a companion site on their World Wide Web server. Husted then created the WWW "edition" of the journal as a series of HTML documents on a PC and uploaded those to a private account for the journal on the university's SUN Cluster (UNIX) where they would be mirrored daily to Penn State's WWW server. Moreover, the flexibility of the WWW format allowed the journal to alter its structure and format easily, in response to reader feedback and professional discussion, thus continually upgrading its appearance, applicability, and usefulness. In consultation with Keown and me, Husted determined that when material was accepted for publication in the *JBE*, it would be uploaded to the FTP site as paginated ASCII text, which was at that time a universally readable format. Husted would then convert copies of this material to HTML documents and have them placed with the journal's other WWW "edition" documents and linked to a current issue "Table of Contents" page. The framework was then in place!

On July 1, 1994, the *JBE* announced its presence on a number of electronic newsgroups, most notably Buddha-L, Buddhist, and Indology. Within a week, despite having no articles online, the journal had approximately 100 subscribers from several countries. After September 1, 1994, the journal issued its first "Call for Papers" on the same networks. By the end of November 1994, the journal counted more than 300 subscribers from twenty-five countries. Up to that point, Husted was manually managing the subscription process. With such a surprisingly large number of subscribers in such a short period, he determined that it would be necessary to automate the subscription and notification process by establishing a *JBE* "listserv" (JBE-L) created on the Penn State University's Listserver. Individuals could now automatically subscribe, while publication notices and journal news could be sent to "JBE-L" and distributed automatically to the hundreds of subscribers.

Gradually, articles began to emerge, buoyed by notices that appeared in *The (London) Times Higher Education Supplement* (on October 14, 1994) and *The Chronicle of Higher Education* (on October 26, 1994). Within a short period, the journal posted its first research papers: James Whitehill's "Buddhist Ethics in Western Context: The 'Virtues' Approach," and Winston King's "A Buddhist Ethic without Karmic Rebirth?" and its first discussion article, Paul Numrich's "Vinaya in Theravda Temples in the United States." In each of these cases, the article took no more than one week from initial receipt until posting in the journal. It also posted "Bulletins" inviting applications for the (visiting) Numata Chair in Buddhist Studies at the University of Calgary, announcing the Numata Lecture Series at the Institute of Buddhist Studies in Berkeley, California, on "Buddhisms in America: An Expanding Frontier," and a bibliography listing scholarly books on Buddhist ethics published in the 1990s. With the appearance of the above titles, many inquiries began to arrive from scholars interested in contributing to the journal.

To facilitate access for European users, the journal established a second full site at Goldsmiths College in London with the help of the college's Computing Services Department. Eventually, an Australian site was established at Coombs Computing Unit of the Australian National University, which was itself mirrored to seven additional sites around the globe, thus assuring all journal subscribers reliable and continuous access to the journal's resources. Later, the Australian site was discontinued due to changes within the Coombs Computing Unit.

Consequently, a project that began as a modest effort to provide scholars interested in Buddhist ethics with a forum for sharing the fruits of their research emerged as a comprehensive, scholarly, electronic journal that was forging the way for other enterprising religious studies scholars to utilize the newest developments in information exchange technology to eliminate the debilitating waiting period for publication, and to move the entire discipline fully into the age of the Internet.

ONGOING DEVELOPMENT

Within a year, the *JBE* had grown to more than 700 subscribers in thirty countries. In an attempt to keep the journal at the cutting edge of developments in electronic publication, the editors decided to expand the offering of the journal. As such, it added several new features to the 1995 edition. The first of these was a section devoted to book reviews of newly published books in all areas of Buddhist studies. Because online book reviews could be generated quite literally within days of a book's publication, the book review section served the worldwide community of Buddhist studies scholars far more effectively than any print journal could hope to do. In addition, the *JBE* created a section on its webpage called "Scholarly Resources," primarily reserved for posting topical bibliographies, but also providing links to other useful tools in Buddhist studies, such as the valuable online resources developed by Charles Muller in Japan, and to major professional societies in Buddhist studies, such as the IABS and the UK Association for Buddhist Studies.

By far the most ambitious project of the journal undertaken in 1995 was the planning and execution of the first online conference in the history of the religious studies discipline. The conference was entitled "Buddhism and Human Rights," and consisted of ten papers posted on the *JBE* site, along with the United Nations "Universal Declaration of Human Rights," and the Dalai Lama's statement on "Human Rights and Universal Responsibility." Between October 1 and 13, 1995, discussion was entertained on the journal's JBE-L listserv. During the two weeks of the conference, the *JBE* home page was accessed 1,350 times, and more than 400 messages were posted on JBE-L. Eventually, the conference papers were collected and published as Volume 2 of the Curzon Press "Critical Studies in Buddhism" series. From a modest initial year of publication, in which four total articles were posted online, the second year yielded eleven articles and the first book review.

In 1996, it became quite apparent that if the *JBE* was to continue to expand its book review section, a separate editor would need to be appointed to manage this complex task, and Mavis Fenn (in Canada) became the *JBE's* Book Review Editor . . . a position she maintained for a number of years. During 1996, the *JBE* published nine articles and sixteen book reviews, but more importantly, adopted a new format for its "official" publications. Seeking to attain parity with traditional print journals, the *JBE* began to publish its articles and book reviews in Adobe Acrobat format, thus allowing both traditional pagination and the inclusion of the foreign language diacritics so important in our discipline. Also in 1996, Damien Keown and I became co-editors of the Curzon series mentioned above, and a link to that series was also posted on the *JBE* site. We maintained editorship of that series, which eventually became part of Routledge, until 2006.

The book review section of the journal continued to expand by leaps and bounds, publishing twenty-six reviews in 1997 and thirty in 1998. The unique expansion of the book review section necessitated staff expansion, with a series of assistant editors being appointed to manage individual sections of the discipline. These assistant editors eventually included James McDermott (South-Southeast Asia, Theravda), Eric Reinders (East Asia), Rob Mayer (Inner Asia/Tibet), and Martin Baumann (Western Buddhism). The publication of articles expanded as well, numbering twelve in 1998. By the end of 1998, the *JBE* had grown to 2,000 subscribers in sixty countries. Moreover, through the diligent work of Lance Cousins, the *JBE* became a host site for the online Pali canon developed by the International Buddhist Research and Information Center (IBRIC) in Sri Lanka.

By 1997, the *JBE's* first technical editor, Wayne Husted, had moved on to another professional position, and the *JBE* needed to departmentalize the various technical aspects of the journal, which had become increasingly complicated and time consuming. The journal was fortunate enough to enlist the skills of Stanley Dunn of Rutgers University, who not only became the Senior Technical Editor of the journal, but also configured a *JBE* server (loaned to the *JBE* from one his research projects and was later replaced by our own Dell PowerEdge 2300 server, purchased for the journal by the Pennsylvania State University), allowing the journal to house and control the entirety of its files and records on its own site. In addition, the journal appointed Christine Baker of Edmonton, Alberta, as its copy editor, although she was replaced in 1999 by Jennifer McCay in Germany; and Daniel McShane of Albany, New York, who had become technical editor, was replaced in Summer 2001 by Kenneth O'Neill of the University of Arizona. In 1998, the *JBE* got a new "facelift," thus keeping its webpage attractive and current. In addition, in 2000 the journal began to employ the Indic Times font, allowing foreign term diacritics in the main HTML texts of all published materials.

In April 2000, the *JBE* sponsored its second online conference, devoted to the topic of "Socially Engaged Buddhism," with Christopher Queen of Harvard University as Honorary Chairman and Convener. Thirteen papers were posted with more than 200 discussion responses posted to the specially designed conference listserv during the week-long event. These papers were collected into a book entitled *Action Dharma: New Studies in Engaged Buddhism*, published in 2003 as part of Routledge Curzon's "Critical Studies in Buddhism" series.

As the *JBE* moved ahead into the new century, it did so with a subscriber base of more than 3,300 individuals, and generated approximately 375,000 "hits" on its site in the six-year period between December 1, 1995, and December 1, 2001. Moreover, it boasted a publication volume quite consistent with the major scholarly journals in Buddhist studies.

Halfway through the first decade of the new century, Keown and I decided—as we each approached retirement—that it would be judicious to find a new, younger staff to edit and manage the *JBE*, and in 2006 we each took emeritus status with the journal. However, before doing so, the journal ran its third online conference in 2005, devoted to the topic of "Revisioning Karma." That conference boasted thirteen exciting papers, and the conference papers were eventually published as *Revisioning Karma—The eBook*, part of yet another new venture undertaken by the *JBE*.

Since 2006, the new editor-in-chief of the *JBE* has been Daniel Cozort of Dickinson College, with able editorial assistance from Christopher Ives of Stonehill College and Barbra Clayton of Mount Allison University in Canada. James Mark Shields of Bucknell University is the book review editor, and the technical work is handled by a staff of area editors and copy editors. The journal is now housed at Dickinson College, and has received a lovely "facelift" that has transformed it into "blog" format, which makes it far more accessible to site visitors. In addition, the Editorial Board has been updated for the new century. Table 5.1 shows the current summary of the *JBE*'s publication of articles and book reviews.

Table 5.1   Current Summary of the *JBE*'s Publication of Articles and Book Reviews

Year	Articles	Book Reviews
1994	4	0
1995	11 + 10 Conference Papers	1
1996	9	16
1997	6	26
1998	12	30
1999	9	26
2000	7 + 13 Conference Papers	19
2001	2	11
2002	3	3
2003	11	5
2004	7	7
2005	5 + 13 Conference Papers	11
2006	11	5
2007	8	4
2008	8	12
2009	5	2
2010	9	7
2011	9	21
2012	14	9

Created by Charles S. Prebish.

A NEW VENTURE

By the end of the previous century, there was not a single scholarly journal devoted solely, or even primarily, to the topic of Western Buddhism. This should hardly be surprising considering the dearth of scholarly journals worldwide that are *exclusively* devoted to the study of Buddhism. Most notably, these include only the *Journal of the International Association of Buddhist Studies, The Eastern Buddhist, Pacific World, The Journal of Buddhist Literature, Journal of the Institute of Buddhist Studies* (Berkeley), *Buddhist Studies Review, Contemporary Buddhism, Chung-Hwa Buddhist Journal, The Pure Land: Journal of the International Society of Shin Buddhist Studies*, and the *Journal of Buddhist Ethics.*

On the other hand, in the decade of the 1990s, significant interest was beginning to emerge in Buddhism's globalization, and a significant part of that interest focused on the development of Western Buddhism as a serious sub-discipline of Buddhist studies (Prebish 2002, 66–81). At the 1998 annual meeting of the American Academy of Religion, for example, a panel devoted to the topic of "American Buddhism at the Millennium" was attended by more than 150 individuals, which made it the largest attendance of any Buddhism-related panel at that year's meeting. It is hardly debatable that the IABS is the flagship professional society for the study of Buddhism throughout the world. Although it sponsors worldwide conferences every other year, until 1999 not a single paper on Western Buddhism had ever been presented. At the Twelfth Conference, held in Lausanne in August 1999 and attended by slightly more than 300 scholars, the "Buddhist in the West" panel was attended by approximately seventy-five scholars, despite being one of seven panels scheduled at the same time. As such, preliminary planning was undertaken for the creation of a new online journal called the *Journal of Global Buddhism* (*JGB*), to be co-edited by Martin Baumann and myself, with Michelle Spuler as managing editor. Following a procedure similar to the one outlined above for the *JBE*, in January 2000, the online *Journal of Global Buddhism* was launched with a mission almost exclusively committed to the investigation of Western Buddhism, as can be seen from a quick glance at the nine subject classifications it considers for publication, shown in Table 5.2.

In addition to the features it shares with the *JBE*, the *Journal of Global Buddhism* initially included special sections devoted to three areas, as shown in Table 5.3.

Table 5.2   Nine Subject Classifications *JBE* Considers for Publication

Historical Studies—Major historical investigations of Buddhist development with a focus on Western countries; developments within individual Buddhist traditions concentrating on historical trends in Western Buddhism.

Transnational Studies—Comparative studies in the development of Western Buddhism; area studies and their interconnectedness; concerns for deterritorialization of locality.

Issues in the Development of Buddhist Traditions—Investigation of membership determination; ethnicity; Buddhist practice(s); democratization; adaptation and acculturation; ecumenical movements; future trends.

Case Studies and Biographical Studies—Investigations of individual Buddhist groups; multiple studies of Buddhist communities within Buddhist traditions and sectarian divisions; studies of leading figures in modern Buddhism, reflecting both Asian immigrant and Western convert communities; studies of leading figures in modern Buddhism, reflecting both Asian immigrant and Western convert communities.

Survey Results and Their Interpretation—Empirical findings resulting from individual investigations; results from journal-sponsored surveys.

Research Bibliographies—Inclusive, broadly based, comprehensive bibliographies; case-specific tradition-based bibliographies; country-specific bibliographies; issue-oriented bibliographies.

(*Continued*)

Table 5.2   (Continued)

Human Rights Issues and Socially Engaged Buddhism—Concerns for all areas
of human rights; issues of equality; justice; freedom; privacy; women's rights;
international codes; peace issues; ecological issues; animal rights; prison reform;
social activism.

Interfaith Dialogue—Similarities and differences between modern Buddhist
traditions and other world religions; cross-cultural hermeneutics.

Theoretical and Methodological Studies—Transcultural transplantation of
Buddhist traditions: models and systematizations; images, projections,
and idealizations of Buddhism; politics of representation; the impact of
globalization; examination of approaches to the study of global Buddhism, such
as diaspora studies.

Created by Charles S. Prebish.

Table 5.3   Features *Journal of Global Buddhism* Shares with the *JBE*

Journal of Global Buddhism Research Projects—The journal functions as an
independent research tool itself, emphasizing surveys, the creation of databases,
empirical investigations, and through the presentation of ongoing research
projects. The focus of the journal's research projects is determined by the
editorial board and/or by independent proposals submitted by scholars working
in the field.

Teaching Resources—This section of the journal focuses on resources for
Web-based courses on Buddhism and distance education courses on Buddhism.
It provides links to all appropriate online sources. This section was initially
edited by Mavis Fenn, who also served as the first book review editor for the
JBE.

Global Buddhist Communities News and Bulletins—This section of the journal
will offer announcements about Buddhist news throughout the world and
within individual Buddhist communities. As the journal developed, this section
was subdivided into "areas," with each area having its own editor. It was also
anticipated that this section of the journal would include community pages and
various popular resources.

Created by Charles S. Prebish.

In 2006 I took emeritus status from the *Journal of Global Buddhism* as
well, elevating Martin Baumann to editor-in-chief. Baumann then appointed
Cristina Rocha of the University of Western Sydney and Jovan Maud of the
Max Planck Institute of Göttingen, Germany, as managing editors. Maud
also serves as technical editor. Franz Metcalf serves as book review editor.
Table 5.4 shows the current summary of the *JGB*'s publication of articles
and book reviews.

Table 5.4 Current Summary of the *JGB*'s
Publication of Articles and Book Reviews

Year	Articles	Book Reviews
2000	5	5
2001	7	3
2002	4	2
2003	3	6
2004	3	6
2005	2	5
2006	0	4
2007	7	2
2008	5	3
2009	12	7
2010	2	3
2011	3	5
2012	6	5

Created by Charles S. Prebish.

THE FUTURE

There are now more than fifty online Buddhist newsletters and popular journals, and while the vast majority of these are indeed "popular" rather than scholarly in nature, the growth in online publication has been spectacular. When one adds the outrageous number of blogs currently operating in cyberspace, the overall numbers become staggering.

Anyone who has perused the vast array of online resources is at once struck by the incredible unevenness of these publications. No doubt, the appraisal of our progress in effective online publication is often measured by the worst of these resources rather than by the best. As a result, a number of religious studies online journals initially worked together to begin a new association designed to establish standards and facilitate excellence in online scholarly publication. That association was known as the Association of Peer-Reviewed Electronic Journals in Religion (APEJR), and its founding members included the *Journal of Buddhist Ethics, Journal of Global Buddhism, Journal for Christian Theological Research, Hugoye: Journal of Syriac Studies, Journal of Hebrew Scriptures, Journal of Religion and Film, Journal of Religion and Society, The Journal of Southern Religion, TC: A Journal of Biblical Textual Criticism*, and *Women in Judaism: A Multidisciplinary Journal*. In its first meeting, held in conjunction with the American Academy of Religion annual meeting in Orlando, Florida, in November 1998, the association established four basic priorities in dealing with issues facing e-journal publication, as shown in Table 5.5.

In addition, it established seven criteria for *full membership* in the APEJR, as shown in Table 5.6.

In 2001 the APEJR established two additional categories of membership to supplement the category of full membership, as listed in Table 5.7.

Table 5.5   Four Basic Priorities in Dealing with Issues Facing e-Journal Publication

1. Confronting the attitude of resistance to electronic journal publications
2. Calling on standard indexing and abstracting journals to acknowledge electronic articles
3. Developing strategies for permanently archiving electronic journals
4. Recognizing the value of electronic publications for tenure and promotion decisions

Created by Charles S. Prebish.

Table 5.6   Seven Criteria for Full Membership in the APEJR

1. The journal has an editorial board consisting of recognized scholars in the field(s) of study pertinent to the journal.
2. The journal has a policy of blind peer review.
3. The journal has been in operation (i.e., articles have been published) for at least twelve months.
4. Two-thirds of current APEJR members must vote to accept a new e-journal for membership (two-thirds of members actually voting, one vote per journal).
5. The journal must continue to publish peer reviewed articles on an annual basis, or more frequently. Journals not continuing to meet the standards set by the APEJR could be removed by a two-thirds vote.
6. The journal must have a registered ISSN number.
7. The journal must be primarily an electronic journal, although it may choose to offer a print version of some or all of its articles as well. The journal must meet the following criteria to be considered "primarily an electronic journal":
   a. The journal's first electronic issue appeared either before or simultaneously with the first print issue.
   b. Subsequent issues of the electronic version of the journal appear at approximately the same time as (or sooner than) the print version.
   c. No substantial portion of the print journal is omitted in the electronic version of the journal (prefaces, editorial notes, acknowledgements, etc., are excluded; also, if an e-journal's articles appear in a printed collection of articles, and additional material appears that is only in print, the journal's status as "primarily an electronic journal" is not affected, since this is a printed collection of journal articles, and not the journal, per se).
   d. Access to the electronic journal is free and unrestricted to everyone on the Web.

Created by Charles S. Prebish.

Table 5.7 Two Additional Categories of Membership

1. *Affiliate membership* is designed to permit new journals that have been in operation for less than a year to participate in the benefits of the association as non-voting members. Member journals that have not published a peer-reviewed article within a year as required may also be granted affiliate membership until active publication is resumed. In any case, affiliate membership shall be extended for a period of no more than one year. A majority of current APEJR members must vote to grant affiliate membership.

2. *Associate membership* is designed for electronic journals that may not meet one or more of the criteria for full membership, but whose quality and/or contribution to electronic publication warrants their association with APEJR as non-voting members. Two-thirds of current APEJR members must vote to grant associate membership, and associate membership can be revoked on the basis of a two-thirds vote.

Created by Charles S. Prebish.

Eventually, as the number of online peer-reviewed journals grew faster, and more comprehensively than the members imagined, the APEJR decided to terminate its operation.

CONCLUSIONS

In his article "Caught in the Belly of a Paradox," Donald Swearer notes, "Because of the paucity of scholarly work in the field of Buddhist ethics, I doubted the wisdom of founding the electronic *JBE* in 1993, but I have been proved wrong" (Swearer 1997, 262). I would contend that other areas of Buddhist studies might fare just as well—or better—than the *JBE* in their own pursuit of electronic scholarly publication.

As peer-reviewed online journals in Buddhist studies complete their second full decade of existence, it is clear that the potential benefits and services of online scholarly publication remain in their infancy. New software now makes it possible to automate virtually all aspects of scholarly print publication, from receiving the initial manuscript, establishing and tracking the blind peer review, and reporting the results of the review to posting pre-prints and incorporating adjustments into the final, officially "published" versions of all articles. While online discussions of articles and free downloads of all journal materials have become routine, a new cottage industry in e-publishing awaits the most industrious e-journal entrepreneurs. Bibliographic materials will become instantly available, and journals will be able to multitask their functions so as to provide both scholarly and popular components to their publication, creating a "one-stop-shopping" site for both scholars and practitioners alike. Inexpensive online conferences may gradually replace the costly and time-consuming international ventures that are currently the staple product of scholarly exchange. Fieldwork research, and the publication of fieldwork results, may be revolutionized by surveys posted, and completed, in online publications. The possibilities are almost limitless. One can only hope that in the mass profusion of electronic exuberance scholars of Buddhism will never lose sight of the fact that Buddhism deals not so much with texts, publications, and data as it deals with Buddhists.

REFERENCES

Hallisey, Charles. 1992. "Recent Works on Buddhist Ethics." *Religious Studies Review* 18(4): 276–285.

Hubbard, Jamie. 1995. "Upping the Ante: budstud@millenium.end.edu." *Journal of the International Association of Buddhist Studies* 18(2): 309–322.

Keown, Damien. 1992. *The Nature of Buddhist Ethics*. New York: St. Martin's Press.

Prebish, Charles S. 1993. "Buddhist Ethics Comes of Age: Damien Keown and *The Nature of Buddhist Ethics*." *Buddhist Studies Review* 10(1): 95–108.

——. 1999. *Luminous Passage: The Practice and Study of Buddhism in America.* Berkley: University of California Press.

——. 2002. "Studying the Spread and Histories of Buddhism in the West: The Emergence of Western Buddhism as a New Sub-Discipline within Buddhist Studies." In *Westward Dharma: Buddhism Beyond Asia*, edited by Martin Baumann and Charles Prebish, 66–81. Berkeley: University of California Press.

Reynolds, Frank. 1979. "Buddhist Ethics: A Bibliographic Essay." *Religious Studies Review* 5(1): 40–48.

Swearer, Donald. 1997. "Caught in the Belly of a Paradox." *Journal of Religious Ethics* 25(3): 253–267.

6 A Virtual Bodhi Tree
Untangling the Cultural Context and Historical Genealogy of Digital Buddhism

Gregory Price Grieve

I like to think, (it has to be!), of a cybernetic ecology, where we are free of our labors, and joined back to nature, returned to our mammal brothers and sisters, and all watched over, by machines of loving grace.

Richard Brautigan (1967)

In January 2009 I—or really, my avatar, Clint Clavenham—sat in the Bodhi Sim: Land of BuddhaDharma under a virtual Bodhi Tree, a digital copy of the tree under which Siddhartha Gautama is said to have awakened and become the Buddha.[1] I was talking with one of the region's builders, Metta, who described Bodhi as "a virtual island in the online world of Second Life dedicated to the teachings of Buddha. A public commons dedicated to Dharma and for the benefit of all." Clearly, I was not in "real life" (actual physical reality), but rather in the virtual world of Second Life, a massive online multiuser virtual platform afforded by digital media (see Chapters 2 and 10, this volume).[2] Using the virtual Bodhi Tree as a touchstone, this chapter asks the seemingly simple question, "What is digital Buddhism?"

Frequently, digital Buddhism is dismissed as inauthentic because it is posed as either an orientalist Western appropriation, or a shallow form of new media (or both). Consider, for instance, the Slovenian Marxist philosopher and cultural critic Slavoj Žižek, who argues that while Western Buddhism presents itself as a remedy against the stresses of networked society, it is actually the perfect ideology, "the imaginary supplement to terrestrial misery." Particularly, "the 'Western Buddhist' meditative stance is arguably the most efficient way for us to fully participate in capitalist dynamics while retaining the appearance of mental sanity."[3] Moreover, in "Cyberspace, or, the Unbearable Closure of Being," Žižek (1997) suggests that one adopt a "conservative attitude" toward virtual reality (166). Žižek's conservative attitude equates virtual reality with postmodernism and maintains, nostalgically, that we are in the midst of a cultural shift away from a modernist mode of calculation, and monological subjectivity tied to Reason. He argues that virtual reality is moving us ever more quickly toward a postmodern

Figure 6.1   Ngram of the phrase "mindfulness" between 1960 and 2000. (Created using Google's Ngram Viewer, March 17, 2014)

mode of simulation, and decentered multiple selves, which are no longer tied to the Real (Žižek 1997, 167–168, 170–171).

The problem with Žižek's analysis, however, is that one can't see the virtual Bodhi Tree for the digital forest. Such ahistorical critique obscures how actual embedded people use digital Buddhism in their everyday lives. Only by examining genuine phenomena can one understand the cultural context and religious history out of which such media practices emerged. Toward this goal, the chapter will trace how digital media, Buddhism, culture, and history have been intertwined in postwar America. I argue that the goal of much digital Buddhism is "mindfulness," which practitioners describe as a spiritualized awareness of the interwoven relation of people and their environment. In this chapter, I tease out the connections between this form of mindfulness pursued online with the evolution of the place of technology in the postwar American imaginaire (Figure 6.1).

We will see that Buddhist expressions of mindfulness meditation that are played out in places like Second Life articulate a convergence of various strands of technology, media, and identity that have come to characterize contemporary American life more generally.

THE ZEN OF SECOND LIFE: A CULTURAL MEDIA APPROACH

Žižek's critique is symptomatic of research on digital religion, particularly studies of Buddhism, which has tended to turn a blind eye to history. On one level, this seems reasonable, because digital Buddhism suffers a double dose of novelty: the digital is a "new media," and Buddhism is often conceived as a recent addition to America's religious landscape. Once one takes the historic turn, one might assume that the place to look for digital Buddhism's historical antecedents would be ancient Asian practices. Once one realizes, however, that the Zen practice found on Second Life bears only a family resemblance to premodern Asian traditions, one needs to look closer to home. Tracing its postwar American genealogy, one finds that the popularity of Buddhism, often in the form of Zen, came about because it functioned to tie anti-technological sentiment together with cybernetic thought. This spiritual "mash-up" should come as no surprise. American popular religion often breeds such strange couplings of religion, media technology, and consumerism (Chidester 2005; Hendershot 2004; McCloud 2004). In fact, from Henry Thoreau's Walden Pond to Henry Ford's conveyer belt, America seems to constantly be falling in and out of love with technology and its relation to a technologically driven consumerism (Ney 1994).

In *The American Encounter with Buddhism*, Thomas Tweed (1992) writes that as Buddhism spreads to new locales, it takes on "the shape and texture of the soil" (xxxiii). To understand the new digital context, this chapter takes a cultural media approach. As Stewart Hoover (2002) writes in *Practicing Religion in the Age of the Media: Explorations in Media, Religion and Culture* that "this is an approach that recognizes the various complexities as they converge in real experience, as they are engaged, constructed, reconstructed, made meaning of and used" (3). Yet defining the Zen of Second Life through the cultural turn proves more difficult than might at first appear, because the practitioners themselves take great pains not to define "Zen." In fact, the Zen of Second Life's chief activity is silent online meditation, which practitioners call *zazen* or just "sitting." During silent online meditation, Residents rest their avatars on virtual cushions and remain inactive in front of their computer screens. However, although silent and inactive, sitting is not a meaningless activity. By concentrating on media practices, the chapter locates silent online meditation in procedures that center on the conscious awareness of breathing. Like the code of a computer program, a procedure is a step-by-step algorithm that emerges from a set of rules for performing a particular operation. Online silent meditation's goal is "mindfulness," which practitioners describe as a spiritualized awareness of the interwoven relation of people and their environment. Mindfulness leads to compassion (*karuna*), a sympathetic understanding of others' suffering.

MINDFUL PROCEDURES: DEFINING THE PRACTICE OF THE ZEN OF SECOND LIFE

Popular convert American practice and online practice, like that found on Second Life, center on several facets of the Buddhist tradition: the therapeutic, the nonhierarchical, the nonviolent, the ecological, and, most importantly, the concept of "mindfulness." Defining the Zen of Second Life was complicated, however, because the practitioners themselves took great pains not to describe it. In fact, if asked for clarification, the community leaders would describe themselves as lay practitioners, saying that they did not have authority, and then they would usually send to the questioner a notecard or a link to other media. For instance, the founder of Hoben, Cassius Lawndale, indicated the YouTube video, "Orientation to Zen 01—Zazen (Zen Meditation)," from the Victoria Zen Center, that states, "Fundamentally, Zen Practice is a very simple activity, just sitting up straight and breathing and paying attention to where you are and what you are doing." Usually "Zen" was explained by Second Life practitioners as a type of practice. For instance, in a notecard handed out on April 23, 2008, entitled "Can I Be Honest With You?" the author describes "Zen" not through a narrative of belief, but through action: "thought turns into speech, which turns into action, which ultimately affects our whole world."[4]

While a *koan* (a story, dialogue, question, or statement used in Zen practice) and guided meditation were sometimes employed, the chief Zen practice was perceived to be conscious breathing. As the "Can I Be Honest With You?" notecard goes on to say, "The first step is to cultivate awareness through mindfulness meditation. Using your breath as a home base for your wandering mind, notice when you get caught up in thought and your attention strays from the breath." Beginners and more seasoned practitioners both employed conscious breathing. Also, when newcomers to the community asked what they should do, conscious breathing was the chief suggestion. For instance, when I first went to meditate, the session leader, Georgina Florida, gave me a notecard entitled, "Joy of Meditation as Nourishment," which states, "Many people begin to practice sitting meditation with the help of this exercise. Even those who have meditated for many years continue to practice it, because the exercise is so effective."[5]

For most practitioners, the goal of silent meditation is "mindfulness," which was seen as making one aware of interbeing and as leading to compassion. Mindfulness translates the term *smrti*, literally, "that which is remembered," and right mindfulness is one part of the Noble Eightfold Path. As a mental factor, it signifies attention to the present, the characteristic of not wobbling, and an absence of confusion and forgetting. While it has a family resemblance to premodern forms, practitioners' understanding of mindfulness enlarged traditional understandings. For instance, when I asked the Second Life Resident Rasa Vibration to describe mindfulness, she responded, hearkening back to Shunryu Suzuki, the Sōtō Zen monk who helped popularize Zen Buddhism in the United States, "I think of the eyes of a child." The community leader TypesZen Sideways defined mindfulness as "de-hypnosis" (Second Life Chat, March 23, 2008). In one of his "GoldenSentences," Mystic Moon, the owner of the Gekkou region, a region of the Zen Buddhist cloud that takes a more mystical approach, described mindfulness as "awareness = " "<——there" (Second Life Chat, January 15, 2009). Mostly, however, when I asked what mindfulness meant, I was not given a definition, but rather, a set of procedures. For instance, the notecard, "Can I Be Honest With You?" goes on to read:

Mindfulness meditation is a straightforward technique for observing all thoughts—good or bad, happy or sad, honest or dishonest. Rather than changing or rearranging anything, we practice simply resting in time and space and noticing how thoughts naturally dissolve on their own. Sitting on the cushion, we soon start to recognize certain repetitive thought sequences. We might think, "There I go again . . ." and then, with a little inner laugh, let go of the thought and come back to the breath.[6]

Yet what does it mean to be mindful? Second Life Zen practice, particularly silent meditation's conscious breathing, is perceived to make practitioners aware of "interbeing," a word coined by the Vietnamese Zen Buddhist monk, Thich Nhat Hanh, to represent the principle of the interconnectedness of all things (Grieve 2011). In this view, everything is codependent, related, and caused by everything else. No single thing stands alone as a discrete entity, whether it is the entire globe or individual selves (Coleman 2002, 121). For instance, a Second Life notecard entitled, "Our True Home," and attributed to Thich Nhat Hanh, reads, "If you continue to look deeply, you will see that in the present moment, you continue to be a rose, a rabbit, a tree, and a rock. This is the truth of interbeing. You are made of non-you elements" (Hanh 2000, 45).

THE ZEN OF SECOND LIFE: A HISTORICAL GENEALOGY

Interestingly, while mindfulness has a family resemblance to classic Asian traditions, it has drifted in the modern period in such a way that its practice now is only tangentially related to earlier forms (Grieve 2011; Griffiths 1986). Much as James Dietrick (2003) has described Engaged Buddhism, modern forms of mindfulness could be considered "the infusion of Euro-American thought into the veins of Buddhist Asia" (253). This does not mean, however, that one has to toss out the baby with the bath water. Just because mindfulness may be a contemporary spiritual practice formed in the interplay between Asian and American popular imaginations, this does not mean that it is any less significant to its practitioners. It may be, to borrow a term from the scholar of popular culture and religion David Chidester, an authentic fake (2005). In what follows, I would like to focus on the historical conditions that have given rise to the kind of Buddhist practice, specifically mindfulness, that one finds now on the Web and in virtual worlds like Second Life. Specifically, the postwar American historical background that makes such phenomena as meditating under a virtual Bodhi Tree not only possible, but desirable.

In postwar America, Buddhism has functioned as a "spiritual mash-up," a form of practice that employs the concept of mindfulness to blend anti-technological sentiment together with cybernetic thought. Spiritualized technology should come as no surprise in the American context. Since the 1860s, America has often employed the myth of technological advances to imagine itself (Ney 1994). Technology's role in America was heightened after World War II, because it was popularly propagandized as the key to Allied victory, and then to winning the Cold War. Yet, technology had a dark side. By 1959, President Dwight Eisenhower had cautioned Congress about the growing power of what he called the military-industrial complex (U.S. Office of the Federal Register 1961, 1035–1040). As seen in popular films, novels, and television, the computer threatened to destroy the human soul, overconsumption to destroy the environment, and the atomic bomb to destroy the globe (Ney 1994, 225–256).

By the mid-1960s, anxiety about the Cold War with Soviet Russia and the growing hot war in Vietnam as well as industrial pollution and social unrest at home led many intellectuals to see technology as the problem and not the cure. Building on romantic strands of orientalism, by the early 1960s, the notion that Eastern mysticism defied "the System" became a foundation stone for many in American counterculture. They perceived Buddhism, particularly Zen, as a politics of consciousness, as a means, like psychedelics, to expand one's mind and thereby reach one's true human potential. During the World War II years, Buddhism had been a dangerous subject. As Robert Spencer writes in *The Social Structure of a Contemporary Japanese-American Buddhist Church*, "The outbreak of the War with Japan was instrumental in disrupting Buddhist organizations (1948: 281; cf. curators). Yet, once Japan was pacified, this disruption of heritage American Buddhism allowed for a "Zen 'boom,'" which saw itself as an antidote to the West's dehumanizing technocracy (Ames 1960; Kapleau 1966). Once Japan was no longer seen as the enemy, the notion that Eastern mysticism defied "the System" became a foundation stone for the many in the 1960s counterculture.

For instance, consider Theodore Roszak's 1968 book *The Making of a Counter Culture: Reflections on the Technocratic Society and Its Youthful Opposition*. Roszak found common ground between 1960s student radicals and hippie dropouts in their mutual rejection of what he calls the "technocracy," the system of corporate and technological expertise that dominates industrial society. For Roszak (1968), the battle against technology was the "paramount struggle of our day" (4). Echoing Jacque Ellul's (1976) notion of an all-encompassing "technique" and Herbert Marcuse's concept of "technological rationality," for Roszak, technology was more than just the physical machines—technology was the systematic tyranny of rationalism, bureaucratic regimentation, and ecological suicide. As Lewis Mumford writes in *The Myth of the Machine*, technology has "achieved a hitherto unattainable level of efficiency. But instead of freeing labor, the royal megamachine boasted of imprisoning and enslaving it" (Mumford 1979, 194). In fact, by the early 1970s, many American Buddhists saw their practice as a strategic way to counter the menace of technology (Prebish 1979, 47). As Thich Nhat Hanh (1974) writes in *Zen Keys*, "Western Civilization has brought us to the edge of the abyss. It has transformed us into machines. The 'awaking' of a few Westerners, their awareness of the real situation has . . . engaged them in the search for new values" (160).

FROM SATORI TO SILICON VALLEY: THE CYBERNETIC
ROOTS OF POSTWAR ZEN

If Buddhism was anti-technological, how did it end up on Second Life? Exhausted in 1985 from the hippie "fragrance of barnyards and hunting camps," Theodore Roszak (1986, 4) gave a lecture entitled "From Satori to Silicon Valley," which revised his argument about the relation between technology and the counterculture. His countercultural heroes were no longer just hippies and beats but computer hackers, among whom Roszak (1986) perceived a new "postindustrial alternative" (5). Instead of opposing all technology, he argued that along with the counterculture's "mystic tendencies and principled funkiness," there had always been a "deep ambiguity . . . a certain world-beating American fascination with making and doing" (Roszak 1986, 15). Roszak (1986) ties these new innovative technologies to an "irrepressible Yankee ingenuity," which he sees in the "rebels and drop-outs [among whom] we can find the inventors and entrepreneurs who helped lay the foundations of the California computer industry" (15). For Roszak, these new technologies were revolutionary because they shared a spirituality with Eastern mysticism. In computers there "was an attractive hope that the high technology of our society might be wrested from the grip of benighted forces and used to restore us to an idyllic natural state" (Roszak 1986, 49–50).

For Roszak (1986), the "reversionary-technophiliac synthesis" of the small-scale computer industry offered a "short cut to satori" (48–49). In late-twentieth-century California, Roszak could tie together what would seem like dispersed fields of knowledge—Zen, computers, and nature—because they are all supported by an underlying cybernetic ideology. Emerging as hostilities ended in World War II, cybernetics promised not just a new science, but as the American engineer and head of the United States Office of Scientific Research Vannevar Bush said, an entire "new relationship between thinking man and the sum of our knowledge" (Bush, 1945). For instance, Bush imagined a device called the Memex (memory + index) that uses a proto-hypertext system, a mechanized device in which an individual stores all his books, records, and communications for quick and easy consultation.

While it has roots back in the Bell Laboratory, the term "cybernetics" was coined in 1948 by Norbert Wiener in his seminal work, *Cybernetics: Or the Control and Communication in the Animal and the Machine*. Wiener (1948) forged "cybernetics" from the Greek *kybernetes*, or "steersman," and defines it as "the entire field of control and communication theory, whether in the machine or animal" (11). Cybernetics researches systems, particularly feedback loops. Emerging from systems theory, information theory, and related sciences, cybernetics pictures the world as a series of systems that contains individuals, societies, and ecosystems, and it is concerned with describing the patterns that form from their emergence. Wiener argued that cybernetics differed from hard empirical sciences, because the focus was not on material form but rather on networks of organization, patterns, and communication made up of users and machines. Such systems can be rain forests, the nervous system, brain and sense organs, and the relationship between mechanical-electrical communication networks, such as computers and their users. "In this view," as Katherine Hayles (1999) writes in *How We Became Posthuman*, "a universal informational code underlies the structure of matter, energy, spacetime—indeed, of everything that exists" (11).

Key to cybernetics and how it differs from preceding conceptions of systems is the "steersman." Rather than being outside the system, the steersman is conceived as an integral part of it and as actually constituted by the system. In *Cybernetics*, Wiener (1948) describes how humans are part of a link of information systems, "in what we shall from now on call the chain of feedback" (114). Cybernetics was not just a scientific theory, but it also comprised a worldview. By countering the disruptive forces of noise and entropy, Wiener saw communication as the organizing force that created the life of individuals and societies (Hayles 1999). As he writes near the end of his autobiography, *I Am a Mathematician*, "We are swimming upstream against a great torrent of disorganization" (Wiener 1964, 324). And as he maintains in the *Human Use of Human Beings*, "We are but whirlpools in a river of ever-flowing water. We are not stuff that abides, but patterns that perpetuate themselves" (Wiener 1950, 96). Wiener originally conceived of cybernetics not as a spiritual metaphysics but rather as a solution for anti-aircraft guns. "At the beginning of the war, the German prestige in aviation and the defensive position of England turned the attention of many scientists to the improvement of anti-aircraft artillery" (Wiener 1948, 11). The problem was that airplanes were much too fast and unproductively wiggly. Only by taking into account the voluntary activity of the pilot as a feedback loop could equations predict an airplane's flight. As Wiener (1948) writes, in what relates to the steersman and what will look forward to postwar Zen and the concept of mindfulness, "we can not avoid the discussion of the performance of certain human factors" (13).

AT HOME IN THE REVERSIONARY-TECHNOPHILIAC SYNTHESIS: A POSTWAR GENEALOGY OF MINDFULNESS

In 1985, by using *satori*, a Japanese Buddhist term for enlightenment, Roszak was looking back to California's countercultural roots. Roszak was also looking forward to the Silicon Valley ideology of the hacker's do-it-yourself, software-driven individualism. By 1985 Roszak had tied much of the Bay Area's "Zen-Taoist mysticism" to a "reversionary-technophiliac synthesis" expressed through cybernetics, computers, and "Eastern spirituality." It was a short skip from a nature religion to becoming a key element of American counterculture. Also, how cybernetic concepts of systems and feedback influenced computers, the counterculture, psychology, and ecology is also clear. Less clear is how a perceived countercultural anti-technological nature religion came to be at the center of corporate networked society.

To be fair, Buddhism is not the only religion to have been adapted for Late Capitalism. Certainly, however, there has been no better relationship between Zen and the corporate world than that best epitomized by the computer industry.[7] Consider, for instance, that in August 2013, North Carolina's Center for Creative Leadership issued a white paper entitled, "Wake Up! The Surprising Truth about What Drives Stress and How Leaders Build Resilience." Written by the senior center member, Nick Petrie, the paper does not claim to have spiritual motives. Instead, it aims "to move beyond traditional approaches and look at where the field [of leadership] is going" (Petrie 2013, 1). Petrie aspires to give leaders tools for dealing with executive "stress and burn out" (Petrie 2013, 2). While Petrie never mentions Buddhism or Zen, "Wake Up!" is clearly indebted to its postwar genealogy—the most obvious evidence being that the "Buddha" is often rendered in English as "Awakened One," and Petrie's use of cybernetic systems is illustrated by such models as "Wide Awake—Attention" (Figure 6.2).

As shown in Petrie's "Wake Up!" the key to understanding how American popular culture moved from cybernetics-influenced Buddhism to a Silicon Valley ideology is mindfulness. Often, mindfulness is understood as a

Wide Awake - Attention

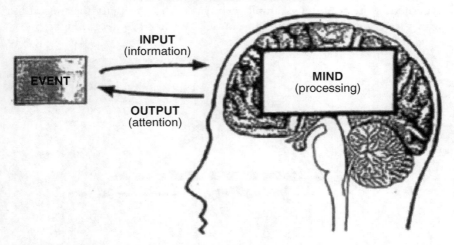

Figure 6.2 "Wide Awake—Attention." The image shows a stylized profile of a human head with a detailed, realistic image of the brain, which encloses a rectangle with the words "MIND (processing)." Just to the right, at the height of what would be the frontal cortex, a shaded rectangle reads "Event." A left-pointing arrow entitled "INPUT (information)" leads from "EVENT" to the brain. Completing the circuit, a second right-pointing arrow entitled "OUTPUT (attention)" leads from the brain back to the "EVENT." (Used with permission of Nick Petrie and Center for Creative Leadership)

thousand-year-old Buddhist technique. Yet a closer look shows that its current formulation originates in postwar America. Following much contemporary discourse which, under the name of mindfulness, superimposes a cybernetic model on neuroscience, Petrie argues that there are negative "waking sleep" ruminations that are opposed to a "good" stress in which your "environment can help you to perform" (Petrie 2013, 7). The key, for Petrie, is to "Wake Up!" by being aware of how you fit into your environment (Petrie 2013, 7). While words such as "smrti" can be found in premodern texts, Petrie's notion of mindfulness has more in common with Wiener's conception of information. Consider that in *Cybernetics*, Wiener (1948) writes, "Information is information, not matter or energy. No materialism which does not admit this can survive at the present day" (132). Similarly, postwar American Buddhism's concept of "mindfulness" is perceived as a type of spiritualized awareness about the world. At the center of cybernetics is a "steersman," aware of and even part of the system that he guides. In a similar fashion, at the center of Zen is a mindful subject who is part of the networked system and is generated by the system as well as being the governor of the system. For Wiener (1948), this steersman is not a free agent but is more of a signalman who regulates switches, "either mechanically or electronically" (114–115).

In postwar America, one can trace the fate of the mindful subject by following the drift of Wiener's use of the home thermostat to model a cybernetic system. For an example, he turns to the "ordinary thermostat by which we regulate the heating of a house" (Wiener 1948, 115; Figure 6.3).

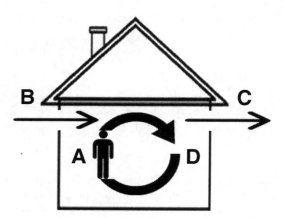

Figure 6.3   Cybernetic system compared to house with thermostat. (a) Steersman sets the temperature, which is (b) affected by input from environment; it (c) outputs to environment, but is regulated by (d) the thermostat. (Created by Gregory Price Grieve)

The outside environment becomes cold and cools the house, and an apparatus senses this and turns on the furnace, which heats the house. The people living in the home, however, are not outside the system. They are the ones that steer the system by choosing the temperature at which to set the thermostat.

THE MECHANICS OF PERCEPTION: STEPS TOWARD ECOLOGY OF POSTWAR ZEN BOOM

The influence of cybernetics is clear on the Beat Generation, a postwar countercultural movement that rejected the status quo of consumerism and experimented with drugs, sexuality, and Eastern religion. The Beats were not against technology per se, but were rather against the technocratic system that they saw as enslaving consciousness. In fact, California's counterculture did not see technology as opposed to Zen, and actually utilized technology as a means of poetic liberation. Consider Gary Snyder's "Look Out's Journal," from his ecological *Earth House Hold: Technical Notes & Queries to Fellow Dharma Revolutionaries* (1969), which consists of the reports of radio transmissions between fellow Zen devotees Kerouac and Whalen during two summers (Williams 2011, 29).[8] In "Crater Shan," dated July 28, Snyder describes a moment that reflects Wiener's metaphor of the "house as consciousness," the digital Zen notion of mindful awareness, and the poetic use of technology: "Down for a new radio, to Ross Lake, and back up. Three days walking. Strange how unmoved this place leaves one; neither articulate or worshipful; rather the pressing need to look within and adjust the mechanism of perception" (4). Consider also Richard Brautigan's 1967 poem, "All Watched over by Machines of Loving Grace" (cited at the top of the chapter), which imagines a utopic system composed of a cybernetic ecology composed of mammals and machines.[9]

In the fifties, Beat and Square Zen were often opposed. Yet as the July 21, 1958, *Time* article, "Religion: Zen: Beat & Square," spells out: "All things bubble along in one interrelated continuum." Along with the Beats, Roszak (1968) also incorporates the teaching of Alan Watts, who he saw as being on hand "to achieve the 'mystic revolution'" (243–244). Echoing cybernetics, Watts explains Zen through notions of systems. Take, for instance, *The Way of Zen*, where he sees delusion (*avidya*) as "really a simple problem of what we now call cybernetics, the science of control" (Watts 1958, 57). Watts never actually cites Norbert Wiener directly, but there are a number of passages in *The Way of Zen* that are copied, sometimes word for word, from Wiener's *Cybernetics* (see Williams 2011, 23, fn 18). Compare, for example, Watts's (1958, 135) description of human self-consciousness as a "'feed-back' system" and his comparing it to the process of a home thermostat (compare to Wiener 1948, 114–115, cited earlier). As Watts (1958) writes:

> Perhaps the most familiar example is the electrical thermostat which regulates the heating of a house. The temperature of the house is thus kept within the desired limit. The thermostat provides the furnace with a kind of sensitive organ—an extremely rudimentary analogy of the human consciousness.
>
> (135)[10]

Much like Thich Nhat Hạnh's concept of interbeing, Watt argues for a religious nondualism, a global skepticism against systems of thought that attempt to dichotomize the world between subject/ego and object/world (Smith 2010, 13; Watts 1958, 55). Zen's cool liberation occurs when one becomes aware that we are composed of fields of thought. As he writes in *The Wisdom of Insecurity: A Message for an Age of Anxiety*, "In such feeling, seeing, and thinking life requires no future to complete itself nor explanation to justify itself" (Watts 1951, 152). Watts (1951, 56, 58) argues that the delusional split arises when one attempts to control the natural flow of the world, which he analyzes through the doctrines of no-self and dependent origination. First, like the digital Zen notion of no-self, for Watts (1958, 56), delusion arises when one forgets the relational nature of the self. As he writes in the *The Tao of Philosophy*, "What you do is what the whole universe is doing at the place you can 'here and now,' and you are something the whole universe is doing in the same way that a wave is something that the whole ocean is doing" (Watts 2002, 18). For Watts (2002, 57–58), suffering came about from ignorance, those "vicious circles" when one forgets that one is part of a larger system.

ZEN AND THE ART OF MANAGEMENT

Yet, how did mindfulness drift from the counter culture to corporate culture? To grasp how a popular cybernetic form of Zen became a late capitalistic ideology, we need to address the 1974 publication of Robert Pirsig's *Zen and the Art of Motorcycle Maintenance* (William 2011). Pirsig offered a post-countercultural perspective, which marked a turning point between the 1960s and 1970s. As Morris Dickstein (1977) writes in *Gates of Eden: American Culture in the Sixties*, Pirsig "reveals a distinct post-sixties outlook," arguing for "systems-analysis rather than dropping out of the system" (274–275). Still, although his message was a watershed, Pirsig's Zen, like the Beats, Alan Watts, and Gregory Bateson, was indebted to cybernetics. For instance, the opening paragraph of Pirsig's novel, a narrative retooling of Wiener's metaphor of a thermostatically controlled house, describes a cybernetic circuit composed of a system of feedback loops, weaving machine, animal and environment (Snyder 1961; Williams 2011, 29). "I can see by my watch, without taking my hand from the left grip of the cycle, that it is eight-thirty in the morning. The wind, even at sixty miles an hour, is warm and humid" (Pirsig 1974, 3).

The key for Pirsig is "Quality," which he sees as the communication that arises when subjects become mindful of the system in which they dwell. For Pirsig, technology and quality are not opposed, nor is technology essentially isolating. "A person who knows how to fix motorcycles . . . with Quality . . . is less likely to run short of friends than one who doesn't. And they aren't going to see him as some kind of object either. Quality destroys objectivity every time" (Pirsig 1974, 351). Yet, as Pirsig asks at the end of chapter fifteen, "what the hell is Quality? What is it?" (Pirsig 1974, 178). "By God," Pirsig discovers soon after, Quality is neither "subjectivity or objectivity, it was beyond both of those categories" (Pirsig 1974, 231). Like Wiener's information, Quality is neither mind nor matter, "it is a third entity which is independent of the two" (Pirsig 1974, 231). Yet, similar to Pirsig, Wiener earlier asks, "What is this Information, and how is it measured?" (Wiener 1948, 61). In 1972, two years before the publication of Pirsig's novel, Bateson defined information as "a difference which makes a difference," and saw it as a way out of the subject/object problem (Bateson 1972, 448). Like binary code itself, a quarter of a century earlier, Wiener perceived information as an event that makes a difference: "one of the simplest, most unitary forms of information is the recording of a choice between two equally probable simple alternatives . . . a choice, for example, between heads and tails in the tossing of a coin" (Weiner 1948, 61). Yet, quality is not simply the flickering of a binary system; for quality to arise, the system must become mindful of itself. Similarly, for Pirsig, echoing Watt's mindful Zen, Quality "is not a thing . . . It is the event at which the subject becomes aware of the object" (Pirsig 1974, 233).

Pirsig's concept of Zen and the metaphysics of Quality quickly found its way into management. What started this trend was in 1978, when Richard Pascale, a consultant at McKinsey & Company and professor of management at Stanford University, published, "Zen and the Art of Management: A Different Approach to Management for the 'Cards-on-the-Table' Executive, Which Works." In his study comparing Japanese and American companies, Pascale found only one significant difference, the quality of communication (1978, 154). Pascale uses the term Zen "to denote these important nuances of interpersonal communication often enshrouded in a veil of mystique" (1978, 154). In fact, he goes on to argue, "the perspective imbedded in Eastern philosophy, culture and values helps make the implicit dimension more visible" (1978, 154). However, on closer inspection, what Pascale is calling "Zen" is in fact a further telescoping of postwar cybernetic thought clothed in Eastern spirituality. Harkening back to Watts's wiggles and Weiner's German aircraft, Pascale (1978) suggests, "Let things flow. 'Success is going straight—around the circle,' says the Chinese adage" (160).[11] Pascale's (1967) reference for this insight, however, is not an Asian source, but rather James D. Thompson's *Organization in Action*, a text that distinguishes between the "rational closed system strategy" and the "flowing natural open-system strategy." Thompson (1967, 4), in turn, bases his distinction on Ross Ashby's (1956) *An Introduction to Cybernetics*, who employs Wiener's metaphors of thermostat and aircraft to describe the two types of systems (see Ashby 1956, 132, 135, 198, 199–200).

Pascale's use of Zen indicates two of cybernetics' key concepts as refracted through popular notions of Eastern spirituality. First, a new "Zen" management style that embraced more flexible models of team culture and innovation and reflected Wiener's steersman, as echoed off Watts's mindful subject, and Bateson's interpersonal communication. Second, the Zen management style leads to the adoption of just-in-time lean administrative methods that resemble cybernetic feedback loops. In the goal of increasing corporate America's efficiency, Pascale's article was the first of myriad management books that used the term "Zen."[12] In a strange feedback loop, however, the Zen that American corporate leaders brought back was a hybrid mix of a militant *bushido* wartime Buddhism, and cybernetic management style that had been introduced by occupation forces after World War II (Matusek 1986; Williams 2011, 42, 45). While Buddhism is often pictured in American popular culture as a peace-loving religion, during World War II, by conflating Zen and the bushido warrior ethic, it contributed to some of the most egregious moments of Japanese militarism (Ives 2009; Victoria 1997). Japan's defeat after World War II, Daizen Victoria argues in *Zen at War*, meant "not the demise of imperial-way Zen and Soldier Zen but only their metamorphosis and rebirth as corporate Zen" (Victoria 1997, 186). While the ethos may have been bushido, however, the management system was a cybernetics that had been introduced by occupation forces after the war.

Consider, for instance, Edwards Deming, who had been invited to Japan at General Douglas MacArthur's request to rebuild war ruined industries, and had within a few years completely transformed the Japanese economy (Williams 2011, 42). Deming's theories relied on cybernetic terms and philosophy, which he had learned during his time at Bell Laboratories. Like Pirsig's motorcycle rider, Deming's manager is a steersman checking a system for quality. Similar to Pirsig's question, however, Rafael Aguayo asks, in *Dr. Deming: The American Who Taught the Japanese About Quality*, "What Is Quality?" (1990, 35–50). Quality is not preference, technological features, or overall design (1990, 37–38). Like Pirsig's event, quality is an attitude toward the work that increases consumer's satisfaction (Dickstein 1977, 50). Expensive new materials or design cannot improve Deming's quality—this would result in a new product. Instead, managers improve quality when mindful of how machines, humans, and environment run together smoothly.

CONCLUSION: THE VIEW FROM THE LOFT

If postwar American Buddhism has had a point, it is to see things more clearly. Sitting under a virtual copy of the Bodhi Tree gives, I suggest, a particular vantage point to understanding digital Buddhism and postwar convert American Buddhism more generally. The chapter has shown that to comprehend Buddhist meditation online one needs to understand that modern practices of mindfulness have grown out of the history of technological developments in the postwar industrialized world. The historic turn demonstrates that such practices are not flawed representations of classic Asian religious traditions, but rather, are a popular post-World War II spiritualizing of cybernetics that has a family resemblance and a cultural feedback relation to Eastern traditions. While it is going too far to say that the Zen of Buddhism on Second Life has absolutely no relationship to Asian practices, its relationship is one of radical adaptation that resulted from cutting and grafting key Buddhist concepts onto cybernetic systems of thought and media practices. In the postwar period, the globalization of such cyber-Zen came about as a perceived antidote to an overly technological society, but in the last-quarter of the twentieth century, "Zen" has drifted to ensnare users further into global capitalism's networked consumerism. As Petrie's "Wake Up!" shows, notions of Buddhism are often the products of corporate management's employment of a postwar cybernetics made palatable by coating it with Eastern spirituality. This pragmatic, individualist, system-oriented thought, which is not hostile to technology and is actually pre-adapted for digital media, plays a part in constituting the Zen of Second Life and networked consumerism more generally.

After untangling the cultural and historic roots, blanket dismissals of digital Buddhism appear both epistemologically confused and politically devious. They are confused because debates of authenticity tend to essentialize Buddhism. Buddhism existed before the second-half of the twentieth century, and it continues to exist after its close. The point of historicizing "Buddhism" in the present moment is not to show that it is the end of a necessary historical process, but rather to point out how a particular people in a particular historic moment used the flotsam and jetsam that has washed up on their cultural shore. Is this authentic? As Theodore Roszak writes, we "leave it up to the Zen Adepts to decide whether anything that deserves to be called authentic has actually taken root in our culture." He further writes, "It is indisputable, however, that the San Francisco Beats, and much of our younger generation since their time, thought they had found something in Zen they needed and promptly proceeded to use what they understood of this exotic tradition as a justification for fulfilling the need" (Roszak 1968, 134).

Questions of digital Buddhism's authenticity are also politically dangerous because they leave out what Slavoj Žižek (1989) calls the sublime object of ideology. For Žižek (1989, 195), ideology operates not simply by deluding people with false consciousness, but rather by creating a fantasy desire that supports an exploitive reality. Rather than shunning the Zen of Second Life as inauthentic and neglecting the study of convert Buddhism more generally, the study of digital religion ought to articulate the attraction for those who practice it and the uses to which they put it. Because in his analysis of digital Buddhism he ignores this kernel of desire, Žižek's attack is, in the end, very un-Žižekian, and resembles Christian theology more than cultural critique. What would a cultural critique of digital Zen entail? Obviously, Digital Zen is often a virtual orientalist practice, which as Justin Chin writes, generates "violence and bigotry directed toward Asian Americans" (Chin 1999, 177; Iwamura 2011). Yet, what about for those convert practitioners? The Zen of Second Life, and postwar American Buddhism more generally, fills a craving for those who use it. Consider, for instance, Jack Kerouac's (1958) statement in *The Dharma Bums*, "Let there be blowing-out and Bliss forevermore" (155).

Understanding the attraction of Digital Buddhism does not mean that we must bracket off and not judge the Zen of Second Life. As Roszak (1968) writes, much Zen was simply a "pretext for license" (136). In other words, is mindfulness a fabricated bliss that lessens the sting of late capitalism, or is it a way of understanding the world around us so that we can make changes to it? For instance, where has Wiener's steersman retreated in all blissful awareness? Where is the systems manager? The mindful Zen subject? Near the end of Petrie's (2013) "Wake Up!" is an image entitled, "Look from the Loft," which "will help you pull all the ideas from this paper together under one roof" (12; Figure 6.4).

Figure 6.4   Look from the loft. "Imagine that the house is your mind and the flood water outside is all the pressures, thoughts, and emotions you face each day" (Petrie 2013, 12). (Used with Permission of Nick Petrie and Center for Creative Leadership)

Echoing Wiener's metaphor of the cybernetic system as a house, the image shows a stylized line drawing of a home, with water cascading in through an open door and dangerously rising up. A silhouette of a small figure dangles from the rafter, as if he has pulled himself above the flood. In the image, the steersman is obviously aware of the system, but the system seems to be in crisis, tearing itself apart. What does a mindful self but impotent subject do when the system is obviously imploding and is no longer sustainable or worthy of sustaining? The Zen of Second Life may make practitioners compassionately aware of a system in crisis and may even make them feel better, but does it give them the tools to change their situation? As Zygmnut Bauman (1993) writes in *Postmodern Ethics*, "The postmodern perspective offers more wisdom; the postmodern setting makes acting on that wisdom more difficult. This is, roughly, why the postmodern time is experienced as living through crisis" (245).

NOTES

1. Now closed, the simulation was launched January 5, 2007 (Tenzin Tuque, January 5, 2007). Comment on "Bodhi Sim launched." *Second Life Forums Archive > Second Life Group Forums > Buddhists of SL* http://forums-archive. secondlife.com/245/e6/158791/1.html accessed January 20, 2014. A You-Tube video can be viewed at "Bodhi—Land of Buddhadharma," uploaded by Danilo Curci, July 26, 2009, *YouTube*, http://www.youtube.com/watch?v=rp NGpB77oO8 accessed February 2, 2012.
2. Linden Lab, "Second Life," http://secondlife.com/.
3. Slavoj Žižek, "The Buddhist Ethic and The Spirit of Global Capitalism," in Europea Graduate School Lecture, August 10, 2012. Transcribed by Roland Bolz and Manuel Vargas Ricalde (English). The European Graduate School, http://www.egs.edu/faculty/slavoj-zizek/articles/the-buddhist-ethic-and-the-spirit-of-global-capitalism/ accessed January 23, 2014.
4. The notecard gives a citation to a September 2007 issue of *Shambhala Sun* and to the author, Cyndi Lee. The actual citation, however, seems to be Cyndi Lee, "Can I be Honest with You?" in *Mindful: Taking Time for What Matters,* http://www.mindful.org/in-love-and-relationships/relating-to-others/can-i-be-honest-with-you accessed January 22, 2014.
5. This seems to be a slightly edited version excerpted from Thich Nhat Hanh, *The Blooming of a Lotus: Guided Meditation for Achieving the Miracle of Mindfulness* (Boston, MA: Beacon Press, 2009).
6. The full text is available here: http://www.mindful.org/in-love-and-relationships/relating-to-others/can-i-be-honest-with-you.
7. As Jaron Lanier (2010) writes, in digital devices such as the iPhone, "A dual message is conveyed. The white void is empty, awaiting you and almost any-thing you project into it. The exception is the surrounding institution, the business, which is not something to be projected away" (212). Consider the cofounder of Apple Inc., Steve Jobs, who Lanier (2010, 211–212) scolds as a trickster guru (see Watts 1951). Before starting Apple, Jobs worked for Atari, designing the game *Breakout* so he could earn enough money to go backpack-ing in India (Lanier 2010). When Jobs returned, he began frequenting the Los Altos Zen Center, meditating and studying under the Zen Master Kobin

Chino Otogowa, whom he later hired as the official *roshi* of the company NeXt and who was even the officiant at Jobs's marriage. From the beginning, as Michael Green (1986) describes in *Zen and the Art of Macintosh*, Apple's marketing and design has been to harness and transcend the "obsessive perfection of the analytical grid" (140). Such mystic technological designs are evident in the iPod and iMac and especially in the iPad, whose design models Creative Worldwide, Inc.'s Zen mp3 player.

8. In a chapter titled "Machines of Loving Grace," Roszak (1986), referring to Brautigan's poem, writes, "For the surviving remnants of the counterculture in the late seventies, it was digital data, rather than domes, archaeologies, or space colonies, that would bring us to the postindustrial promised land" (39).

9. The poem was originally handed out on the streets of Haight-Ashbury in the summer of 1967. A copy of the handbill can be found at http://www.redhouse books.com/galleries/freePoems/allWatchedOver.htm (reprinted in *The Pill versus the Springhill Mine Disaster,* copyright 1968 by Richard Brautigan, http:// www.brautigan.net/machines.html); Brautigan (2971, 240).

10. Alan Watts was probably introduced to cybernetics through Bateson, whom he knew from Esalen, a countercultural retreat center in Big Sur (Kripal 2007). For instance, in *Psychotherapy, East and West*, citing Bateson, Watts (1961) posed Zen as a type of "psychotherapy, as a problem of communication, 'the social matrix of psychiatry'" (123).

11. That Pascale's "Zen and the Art of Management" was *de facto* about cybernetic management is clear if we look at the trajectory of his later work. Consider, *Surfing the Edge of Chaos: The Laws of Nature and the New Laws of Business,* where he argues that managers should turn their companies into agile adaptable "living systems" (Pascale, Milleman, and Gioja 2001). The book was a popularization of Pascale's (2011) article "Intentional Breakdowns And Conflict By Design," which argued, "According to an obscure tenet of cybernetics, the Law of Requisite Variety: 'Any system must encourage and incorporate variety internally if it is to cope with variety externally.' In other words, it takes variety to manage variety" (13).

12. For instance, Williams (2011) lists thirty-three management books that use "Zen" in their name, and a total of eighty-seven "Zen and the Art of" titles (57–70). While Pascale's article was influential, however, the over determination of "Zen" can be traced to corporate America's anxiety with Japan in the early 1980s (Williams 2011, 41–43). By the late 2010s, after the deflating the of Japanese economic bubble, and American outsourcing of manufacturing to China starting in the 1990s, it is hard to imagine the overarching concern Western corporate managers had for Japan. Consider, for instance, the May 23, 1983, article in *Business Week*, "Chip Wars: The Japanese Threat," or documentaries such as NBC's *If Japan Can, Why Can't We* (1980), and PBS's *Japan: The Electronic Tribe* (1987) (Williams 2011, 42). The consensus was, as John Micklethwait and Adrian Wooldridge (1996) write in *The Witch Doctors: Making Sense of the Management Gurus*, that, "Japanese manufacturing trounced American ones in the 1980's because they embraced 'quality'" (18). As reflected in the popular culture, this anxiety about quality and a Japanese spiritual discipline is evident in such films as Ron Howard's 1986 comedy *Gung Ho*, which tells the story of a Japanese corporate take over of an American car factory. For instance, in a scene after the auto factory has been re-opened, a white-coated Japanese inspector tells a blue-collar line worker that his car is defective (31:40). The worker replies, "That's the dealer's problem. Every car can't be perfect." The inspector states, "In Japan, if there is defect, worker is ashamed. He stays [the] night to fix. In Japan, [the] goal is zero percent defect."

REFERENCES

Aguayo, Rafael. 1990. *Dr. Deming: The American Who Taught the Japanese about Quality*. New York: Simon and Schuster.

Ames, Van Meter. 1960. "Current Western Interest in Zen." *Philosophy East and West* 10(1/2): 23–33.

Ashby, William Ross. 1956. *An Introduction to Cybernetics*. New York: Chapman & Hall.

Bateson, Gregory. 1972. *Steps to an Ecology of Mind*. Chicago: University of Chicago Press.

Bauman, Zygmnut. 1993. *Postmodern Ethics*. London: Wilely.

Brautigan, Richard. 1967. *All Watched Over by Machines of Loving Grace*. San Francisco: The Communication Company.

Bush, Vannevar. 1945. "As We May Think." *Atlantic*. http://www.theatlantic.com/magazine/print/1969/12/as-we-may-think/3881/. Accessed January 24, 2014.

Chidester, David. 2005. *Authentic Fakes: Religion and American Popular Culture*. Berkeley: University of California Press.

Chin, Justin. 1999. *Mongrel: Essays, Diatribes, + Pranks*. New York: Macmillan.

Coleman, William James. 2002. *The New Buddhism: The Western Transformation of an Ancient Tradition*. London: Oxford University Press.

Deitrick, James. 2003. "Engaged Buddhist Ethics: Mistaking the Boat for the Shore." In *Action Dharma: New Studies in Engaged Buddhism*, edited by Christopher Queen, Charles Keown, and Damien Keown, 252–269. New York: Routledge.

Dickstein, Morris. 1977. *Gates of Eden: American Culture in the Sixties*. New York: Penguin Books, 1977.

Ellul, Jacques. 1976. *The Ethics of Freedom*. New York: Wm. B. Eerdmans Publishing Company.

Green, Michael. 1986. *Zen and the Art of Macintosh*. New York: Running Press.

Grieve, Gregory. 2011. "Do Human Rights Need a Self? A Skillful Reading of Engaged Buddhism, Literature and the Heroic Compassion of the Samsaric Subject." In *Human Rights and Literature*, edited by Elizabeth Swanson Goldberg and Alexandra Schultheis, 247–261. Philadelphia: University of Pennsylvania Press.

Griffiths, Paul. 1986. *On Being Mindless: Buddhist Meditation and the Mind-Body Problem*. La Salle, IL: Open Court.

Hanh, Thich Nhat. 1974. *Zen Keys*. New York: Random House.

———. 2000. *Going Home: Jesus and Buddha as Brothers*. New York: Riverhead Trade.

———. 2009. *The Blooming of a Lotus: Guided Meditation for Achieving the Miracle of Mindfulness*. Boston: Beacon Press.

Hayles, Katherine. 1999. *How We Became Posthuman: Virtual Bodies in Cybernetics, Literature, and Informatics*. Chicago: The University of Chicago Press.

Hendershot, Heather. 2004. *Shaking the World for Jesus: Media and Conservative Evangelical Culture*. Chicago: University of Chicago Press.

Hoover, Stewart. 2002. "The Cultural Construction of Religion and Media." In *Practicing Religion in the Age of the Media: Explorations in Media, Religion and Culture*, edited by Stewart Hoover and Lynn Schofield Clark, 1–6. New York: Columbia University Press.

Ives, Christopher. 2009. *Imperial-Way Zen: Ichikawa Hakugen's Critique and Lingering Questions for Buddhist Ethics*. Honolulu: University of Hawai'i Press

Iwamura, Jane Naomi. 2011. *Virtual Orientalism: Asian Religions and American Popular Culture*. Oxford: Oxford University Press.

Kapleau, Philip. 1966. "Report from a Zen Monastery, 'All Is One, One Is None, None Is All.'" *New York Times*, March 6, 1966.

112   *Gregory Price Grieve*

Kerouac, Jack. 1958. *The Dharma Bums.* New York: Penguin.
Kripal, Jeffrey J. 2007. *America and the Religion of No Religion.* Chicago: The University of Chicago Press.
Lanier, Jaron. 2010. *You Are Not a Gadget: A Manifesto.* New York: Alfred A. Knopf.
Lee, Cyndi. "Can I be Honest with You?" *Mindful: Taking Time for What Matters.* http://www.mindful.org/in-love-and-relationships/relating-to-others/can-i-be-honest-with-you. Accessed January 22, 2014.
Matusek, Paul. 1986. "Corporate Zen: Zen—Mediation in Japanese Companies." *Bonner Zeitschrift für Japanologie* 8: 170–176.
McCloud, Sean. 2004. *Making the American Religious Fringe: Exotics, Subversives, and Journalists, 1955–1993.* Chapel Hill: University of North Carolina Press.
Micklethwait, John, and Adrian Wooldridge. 1996. *The Witch Doctors: Making Sense of the Management Gurus.* New York: Times Books.
Mumford, Lewis. 1979. *The Myth of the Machine: Technics and Human Development.* New York: Harvest/HBJ Book.
Ney, David. 1994. *American Technological Sublime.* Boston: MIT Press.
Pascale, Richard. 1978. "Zen and the Art of Management: A Different Approach to Management for the 'Cards-on-the-Table' Executive, Which Works." *Harvard Business Review.* br.org/1978/03/zen-and-the-art-of-management/ar/1. Accessed January 26, 2014.
———, Mark Milleman, and Linda Gioja. 2001. *Surfing the Edge of Chaos: The Laws of Nature and the New Laws of Business.* New York: Crown Business.
Petrie, Nick. 2013. "Wake Up! The Surprising Truth about What Drives Stress and How Leaders Build Resilience." www.ccl.org/leadership/pdf/research/WakeUp.pdf. Accessed June 23, 2014.
Pirsig, Robert. 1974. *Zen and the Art of Motorcycle Maintenance: An Inquiry into Values.* New York: Bantam Books.
Prebish, Charles. 1979. *American Buddhism.* North Scituate, MA: Duxbury Press.
"Religion: Zen: Beat & Square." 1958. *Time.* Monday, July 21.
Roszak, Theodore. 1968. *The Making of a Counter Culture: Reflections on the Technocratic Society and Its Youthful Opposition.* New York: Doubleday.
———. 1986. *From Satori to Silicon Valley.* San Francisco, CA: Don't Call it Frisco Press.
Smith, David. 2010. "The Authenticity of Alan Watts." In *American Buddhism as a Way of Life,* edited by Gary Storhoff and John Whalen-Bridge, 13–39. Albany, NY: SUNY Press.
Snyder, Gary. 1961. "Buddhist Anarchism." *Journal for the Protection of All Beings* 1: 1–13.
———. 1969. "Buddhism and the Coming Revolution." In *Earth House Hold: Technical Notes and Queries to Fellow Dharma Revolutionaries.* San Francisco, CA: New Directions.
Spencer, Robert F. 1948. "Social Structure of a Contemporary Japanese-American Buddhist Church." *Social Forces* 26(3): 281–287.
Thompson, James. 1967. *Organization in Action.* New York: McGraw Press.
Tweed, Thomas. 1992. *The American Encounter with Buddhism: 1844–1912.* Chapel Hill: The University of North Carolina Press.
U.S. Office of the Federal Register. 1961. Eisenhower, Dwight D. (Dwight David), 1890–1969, United States. President (1953–1961: Eisenhower). Washington, DC: Office of the Federal Register, National Archives and Records Service, General Services Administration.
Victoria, Daizen [Brian]. 1997. *Zen at War.* New York: Routledge.
Watts, Alan. 1951. *The Wisdom of Insecurity: A Message for an Age of Anxiety.* New York: Pantheon Books.

————. 1958. *The Way of Zen*. New York: Pantheon.

————. 1961. *Psychotherapy, East and West*. New York: New American Library.

————. 2002. *The Tao of Philosophy*. North Clarendon, VT: Tuttle Publishing.

Wiener, Norbert. 1948. *Cybernetics, or Control and Communication in the Animal and the Machine*. New York: The Technology Press.

————. 1950. *Human Use of Human Beings*. New York: Houghton Mifflin.

————. 1964. *I Am a Mathematician: The Later Life of a Prodigy*. Cambridge, MA: MIT Press.

Williams, John. 2011. "Techne-Zen and the Spiritual Quality of Global Capitalism." *Critical Inquiry* 37: 17–70.

Žižek, Slavoj. 1997. *The Plague of Fantasies*. London: Verso.

————. 2012. "The Buddhist Ethic and The Spirit of Global Capitalism." In *European Graduate School Lecture, August 10, 2012*. Transcribed by Roland Bolz and Manuel Vargas Ricalde (English). The European Graduate School. http://www.egs.edu/faculty/slavoj-zizek/articles/the-buddhist-ethic-and-the-spirit-of-global-capitalism/. Accessed January 23, 2014.

Part III

Buddhism, Media, and Society

7 The Madhyama Is the Message
Internet Affordance of *Anatman* and *Pratitya Samutpada*

Daniel Veidlinger

It may come as no surprise that religion is a very popular topic on social networking sites. In fact, in 2009 on MySpace.com, which was the most prominent social networking site before Facebook arrived on the scene, Jesus Christ was mentioned as an interest in three times more profiles than was Britney Spears, and Buddhism was equally as trendy as the pop singer. MySpace featured a great deal of information about people's spirituality when I examined the data in over a million profiles in 2009 and happily for the sake of comparison, a major survey of religion in America conducted by the Pew Forum on Religion and Public Life (2007) had just a few years earlier also produced valuable data about the religious affiliations of Americans across the country. Interestingly enough, the data from the offline survey matched almost exactly the data that could be found on MySpace. For instance, the percentage of MySpace users in America who wrote that they were Catholic was virtually the same as those who told the Pew survey they were Catholic. Likewise for Jews, Hindus, and most other religions. However, one religion was cited in more than two and a half times as many MySpace profiles as one would expect based on the Pew survey results. That religion was Buddhism.

This chapter will look at whether it is possible that there is something about being connected to others online that may lead people to display an affinity for Buddhism. In other words, does the Internet make you Buddhist? In addition to the MySpace profiles, I had the opportunity to study several million profiles from Facebook in May 2009, which revealed more data about the position of Buddhism among social network users in America. The analysis of the interests that were cited in the North American Facebook profiles showed once again that people in this kind of online environment appear to be far more interested in Buddhism than one would expect based upon knowledge of the general patterns of offline religious affiliation. Interestingly, the king of social networking, Mark Zuckerberg, creator of Facebook, in September 2010 listed only a few interests in his own profile, one of which was "Eliminating Desire" (Vargas 2010, 54), which may be a cryptic reference to an abiding interest in Buddhism, as had one of his heroes, Steve Jobs.[1] As I will show further on, we are now coming to the point where we can say that Buddhism is gaining popularity among Internet users much faster than any other major world religion.

How can we account for these factors? Is it possible that Internet usage, or in particular the experience of using Social Networks, can foster an interest in Buddhism in the user? The debate about whether technology itself can shape human thought and behavior has a long and varied history,[2] with some people arguing that technology *allows* certain behaviors but does not actually *cause* them, and others holding a stronger version that gives causal agency to technology (Bimber 1994). This debate, however, misconstrues human agency. Much like the argument over gun control, the human decision to actually pull the trigger, or click the mouse, only creates the illusion that the choice belongs to humans. For instance, although gun advocates often say, "Guns don't kill people, people kill people," the fact is that the more guns there are in a society, the more gun deaths there are. In a similar fashion, the more computers there are, the more this technology shapes society and religious practices in certain ways (Campbell 2005).

Early academic study of mass media as pioneered by thinkers such as Marshall McLuhan (1964) and Walter Ong (1982) has suggested that the way we receive information does, in fact, influence the way it is processed and affect the way people within that communications nexus see themselves and the world around them. McLuhan's famous dictum, "The medium is the message,"[3] sums up this approach succinctly and, though controversial, it has informed a great deal of innovative research in the field. With this background, we can then begin to ask whether the Internet affords all religions equally, or whether the effects that this particular mass medium has can influence society in a particular religious direction. Cowan and Dawson (2004) were among the first to identify a need "to discern whether the technological and cultural aspects of the Internet are better suited to the advancement of one style or type of religion over another" (11). This chapter argues that the Internet affords the Buddhist notions that the personal ego is merely a tissue of conditioned mental and physical elements (*anatman*) that are sustained through an interconnected web of dependent origination (*pratitya samutpada*). It posits that the Internet has this effect because advances in communication technologies have allowed humans to interact more intimately with a greater number of other people over vaster distances than ever before and this interaction problematizes our understanding of the limits of the self.[4] In order to add further support to this contention, besides analyzing millions of profiles on social networks to discern what people were saying about their religious beliefs and leanings, I also conducted a detailed survey about religious beliefs and online usage behaviors that will be described later. This survey strongly suggests that there is a direct link between using the Internet and endorsing the ideas of selflessness and dependent origination.

My research is significant because it suggests that in communicative environments such as the Internet, some of the ideas that are most prominently found in Buddhism have a propensity to take hold. For those raised in a religious or philosophical tradition that celebrates the individuated subject and sees the world in dualistic terms of self and other, telematic communications that deepen inter-subjective connectivity and blur our personal borders engender a growing cognitive dissonance, which can be reduced through the adoption of the kind of ontology found in Buddhism. This points to a continued interest and acceptance of these key ideas of Buddhism as the Internet and social networking permeates our society more fully and is likely to affect the spiritual development of humanity to a considerable degree in the years to come.

METHOD: SOCIAL MEDIA SURVEY AND ANALYSIS

My research for this inquiry consists of two parts. First, I performed a content analysis of social network profiles by downloading 1,182,800 MySpace profiles and using parsing software to tease out a list of interests as well as religious affiliations of the users who produced the profiles. I also used Facebook's ad-targeting system to tell me how many of their users claimed to belong to the different religions of the world and how many had various other interests related to my inquiry. For the second part, in order to get a fuller picture of the specific beliefs that might underlie the apparent outsized interest in Buddhism online, I conducted a survey of religious beliefs among Internet users that was aimed at discerning whether there are correlations between Internet usage and religious ideology. The survey contained a number of questions where the subjects were requested to indicate how much they agreed with the statement at hand, and it also collected demographic information and asked the subjects to indicate how much time they spent on the Internet and on social networks and to rate the degree of their involvement (see the Appendix).

The survey was distributed to a random sample of Facebook users. The method of delivery was through an advertisement that was built using Facebook's self-serve ad-creation system as found at http://www.facebook.com/ads/create/. The advertisement was displayed randomly to all users of Facebook during two timeframes, the first during May 2010 and the second during November 2010. A total of 2,972,167 impressions of the advertisement were delivered leading to 878 clicks. When the Facebook users clicked on the ad, they were taken to the online survey, and 309 people actually completed the survey. The data was then collected automatically into a spreadsheet that was used to compile the results.[5] The subjects were asked to rate the degree to which they endorse these ideas found in questions 7–21 on a scale of 1 to 9, with 1 indicating strong disagreement, 5 a neutral attitude, and 9 strong agreement. For the amount of time spent on the Internet each day (Q1), subjects were given a choice ranging from one to ten hours. For the question about how much they participate in producing Internet Culture (Q3), subjects were prompted to think in terms of how many blog postings, status updates, and other user-generated instances of content they produce. They were then given five choices ranging from "not really, a little, a fair bit, a lot, it's my main activity."

The responses were analyzed to see if there were correlations between certain answers. The scale used is a standard Pearson correlation index ranging from –1 to 1, where a score of 1 indicates that the two sets of data are perfectly correlated, with one following the ups and downs of the other exactly: as the former increases, there will be a corresponding increase in the second. A score of –1, therefore, means that they are inversely related, such that a high score in one invariably means that there will be a very low score in the other. A score of 0 means that there is no appreciable correlation between the two datasets, suggesting that knowledge of one set of data will predict nothing about the data that will be found in the second set.

The results of the survey do indeed suggest that there is a statistically significant correlation between Internet usage and certain religious ideas. It is well known in statistics that a correlation between sets of data does not necessarily imply that one affects the other, and this point is to be kept in mind while reading the following information. But in the absence of other ways to explain the correlations, it is appropriate to assume that the reason two sets of data are correlated is that the processes represented by one set of data have some direct effect on the other. I will discuss the possible reasons for the results after I have presented them. The discussion will demonstrate that it is certainly reasonable to assert that the connections and correlations are, in fact, a result of Internet usage and not a product of some other factor.

THE BUDDHIST CORE: *ANATMAN* AND *PRATITYA SAMUTPADA*

Before discussing how the Internet might affect the reception of Buddhist ideas, it is necessary to examine just what is meant by "Buddhist ideas." There are in Buddhism, as in all world religions, many different notions about what the teachings of the religion are. For the purposes of the present inquiry, since this volume focuses on Buddhism and digital media, I will use a principle in information theory to sift out the "key Buddhist ideas." Information is not just any data, but rather information must provide something new that one does not already know, that is not redundant (Shannon 1948). On that score, the features of Buddhism that are distinctively Buddhist and that cannot be found in any other tradition are the ideas of impermanence, no-soul, and dependent origination. These ideas are exclusive to Buddhism, whereas many other ideas found in Buddhism, such as the importance of having compassion, honoring the founder of the religion, belief in deities who can help one achieve heavenly states—all these can be found in many, if not most, other religions. This approach supports Japanese Buddhologist Matsumoto Shiro, who says, "Buddhism is the teaching of non-self and the teaching of causality . . . the crucial point is the denial of any eternal, substantial, underlying basis or locus on which everything else depends upon or arises from" (quoted in Swanson 1997, 7).

At its core there are two key Buddhist concepts: *anatman* and *pratitya samutpada*. In Buddhist ontology, the idea of *anatman* posits that there is no permanent soul. Rather, the human personality consists of interactions amongst the five aggregates or *skandhas*—body, feeling, perception, mental formations, and consciousness—that together constitute our psycho-physical complex, and are in a constant state of flux from moment to moment. The dynamics of this system give rise to the sensation that there is a self or soul lurking within that is the source of our true identity and the witness to our experiences, but this is not in Buddhism's view a correct apprehension of reality. The Buddhist notion of *pratitya samutpada* holds that things do not exist in and of themselves, but rather arise due to other causes and conditions, which are in turn dependent on yet other causes, creating an unending, interdependent network of causes that form our reality, much like a spider's web, with each part sustaining the other. Nothing, in this view, can be truly separated from the conditions that gave rise to it, and this has led to a profound emphasis on compassion in the Buddhist tradition.

The networked nature of the Internet is capable of bringing these Buddhist ideas to life in an explicit way that no other technology has until now been able to do. The idea that we affect each other through our actions in some way, regardless of whether we live in close proximity, is much easier to apprehend through using the Internet than through daily life without this extension of our reach. Sudhana's famous vision of Indra's Jeweled Net found in the *Avatamsaka Sutra* is one of the best and most well-known examples of this idea in the Buddhist literature. As Francis Cook describes it:

> Far away in the heavenly abode of the great god Indra, there is a wonderful net which has been hung by some cunning artificer in such a manner that it stretches out infinitely in all directions. In accordance with the extravagant tastes of deities, the artificer has hung a single glittering jewel in each "eye" of the net, and since the net itself is infinite in dimension, the jewels are infinite in number. There hang the jewels, glittering like stars in the first magnitude, a wonderful sight to behold. If we now arbitrarily select one of these jewels for inspection and look closely at it, we will discover that in its polished surface there are reflected *all* the other jewels in the net, infinite in number. Not only that, but each of the jewels reflected in this one jewel is also reflecting all the other jewels, so that there is an infinite reflecting process occurring.

(Cook 1977, 2)

Another good reason to consider the ideas of *anatman* and *pratitya samutpada* to be among the core defining ideas of Buddhism is that, whatever the scholar of Buddhism might say about the position of these ideas within Buddhist doctrine, the people who responded to my survey do appear to believe that they are closely associated with Buddhism. Those who self-identified on Q25 as Buddhist endorsed these ideas as expressed in Q13 (The self is an illusion) and Q17 (The universe is an interdependent web) more strongly than they were endorsed by the adherents of any other religion. The average Buddhist endorsement of Q13 was 8.11 with a standard deviation of 1.69, and of Q17 was 8.67 with a standard deviation of 0.71. The next highest score for Q13 was held by Muslims at 7.43, and for Q17 was held by Wiccans at 7.00. Since these were out of a scale of 9, with 9 indicating "Strongly Agree," the Buddhist score is about as high a score as a proposition in this kind of survey is likely to get. Indeed, on the entire array of fifteen doctrinal questions across all the major religions, there were only two scores that were higher than 8.67: Both Protestants and Catholics had the same score of 8.81 for the idea that "There is a Divine Being who created the Universe" (Q8); and Muslims apparently feel that "Helping others is my ultimate goal" (Q12), because it received a score of 8.86. This makes it quite clear that regardless of the actual prominence of these ideas within the texts or the lived history of Buddhism in Asia, modern American Internet users who identify themselves as Buddhist seem to agree also with these ideas most strongly. It also must be noted that the Buddha himself identified dependent origination with the deepest meaning of the Dharma, declaring, "Whoever sees dependent origination sees the Dharma; whoever sees the Dharma sees dependent origination" (*Majjhima Nikaya*.I.191). It is now time to look in more detail at the evidence that I have gathered to show that using the Internet is associated with greater adherence to Buddhism or its associated key ideas.

SOCIAL NETWORK STATISTICS

My analysis of social media uncovered a good amount of evidence to suggest that something is happening online that is moving people in the direction of Buddhism. I will first present the data that I found in American Facebook and MySpace profiles, and then move on to look at the online survey that I conducted. I analyzed Myspace.com in March 2009, when it was still a leading social network, and in this case, as I have already said, the religious affiliation figures were remarkably similar to what was found in the Pew survey with the notable exception of Buddhism. For my study, 1,182,800 profiles were examined and the results are shown in Table 7.1.

Table 7.1 Religious Affilitation on MySpace.com Compared to Results of Pew Religious Landscape Survey

Religion	MySpace Adherents	Proportion	Pew survey
Catholic	305963	25.90%	23.90%
Other Christian	687119	58.10%	52.20%
Jewish	18493	1.60%	1.70%
Muslim	11280	0.90%	0.60%
Hindu	6545	0.50%	0.40%
Secular/Atheist	110482	9.30%	16.10%
Wiccan	20728	1.70%	n/a
Buddhist	22188	1.90%	0.70%

Created by Daniel Veidlinger.

From Table 7.1 one can see that, aside from Wiccan (see Grieve 1995), which was not reported on the Pew survey, the religion whose popularity was by far the greatest in comparison to the Pew survey was Buddhism, with a 271 percent increase in self-reported adherents above what the Pew survey found. This is not a one-off anomaly, because a similar bias toward Buddhism can be seen on Facebook as well.

On Facebook in 2009, there were 423,380 people who self-identified as Catholic and 16,300 who identified as Buddhist, giving a ratio of 26:1 in favor of Catholicism. However, the major survey of 35,000 people conducted by the Pew Forum on Religion & Public Life between May 8 and August 13, 2007, put the Catholic population of the United States at 70,000,000 or 24 percent of the population and the Buddhist population at 2,037,000 or 0.7 percent of the population.[6] This produces a ratio of 34:1 of Catholics versus Buddhists through the Pew study, as opposed to 26:1 through the Facebook figures that I obtained. Accordingly, on Facebook there is a significantly higher presence of people defining themselves as Buddhist when marked against those defining themselves as Catholic compared to the Pew study. If we look at the *interests* of people on Facebook, the differential between what one might find in the offline and online worlds is even more pronounced. There were 13,840 people who mentioned Catholicism as one of their interests, but a staggering 29,220 mentioned Buddhism as an interest. This suggests that while people identify themselves formally as Buddhist in this environment more commonly relative to the offline population as a whole, they show an order of magnitude greater *interest* in Buddhism. The number of those who were interested in Buddhism was almost double the number of those identifying as Buddhists, whereas the interest in Catholicism was far less than the number of adherents. For comparison, the number of people interested in "Judaism" was ten times smaller than the amount of people describing themselves as Jewish. "Christianity" was cited by 91,600 people as an interest, which is almost twenty times smaller than the 1,764,700 people who identified as Christian. Note that this number is only three times greater than the total number of those who are interested in Buddhism, even though the number of adherents is dozens of times that of Buddhism.

SURVEY RESPONSES ENDORSING *ANATMAN* AND *PRATITYA SAMUTPADA*

With the social network profiles as a background, it is now time to focus on the survey to get a more nuanced understanding of what might be occurring online with respect to Buddhist ideas. In the survey responses, there was a significant degree of correlation between Internet usage and religious beliefs in only a few of the cases, and these bear very strongly on core ideas of Buddhism. The highest correlation scores were in fact between Internet usage and the following two beliefs: "The individual is an illusion: All things are actually Interconnected on a deep level" (Q13) and "The Universe is an Interdependent Web of Being" (Q17). Not only were these the two highest-scoring correlations, but they were, in fact, the only beliefs that were significantly correlated with Internet usage at all. The only other beliefs from among the many that were queried in this survey that showed any appreciable correlation with Internet usage was "I believe in Cosmic Justice—i.e., Karma . . . etc . . ."(Q15), with a score of 0.131,with hours spent on the Internet (Q1), and 0.170 with production of Internet Culture (Q3), and "It is possible that Religions other than my own may be True" (Q21), which correlated with Q1 at a score of 0.137.

The correlation scores for Q13 and Q17 with Internet usage were the most significant of all the questions from a statistical point of view, taking into consideration the number of respondents to the survey as noted in Table 7.2.

Table 7.2   Correlation of Internet Involvement with Key Buddhist Ideas Using Pearson Index

Survey Question	Survey Question	Correlation Score
Internet Usage (Q1)	Individual is an illusion (Q13)	0.213
Internet Usage (Q1)	Interdependent Web (Q17)	0.162
Producing Internet Culture (Q3)	Individual is an illusion (Q13)	0.235
Producing Internet Culture (Q3)	Interdependent Web (Q17)	0.219

Created by Daniel Veidlinger.

If we look at the average score for some of the questions, and then look at the averages for specific segments within the population, we can learn more about trends and tendencies among the subjects. Respondents were asked what religion they would like to learn more about (Q27), and the top responses were Christianity, Judaism, Islam, and Buddhism, in that order. But, if we calculate the average time spent on the Internet of these segments, we find some telling results. The overall average amount of time per day spent on the Internet among all 309 respondents was 3.81 hours. Among people with an interest in learning about different religions, we find that those who said they were most interested in learning more about Buddhism (n = 24) were on the Internet for a remarkably high average of 5.43 hours every day. This is over 40% more Internet usage every day than the average person, suggesting a connection between using the Internet and coming to an interest in Buddhism. For comparison, the average time spent by people who were becoming interested in Christianity (n = 31) was 3.03 hours, Judaism (n = 15) 3.43, and Islam (n = 14) 3.25, all of which are slightly below the average. All of those interested in Buddhism said that they participate in producing Internet culture "A fair bit" or "a lot," except for one who said "a little," whereas among those interested in the other religions, many instances of "Not Really" are seen.

DISCUSSION: THE SIGNIFICANCE OF IMMERSION

These results suggest that people who use the Internet express an increased interest in Buddhism. This striking result must be explained, and the possibility that Internet use is actually a factor in creating the observed interest in Buddhist ideas must be investigated. In the 1990s, it was the case that North Americans who tended to be interested in Buddhism came from the same demographic group as did Internet users, namely upper-middle-class educated whites (Prebish and Tanaka 1998). Therefore, results such as those that I have shown could be understood as simply a reflection of the pre-existing tendencies of a particular demographic group, rather than a result of the effects of actually using the Internet. However, in recent years, the Internet has permeated society to such a degree that there are no longer any significant differences between its usage in different demographic groups.[7] Therefore, we should look to the significance of "immersion" in creating the observed effects.

"Immersion" creates an experience of "being there" "that organizes sensory information in such a way as to create a psychological state in which an individual perceives himself or herself as being present or having 'presence' in them" (Blasovich 2002, 129). Most people have experienced the sense of being sucked into a good movie while watching the screen. One forgets about the world outside the theater and becomes completely involved in the events impinging the senses. Online, immersion occurs when the actual world is sufficiently muted, and the virtual world sufficiently heightened, creating a feeling that one is no longer in the actual world (Grieve and Heston 2011). When subjects are using the Internet for extended periods of time, especially when participating in a virtual world such as Second Life or a social network in which they are projecting a representation of themselves into the online world, they may feel drawn into the computer such that the boundary of their self-identity is extended beyond the physical body and into the more expansive cybernetic world on the screen. Upon reflection, this would problematize the view that there is a constant and unchanging, unitary, embodied entity that is their essential identity or self, for if so, how could it extend to the computer and beyond?

Recent developments in cognitive science can be used to explain the effects on a user's psychology of this process and to bolster the traditional Buddhist view about the lack of a self by shedding light on precisely why and how the illusion of an embodied, independent self emerges, and consequently how it can be deconstructed. Research into the etiology of the cognitive sense of selfhood shows such remarkable accord with traditional Buddhist understandings of this phenomenon that Thomas Metzinger, founder of the Association for the Scientific Study of Consciousness, can commence his provocative book *The Ego Tunnel: The Science of the Mind and the Myth of the Self*, with an echo of the Buddha, " I will try to convince you that there is no such thing as a self . . . There is no thing, no indivisible entity that is *us*" (Metzinger 2009, 1).

Metzinger points out that the integration of variegated sensual stimuli into one coherent mental image of the world and the body's place within it is crucial for the construction of a sense of self. As Buddhism posits, different kinds of consciousness arise based on aural, visual, tactile, and other stimuli, but of course these must all be reconciled so that the mind knows that, for example, the sweet smell hitting the nose, the red petals exciting the eyes, and the sharp thorns digging into the hands are all coming from the same object. Based on this input, a phenomenal model of a rose arises in the mind. In like manner, the sensing of one's own body allows for the notion of an embodied self to arise in the mind.

This phenomenon has been implicated in experiments conducted by Botvinick and Cohen (1998) through which subjects were made to perceive a rubber hand placed on a desk as being part of themselves. This "rubber-hand illusion" consists of a box into which is placed the healthy subject's left hand and arm up to the elbow so that the subject cannot see it. A realistic-looking rubber hand is then placed on the table in front of the subject and it is stroked with a probe while the hand in the box is simultaneously stroked in exactly the same way. After a few minutes, the subject begins to perceive the rubber hand as part of his or her own body. There is even a sensation commonly reported in which the position of the real arm is perceived as changing such that it is connected to the rubber hand. Metzinger has successfully replicated these results using a full-body mannequin, which he says comes to be endowed with "mineness," a conscious sense of ownership on the part of the subject (Metzinger 2009, 5–6). In these cases, just as the Buddhist view sees consciousness as the charioteer who controls and organizes the other faculties, so it seems that consciousness brings together the different stimuli from the various senses and integrates them into a phenomenal model of the self that is coherent and located in space and time. But this model is only an illusion that appears real; it can be tricked when tactile and visual stimuli are displaced, as in the experiment above. The Internet may be able to trick the mind into perceiving that one's identity extends into the cyberworld, an effect which would presumably become more pronounced the more time one spends online staring at the screen, and projecting one's identity onto it through producing pictures and videos of oneself, writing text, chatting with friends and especially using an avatar. This experience would naturally tend to make one think more critically about what exactly the individual self is, and upon coming across Buddhist ideas on this matter, surely a person with such experiences would find them more appealing than someone who has not questioned the self in this way.

Some further light can be shed on this issue by Joanna Macy, who has written about the constructed nature of the self from the perspective of systems theory. She points out that because the human being is an open system, it is formally speaking impossible to delineate precisely where the self ends and the other begins. In the case of a blind man walking with a stick, for example, the stick forms an integral part of the system that is taking in information and processing it in order to guide the person through the terrain. The entire circuit that delineates the organism in this case must include the cane, as it surely would the eyes for a seeing person. "The self is a metaphor," she writes:

> We can decide to limit it to our skin, our person, our family, our organization, our species. We can select its boundaries in objective reality. As the systems theorists see it, our consciousness illuminates a small arc in the wider currents and loops of knowing that interconnect us. It is just as plausible to conceive of mind as coexistent with these larger circuits, the entire "pattern which connects."

(Macy 1991, 188–189)

The experience of using Internet technology itself could on this understanding stimulate the apprehension of insights such as this in the user more readily than many other activities, making them more receptive to Buddhism.

The computer is substantially different from any other tool that we use because it is able to process information in a way that can appear to be very like the way a human being processes and analyzes data. It may be that the more one uses a computer, the more one has a tendency to associate the way it operates with the way a human being operates, and to deconstruct thereby the sense that there must be an unchanging soul that animates the mind.

Even back in a 1984, pioneering sociologist of technology Sherry Turkle found in a study of college students that "the idea of thinking of the self as a set of computer programs is widespread among students" (Turkle 1984, 289), especially those who had some familiarity with computers. Based on discussions that she had with computer users, Turkle echoes the Buddhist idea of *anatman* in suggesting that:

> A model of mind as multiprocessor leaves you with a "decentralized" self: there is no "me," no "I," no unitary actor. Mark expressed this when he admonished me not to talk about my mind as though "I" was thinking . . . But theories that deny and "decenter" the "I" challenge most people's day-to-day experience of having one. The assumption that there is an "I" is solidly built into ordinary language, so much so that it is almost impossible to express "anti-ego" theory in language. From the moment that we begin to write or speak, we are trapped in formulations such as "I want," "I do," "I think."
>
> (Turkle 1984, 290–291)

In addition to the effects on the conception of the self that may lead to an appreciation of Buddhist notions of the mutability of the self, the Internet doubtless fosters in the user a deeper understanding of the idea of interdependence than does any other technology. The striking image of Indra's Jeweled Net presented already has many obvious parallels in the architecture of the Internet, which through copious usage can affect the way the user perceives the world in general. As one lives more and more of one's life on the Internet, it becomes progressively more difficult to see each person, thing, or event as isolated in space and time and bearing no connection to other things. The seminal Buddhist teaching of dependent origination, which the Buddha identified with the deepest meaning of the Dharma,[8] is itself then reflected in the Internet. In modern times, Sudhana might have beheld a web of computer screens, with each screen reflecting every other screen.

CONCLUSION

This chapter has used MySpace and Facebook profile data to show that the more time one spends on the Internet, and in particular on social networking sites, the more likely one is to have an affinity for Buddhism. While citing "Buddhism" as an important part of one's religious identity or as an interest in one's life does not in itself tell us anything about exactly what aspects of Buddhism one finds attractive, the survey about religious beliefs and online behavior that I conducted suggests that the Internet affords a conception of the individual self as illusory, replacing an unchanging self with a sense of interconnectedness and interdependence. These ideas dovetail well with the core Buddhist notions of *anatman* (no-self) and *pratitya samutpada* (dependent origination), and are likely to play an important role in the attractiveness of Buddhism to the wired segments of society. Just as the printed word helped to usher in the age of Protestantism[9] as well as biblical literalism, so too the Internet may stimulate the rapid growth of Buddhism in the coming years. Does this mean that the Internet causes people to become Buddhist? That depends on how one conceives of the notion of causality, but it does suggest that the Internet is a key factor in what may be a gradually changing mindset from one in which each person sees oneself as an independent agent unconnected to others to a mindset in which an appreciation for the mutability of the self and the interconnection of people and things around the globe is more pronounced.

Appendix
Survey Questions

1. How many hours per day do you spend on the Internet?
2. How many hours per day do you spend on Social Websites?
3. How much do you participate in producing Internet Culture?
4. Do you agree to the terms of this survey which will be used for academic research?
5. How Frequently do you Meditate?
6. How Frequently do you Pray?
7. There is an eternal Soul that continues after the body dies.
8. There is a Divine Being who Created the Universe.
9. Reaching a permanent state of bliss is my ultimate goal.
10. We must have Compassion for all other Beings.
11. We must conquer our desires in order to reach an advanced stage of spirituality.
12. Helping others is my ultimate goal.
13. The individual is an illusion: All things are actually Interconnected on a deep level.
14. God is separate from Creation.
15. I believe in Cosmic Justice.
16. I believe in Reincarnation.
17. The Universe is an Interdependent Web of Being.
18. All people regardless of race, gender or religion have a chance of achieving Salvation.
19. All beings have a divine spark of God inside them.
20. I believe in my Sacred Texts even when they disagree with Science.
21. It is possible that religions other than my own may be True.
22. What is Your Age?
23. What is Your Gender?
24. What belief system were you born into?
25. What belief system do you currently identify with the most?
26. What is your level of religiosity?
27. What religion would you like to learn more about?

NOTES

1. "Job's engagement with Eastern spirituality, and especially Zen Buddhism, was not just some passing fancy or youthful dabbling. He embraced it with his typical intensity, and it became deeply engrained in his personality" (Isaacson 2011, 35).

2. An early example of thinking that took seriously the ability of technology to shape the way people think can be found in the work of pioneering French socialist Constantin Pecqueur, who wrote in admiring terms about the lofty possibilities of the railways. Even before the radio and telephone opened up new possibilities for communication among people across great distances, the train allowed people to communicate with others more easily and quickly by transporting not just their voice but their bodies quickly over vast expanses:

   > By causing all classes of society to travel together and thus juxtaposing them into a kind of living mosaic of all the fortunes, positions, characters, manners, customs, and modes of dress that each and every nation has to offer, the railroads quite prodigiously advance the reign of truly frater-nal social relations and do more for the sentiments of equality than the most exalted sermons of the tribunes of democracy. To thus foreshorten for everyone the distances that separate localities from each other, is to equally diminish the distances that separate men from one another. (cited in Schivelbusch 1986, 70–71)

3. This phrase can be found in McLuhan's Understanding Media: The Extensions of Man (1964) which, though many of its claims have remained highly controversial, is commonly regarded as having laid the foundation for modern media studies.

4. Like all religions, Buddhism is a rich field that contains many varied beliefs and practices, some of which are even so different as to be contradictory. For example, some early texts suggest that one's deeds and karma follow one inevitably "like a cart following an ox," whereas some Mahayana schools hold that a Bodhisattva can alleviate an individual's karmic burden. Therefore, defining what counts as Buddhism is notoriously difficult, and is a subject that cannot be examined here. When an individual in America cites Buddhism as the religion that most influences them in their social network profile, they can mean many different things by this statement, such as that they meditate regularly, or that they attend worship services at a local Buddhist temple, or that they have read "What the Buddha Taught" and really enjoyed it, or a whole host of other possible definitions, as outlined by Nattier (1998), Prebish (1979), Numrich (2003), and others. This chapter focuses on two elements that have traditionally been considered by both Theravada and Mahayana Buddhists as seminal defining aspects of the Buddha's Dharma: *pratitya samutpada* (often translated as "dependent co-origination") and the associated idea of *anatman* (no-self) that is essentially a corollary of the former notion. The Buddha himself identified *pratitya samutpada* with the deepest meaning of the Dharma, declaring, "Whoever sees dependent co-origination sees the Dhamma; whoever sees the Dhamma sees dependent co-rigination" (*Majjhima Nikaya*.I.191), which is as good a reason as any to focus on this idea as a key expression of Buddhism in this chapter.

5. It is important to point out two possible factors that could in theory skew the results of this survey. There is a self-selection bias to the results, but this is present in any study where the subject is motivated to fill out the survey only based on his or her own desire to do so. Another problem is that for

privacy reasons, the IP addresses of the computers through which the survey was viewed were not tracked. This has lead to the possibility that one person could have filled out the survey multiple times, thus skewing the results, although since there would be absolutely no motivation to do so, it is unlikely that this happened.

6. Another major study conducted in 2001 of over 50,000 people (American Religious Identification Survey) found only 1,082,000 Buddhists making up less than 0.5 percent of the population. For most of the following pages, I will use the Pew study because the ARIS, although conducted on more people, almost certainly underestimates the total number of Buddhists.

7. For a recent May 2013 survey of the demographics of Internet users, see the report of the Pew Internet and American Life project (http://pewinternet.org/Trend-Data-%28Adults%29/Whos-Online.aspx). Here, 85 percent of people surveyed use the Internet and when it is broken down by demographic group, 86 percent of whites, 85 percent of blacks, and 76 percent of Hispanics were online. These results cannot account for the effects that I have documented.

8. The Buddha said "whoever sees dependent origination sees the *dhamma*, whoever sees the *dhamma* sees dependent origination" (*Majjhima Nikaya* I.191).

9. For a good summary of research into the effects of printing on all aspects of Protestantism, from the dissemination of Luther's ideas through printed works, to the focus on reading the Bible, the loosening of clerical control over domestic life, and the bringing of spirituality into the home along with Bibles and prayer books, see Eisenstein (1980), especially chapter 4, "The Scriptural Tradition Recast: Resetting the Stage for the Reformation."

REFERENCES

Bimber, Bruce. 1994. "Three Faces of Technological Determinism." In *Does Technology Drive History?*, edited by Leo Marx and Merritt Smith, 79–100. Cambridge, MA: MIT Press.
Blascovich, J. 2002. "Social Influence within Immersive Virtual Environments." In *The Social Life of Avatars: Presence and Interaction in Shared VirtualEnvironments*, edited by R. Schroeder, 127–145. London: Springer-Verlag.
Botvinik, M., and J. Cohen. 1998. "Rubber Hands 'Feel' the Touch That Eyes See." *Nature* 39(1): 756.
Campbell, Heidi. 2005. *Exploring Religious Community Online: We Are One in the Network*. Oxford: Peter Lang.
Cook, Francis H. 1977. *Hua-Yen Buddhism: The Jewel Net of Indra*. University Park, PA: Penn State University Press.
Cowan, Douglas, and Lorne Dawson, eds. 2004. *Religion Online: Finding Faith on the Internet*. New York: Routledge.
Eisenstein, Elizabeth. 1980. *The Printing Press as an Agent of Change*. Cambridge, UK: Cambridge University Press.
Grieve, Gregory. 1995. "Imagining a Virtual Religious Community: Neo-Pagans on the Internet." *Chicago Anthropology Exchange* 7: 98–132.
Grieve, Gregory, and Kevin Heston. 2011. "Finding Liquid Salvation: Using the Cardean Ethnographic Method to Document Second Life Residents and Religious Cloud Communities." In *Virtual Worlds, Second Life, and Metaverse Platforms: New Communication and Identity Paradigms*, edited by Nelson Zagalo, Leonel Morgado, and Ana Boa-Ventura, 288–305. Hershey, PA: IGI Global.
Isaacson, Walter. 2011. *Steve Jobs*. New York: Simon and Schuster.

Macy, Joanna. 1991. *World as Lover, World as Self*. Berkeley, CA: Parallax Press.

McLuhan, Marshall. 1964. *Understanding Media: The Extensions of Man*. New York: Mentor.

Metzinger, Thomas. 2009. *The Ego Tunnel: The Science of the Mind and the Myth of the Self*. New York: Basic Books.

Nattier, Jan. 1998. "Who Is a Buddhist?" In *The Faces of Buddhism in America*, edited by Charles Prebish and Kenneth Tanaka, 183–195. Berkeley: University of California Press.

Numrich, David. 2003. "Two Buddhisms Further Reconsidered." *Contemporary Buddhism* 4(1): 55–78.

Ong, Walter. 1982. *Orality and Literacy: The Technologizing of the Word*. London: Methuen.

Pew Forum on Religion and Public Life. 2007. *US Religious Landscape Survey*. http://religions.pewforum.org/pdf/report-religious-landscape-study-key-findings.pdf. Accessed August 17, 2012.

Prebish, Charles. 1979. *American Buddhism*. Belmont, CA: Wadsworth.

Prebish, Charles, and Kenneth Tanaka. 1998. *The Faces of Buddhism in America*. Berkeley: University of California Press.

Schivelbusch, Wolfgang. 1986. *The Railway Journey*. Berkeley: University of California Press.

Shannon, Claude. 1948. "A Mathematical Theory of Communication." *Bell System Technical Journal* 27(3): 379–423, 623–656.

Swanson, Paul. 1997. "Why They Say Zen Is Not Buddhism: Recent Japanese Critiques of Buddha Nature." In *Pruning the Bodhi Tree*, edited by Jamie Hubbard and Paul Swanson, 3–29. Honolulu: University of Hawaii Press.

Turkle, Sherry. 1984. *The Second Self: Computers and the Human Spirit*. New York: Simon and Schuster.

Vargas, Jose Antonio. 2010. "The Face of Facebook." *The New Yorker*, September 20, 54–64.

8 Buddhist Apps
Skillful Means or Dharma Dilution?

Rachel Wagner and Christopher Accardo

Cecil Holmes remarks, "when a faith as ancient as Buddhism comes to the United States, it follows a mixture of patterns: It keeps what is necessary for its integrity and it also Americanizes. Americanizing includes making use of available media to explain and explore the faith's tenets" (Holmes 2010, 53). Drawing on the wisdom of those Buddhist-informed communications scholars who call for an awareness of contingency and contextualization, we find that dharma teachings are, in fact, very much shaped by their digital environments. Indeed, the iPhone, with its personalized programs and noise-walling headphones, is perhaps the most poignant icon of American individualism today. Seeking innovative ways to spread the teachings and practices of Buddhism, programmers have begun in recent years to translate elements of Buddhist belief and practice into the form of apps, and in so doing the message has necessarily been altered by the medium.

As Buddhist teachings and practices are transformed into digitized, structured programs experienced largely individually, and as they are consumed via iPhones, iPads, and other mobile devices, they are increasingly experienced alone rather than in community. Therefore, some of the most compelling questions about Dharma delivery via apps have to do with the individual versus the communal nature of Dharma practice in America. Apps are also increasingly commercialized, accessible by design only via a corporation-controlled device and software-delivery system. Apps, then, are subject to the ideological rhetoric imposed by programming structures that shape user experience of the teachings received through them. Whereas many might argue that the Dharma should be free, a Buddhist app can be purchased—usually for about 99 cents.

As Buddhist practice increasingly takes place online, the space of meditation itself is re-contextualized into the blur and motion of contemporary urban life, such that practice often becomes something that people do while they are doing something else. With little to no time for quiet meditation, the Dharma becomes a stream running alongside multiple other streams, something scheduled amid other digital activities, something piped through earplugs, consumed while commuting, and, at times, channeled through games. It is processed in the same physical way that we consume music, hear the news, or send our email. It becomes, in essence, one of many competing components in our lives, transformed by the medium that delivers it and less often taking us out of daily life but instead being scripted to flow within it—even as the technology separates us via software, hardware, and plastic nodes in our ears from those people and things that flow by around us.

It is important, however, not to become too sentimental in our view of traditional Buddhism in Asia and overlook the historical continuities of the above-mentioned issues that confront digital Buddhism in the modern world. Each one of the potential impediments to Buddhist practice that emerge in the current digital age—commercialism, the burying of the Dharma within the din of everyday life, and individualism—is by no means unprecedented in pre-modern Asian contexts. Merchants have been taking advantage of the crowds who gather at sacred Buddhist sites in Asia for centuries, attempting to sell their wares to pilgrims who have journeyed to honor the Buddha and his teachings. Anyone who has visited a Buddhist temple in Asia has noticed that the hustle and bustle of daily life is by no means abated on these premises, and during recitation of scriptures by the monks, there is often a loud din of people in the congregation who are openly chatting about the various issues of interest to their lives with friends who are also at the ceremony. In fact, the Buddha recognized early on the difficulty of truly finding time to dedicate to meditation and the pursuit of Nirvana. For this reason, the Buddha recommended the monastic rather than the householder's path for anyone intent on practicing the Dharma to the fullest extent.

Finally, we must also recognize that individualism is not necessarily an impediment in progress toward the goals of Buddhism. While selfishness certainly pulls one away from the Buddhist ideals, doing something at one's own pace, and on one's own, is something else entirely. In fact, there has been a tension within the Buddhist tradition from its inception between the isolated individual on a quest to reach Nirvana and the community of believers. On one hand, the third jewel of Buddhism, equal in importance to the Buddha and the Dharma, is the *sangha*, which literally means "the community." Much of Buddhist law as found in the *Vinaya* is concerned with how to live in harmony as a community, specifically as monks and nuns, but there are also a great many texts in the tradition that focus on the importance of harmonious social life, such as the *Sigālaka Sutta* of the *Dīgha Nikāya*. On the other hand, one of the most beloved early poems in the Buddhist tradition is the *Khaggavisana Sutta* (Sutta Nipāta 1.3) that enjoins the aspirant to wander alone like a rhinoceros in verses such as the following: "For a sociable person there are allurements; on the heels of allurement, this pain. Seeing allurement's drawback, wander alone like a rhinoceros."[1] We might also note that in early Buddhism there was a notion that some people might wish to practice the Dharma in a more advanced way than others, and for them was recommended thirteen *dhutangas* or ascetic practices. One of these practices was to live alone in the forest, away from society, which was regarded as making it possible to reach Nirvana more quickly.[2] Therefore, we must keep in mind in what follows that the issues that are raised are not totally different in kind from those that Buddhists have been wrestling with for centuries, but they are certainly more pronounced and pervasive in the modern digital environment.

In order to analyze the group that we might call "Buddhist apps," a certain amount of generalization is immediately required. Apps are technology in motion, perhaps more so than websites, or even virtual religious structures in worlds like Second Life. The set of Buddhist apps changes every day as new ones enter into the flow of consumption through sites like the iTunes store, and others disappear. Thus, we can appropriately say, with some degree of Buddhist-derived wisdom, that research about Buddhist apps is overwhelmingly contingent, dependent, incomplete, and transient. Nonetheless, even a snapshot view is telling. A search for "Buddhism" in the iTunes store yielded 323 apps on June 11, 2013.[3] The apps were sorted according to the iTunes system, falling under various categories selected by the app developer from a list offered by Apple. The 323 apps we looked at fall into the following Apple-designated categories and distributions: books (70); lifestyle (116); education (27); reference (22); health and fitness (27); entertainment (15); games (5); travel (9); music (6); utilities (8); photo & video (2); social networking (4); business (3); medical (4); navigation (3); productivity (1); news (1).

The strong preference in Buddhist apps is for the category of "lifestyle," with "books" coming in at a close second. In the set of Buddhist apps we examined that were labeled "lifestyle," the diversity was immense, including prayer prompts; a "karma tracker;" Buddhist digital "wallpaper;" instruction for meditation; digital gongs for use in meditation practice; prayer beads; as well as a host of different dharma-related resources, some also textually based. Designers label the apps themselves, driven by different motives and levels of knowledge and experience with Buddhist practices. Perhaps the flexibility of the label "lifestyle" helps to explain why it has surged in popularity as the category for all kinds of religious apps in recent years.[4]

The apps also come from a large range of traditions. Many are in English, but others are in Chinese, and a few in Tibetan. Some are designed for sanghas, others specifically for individual use, and some for either of these. Some draw on specific historical precedents, but others offer what they see to be a modern, hip, urban distillation of Buddhist principles; others mix Buddhism with a tradition-less (or poly-traditional) "New-Age." It is with these kinds of problems in mind that Asian communications scholar Yoshitaka Miike (2010) proposes that when examining cultural phenomena, "rather than scrutinizing the person, text, and document and treating them as if they were objects of analysis and critique, we must attend genuinely to them as subjects of voices as they tell their own stories about their cultural worlds" (4).

In the case of apps, this would mean paying careful attention to who produced every single app, under what conditions, for what audience, and within what particular historical and cultural context. Yet to fully acknowledge all of these individual contexts would require that we scrap altogether the project of considering larger trends in Buddhist apps. If we *must* engage in such generalizations, we should recognize their inherent limitations. As a gesture toward the contextual study that Miike proposes, we should also pay careful attention to what non-Western theorists of communications and app designers have to say about Buddhism, a tradition that many of these theorists call their own. So, instead of considering a large set of apps for trends and transformations over time, we ask a more general question, one that sets the stage for our subsequent analysis of specific apps: What might a Buddhist perspective on communications theory reveal about the use of "Buddhist" apps in a largely Westernized, digitized American context? We can first observe that communications theory, especially when it is coupled with Buddhist insights, exposes what we already suspected but often like to ignore: that when we study Dharma embedded and communicated in the context of portable devices, it can indeed be shaped by its environment.

A BUDDHIST APPROACH TO COMMUNICATIONS THEORY

Satoshi Ishii offers what he considers to be one of the first "religio-philosophical communication models" based specifically on the principles of Buddhism. For Ishii, twentieth-century communications theory has focused predominantly on "human-to-human and human-to-machine activities," and neglected religious communication activities, such as prayer that should be understood as a form of communication as well: "Existentially and ontologically, however, the fact must not be forgotten that human existence is possible by communicating not only with other human beings and machines but also with supernatural beings and natural beings in the triworld" (Ishiii 2001, 9). That is to say, when thinking about the various forms of communication, researchers should include transcendental modes of communication with perceived other worlds or higher modes of being.

In referring to the "tri-world," Ishii is describing "communication" with what he calls the "cosmic Dharma," which can be understood to be the totality of all things, both "here" and "there," both other and immanent. Here, communication is not with a transcendent entity—that is, with the Divine Other as conceived in the mainstream Western sense—but rather "with" the ultimate awareness of enlightenment. Meditation can in this sense be viewed as a form of communication, even though it is quite different from Western ideas of prayer. Meditation involves coming to know the true nature of the cosmos, and, as such, it involves the transfer of something, albeit not in linguistic form, between the meditator and the cosmos. That is to say, for Ishii, communication can be a mode of seeking enlightenment, and seeking enlightenment is a form of communication. At least theoretically, then, using an iPhone to aid in the quest for enlightenment seems reasonable, if the "communication" enabled by it involves engagement with the "cosmic Dharma." In a similar approach applied to Hindu *moksha*, Nirmala Mani Adhikary (2010, 76) argues that communications can be a form of acceptable yoga with the ability to lead to *moksha*. In fact, the word *yoga* itself comes from the Sanskrit meaning "to unite" and has always connoted a connection between the aspirant and some higher power.

For both of these theorists, communications can be seen as spiritual discipline, suggesting that apps—as fixed or ritualized forms of communication with the principles of liberation—may function as disciplines as well. However, Ishii's remarks also invite us to ask to what extent the use of mobile devices for Dharma delivery may affect the ways we process those teachings. We normally use mobile devices for the sending and receiving of messages from other human beings about daily affairs (via cell phone use and through various messaging technologies). So, today, are we more inclined to focus on the communication of human to human, or even human to machine, than we are on the human to the "tri-world," or world of enlightenment?

Joonseong Lee, like Ishii, argues for a deep contextualization of communications practice and argues that engagement with virtual reality entails, for Buddhist-informed theory, a recognition of the fluidity between what we normally consider the "virtual" and the "real." Considering the Buddhist use of blogs in spiritual practice, Lee considers how cyberspace has what he recognizes as essentially Buddhist properties: it has "immanent, nonlinear, relational, and contextual characteristics" (Lee 2009, 98). Lee (2009) proposes that "the immanent characteristics of cyberspace influence the self-cultivation by the priests" (98) in various ways. Pointing toward the common tendency by Western-influenced scholars like Heidi Campbell to view the Internet as a separate space, Lee wishes to "avoid the dichotomized boundary of real space and cyberspace, which we believe reflects only a limited capacity to appreciate the notion of space" (98). Instead, he proposes we think of "inside-and-outside cyberspace," a notion that reveals how one's "practice-oriented spirituality" affects how one interacts online. In other words, we simultaneously exist as manifest selves online *and* offline—not one or the other.

If the screen of the device does not represent a "there" that is distinct from "here," that is, if we don't view the virtual "world" as distinct from the real world, then the use of apps will be driven not by a desire to interact with the transcendent *through* the device (as sometimes happens with popular Christian prayer apps, for example). Rather, technology in this Buddhist sense will be judged according to its ability to support lived cultivation of awareness, a skill that can be honed both online and offline with proper devotion. This deconstruction of the assumption of static dualisms between here/there, sacred/profane, and online/offline is one of the most powerful changes that Western-informed researchers of "Eastern" uses of technology must confront.

Robin Barooah, creator of the Buddhist app *Equanimity*, sees a compelling association between virtual reality and Buddhist teachings, hinting at the continuity across spaces:

> The concept of virtual reality has an interesting relationship to Buddhist ideas. Essentially, Buddhism holds that we are all experiencing a virtual world constructed by our own minds (or in some ways of saying it, the mind "is" the virtual world). Enlightenment is reached when we understand the process by which this virtual world is created and "see through" it to how things really are. When Buddhists talk of the mind or the self being an illusion or not real, partly what they are saying is that these things are processes rather than independent objects. Virtual reality demonstrates to us our capacity to become immersed in artificial worlds, and to temporarily forget the process by which we created them. Perhaps if they are not too intoxicating, the threshold between worlds will provide a guidepost to recognizing what is ultimately real and what is transient.
>
> (Barooah, e-mail correspondence with the
> author, July 31, 2011)

Barooah is right that virtual reality has the ability to make us more aware of our fascination with constructed worlds of all kinds (including our own). Certainly, contingency characterizes the programmed worlds that we enter into online as well as the programmed worlds that we co-construct in our day-to-day lives. But it would be a mistake to assume that all engagement with virtual reality is the same. Our engagement with virtual worlds—especially rigid programs like iPhone apps—invites careful scrutiny, especially for the individualism the devices invite as well as the implicit shaping of behavior that apps can encourage through ritualized modes of encounter.

THE iPHONE IS THE MESSAGE

Most people have heard a version of Marshall McLuhan's prescient pronouncement, "the medium is the message," uttered long before iPhone and Twitter were everyday words. Today, we have a host of new mediums, all of which profoundly shape the messages they deliver. If the technology that we utilize—our iPhones, iPads, laptops, PCs—offer religious engagement via coded, scripted, programmed encounters, then we must ask in what way the very programs we access may be *shaping* those religious practices. Media theorist Ian Bogost calls such ideological engagement with technology "procedural rhetoric," and defines this as "the practice of persuading through processes in general and computational processes in particular." Procedural rhetoric, says Bogost (2007), is "a technique for making arguments with computational systems and for unpacking computational arguments others have created" (3). "Procedural rhetoric" consists of those "processes [that] define the way things work: the methods, techniques, and logics that drive the operation of systems" (Bogost 2007, 36).

To examine procedural rhetoric, then, is to look at how arguments are addressed to users via the things they are *doing* in interaction with a program (or app). It is to understand how persuasion operates via deliberately scripted user performance. In the case of Buddhist apps, then, we are invited to ask how the vessel for the Dharma—the program driving the app as well as the hardware that we mobilize while using it—affects the teachings we receive. What is the procedural rhetoric at work in a given Buddhist app? How does the medium of the smartphone itself shape the teachings received through it? One of the most powerful implicit messages that the iPhone sends for those utilizing Buddhist apps is that the Dharma can be learned alone, most likely with headphones on, and possibly even while working out at the gym or commuting to the office, even if the app isn't explicitly designed for this purpose.

iPhones are deeply personalized devices: the user determines how and when an app will be used—not one's community. The Dharma, says the medium of the iPhone app, is more inclined to be seen as something you squeeze in between other things you should be doing. It is a personal, private thing. As we proposed earlier, this individualized functionality raises a fundamental point that has dogged Buddhism more generally over its history, which is whether Buddhism should be an individual practice or something done in community. The Mahayana ideal of the Bodhisattva who vows to help all beings reach enlightenment has been used to criticize the Hinayana ideal of the individual Arhat who strives for enlightenment on his or her own. Whatever position one takes on the debate about the most appropriate relationship between the individual and the community, it should be understood that being separated from the community has never been viewed as necessarily being an impediment toward progress along the Buddhist path; even the well-known story of the Buddha's life has him meditating alone under a tree to reach full enlightenment. So the key problem is not perhaps whether one is participating in a community of practitioners or as an individual, but rather whether one is individualistic. If one thinks only of oneself, and sees oneself as having an immutable self that one "owns," and does not realize the impermanent and ephemeral nature of the individual identity and indeed of all things, then regardless of whether one is in community or not, the practice of Buddhism will not go far. Whether apps incline one toward that way of thinking or not is something that must be considered in any analysis of their role in digital Buddhism.

Not only are these issues of individual versus community not new to the modern instantiations of Buddhism, but it is also possible to assert that a given app could act like many Buddhist traditional practices which integrate the seemingly mundane with the spiritual. Considering the Tibetan traditions of Buddhism, we can see how non-digital spiritual tools like *malas*[5] and *mantras* can turn daily routines into spiritual practices, connecting the practitioner to all levels of the "tri-world," merging notions of sacred space and time. In a spiritual world where there are prayers for eating, drinking, driving, and even seemingly un-sacred (or at least impolite) bodily functions, it seems plausible that an app could likewise be integrated into the day-to-day, connecting the sacred to the routine rather than dividing them. However, on the most practical level, we must acknowledge that an app's interface does not usually facilitate this interconnection: the practitioner will likely have to engage with a screen or listen with headphones. While a physical *mala* or vocal/thought prayer can be used while interacting with the world, an app is more likely to turn the world into something on the periphery of the digital program. And, we're sure most app makers would agree, the user should certainly not be using these apps while driving, walking, or in places where the most basic awareness of surroundings is required.

While these apps may be seen as "tools" for practice, they are tools with obvious limitations. The heart of Buddhist practice in all traditions is the application of dharma and meditation in order to enact meaningful change in perspective and action in the "real world," or in the human realms of the "tri-world." The fruits of formal practice should ideally be seen in the informal daily arenas; or, in the vernacular of many practitioners, the most important part of practice is not what happens on the meditation cushion, but off. While spiritual tools may act as aids, the ultimate goal is for positive change to be replicable even if the practitioner has left their spiritual toolbox elsewhere. In a sense, the spiritual tool becomes a symbol connecting the practitioners to their practice: the physical presence of a *mala* can be a reminder of calm even without physical manipulation, and *mantras* need not be said aloud. But can an app, like a mala or mantra, also operate as a tool and symbol even when the iPhone is off? In this way, we could call a Buddhist app particularly successful if the practitioner can benefit without its immediate use. Considering that many of these apps offer a virtual serenity of calming flowers, tinkling bells, and inspirational quotes and images in the confined womb of a small screen and headphones, it is likely that internal equanimity is a state realistically attained as easily without the app. If one insists on integrating a mobile device and its programming into practice, then the medium can become the message, and the iPhone is in danger of becoming a personalized Dharma tool that can replace traditionally prescribed tools.

ME, MYSELF, AND iDHARMA

The movement of so much information to the individual user of an iPhone or mobile device to the exclusion of almost all obligatory behavior in relationship with others marks the iPhone as one of the most connected and also the most isolating of contemporary devices. One may send emails and make

phone calls from an iPhone, but we also receive as much streaming entertainment, news stories, YouTube videos, cartoons, Facebook updates, and
Twitter feeds as we might wish. And most of it is received in an incredibly
personal way, demonstrated via the hardware interface of the tiny, personalized screen. Drawing on Harvey Aronson's *Buddhist Practice on Western
Ground*, Holmes (2010) notes, "American society's strong emphasis on the
external and on individuality contrasts with traditional Buddhist teachings"
(55). So whereas American Buddhism has always tended to be individualized, mobile devices increase this tendency.

The individualizing tendency of smartphones extends beyond Buddhism.
In *Godwired: Religion, Ritual and Virtual Reality*, Rachel Wagner (2012)
argues that today's fascination with the iPod and the iPhone reveals what
she calls the "iPod self," such that our personal mobile device is a visible
metaphor for the fluidity of the contemporary self, with apps that are chosen and eventually deleted, an external representation of the values systems
we "run" on our embodied selves:

> The iPod is one of the most poignant of these indices of meaning avail-
> able today, and I propose, in some ways an apt (app) model for the
> hybrid, wired, and plural self engaged in what Rehak calls "play with
> being" (123). Apple's iPod (as well as almost any smartphone) con-
> tains within it a number of different applications or apps, chosen by
> the owner, who cobbles them together much like a bricoleur. It is also
> fair to say, at least in some respects, that the choices of apps say some-
> thing about the identity of the iPod owner, reflecting in a palpable way
> the identity formation work described by [Diana] Eck, [Lynn Schofield]
> Clark and [Wade Clark] Roof.
>
> (Wagner 2012, 111)

The iPod or the iPhone is one of the most personal, intimate devices we use.
After all, one might say that the "I" in iPhone is "me." Rarely does anyone
else use one's iPhone, and if they do, the owner may become uncomfortable.
We all have deeply personal information embedded on our mobile devices,
including passwords and logins, as well as private apps for tracking things
like moods and health issues.

In terms of the larger characteristics of American culture, this cultivated
individualism is fairly common, but not necessarily conducive to Dharma
development. Many of the apps appeal especially to religious seekers. Many
individuals who dabble in Buddhism do not necessarily follow recognizable
or prescribed Buddhist practices, but instead view the Dharma as a spiritual
buffet from which they may pick and choose. A typical practice may have a
little Vipassana here, some Tibetan *tong-len* compassion practice there, and
a sprinkle of Zen bodhisattva prayers and prostrations done in front of a
Thai Theravadan representation of the Buddha, which may reside alongside
images of the Vietnamese Thich Nhat Hanh, the Tibetan Dalai Lama, and

maybe even figures from other religious traditions or personal totems. Many apps appeal to this form of eclecticism, and may be off-putting or seem muddled to traditional Buddhists.

One of the most eclectic and individualized apps is iShrine Virtual Buddhist Shrine (jChicken.com, 2009). Users are able to select from a list of cross-traditional items to display, allowing the practitioner to engage with items that were scanned from what the creator calls "a genuine Buddhist altar." But users don't need to go anywhere where they might encounter other practitioners. The simulacrum of the altar becomes everyone's personal, portable altar, "a realistic and interactive Buddhist altar in the palm of your hand," all the more personal since it allows one to potentially create an unlikely altar—one that exhibits an eclectic blend of Zen, Tibetan, and Theravadan Buddhist symbols.

Despite the potential problems associated with eclectic apps, for some self-identified Buddhists, the more tradition-specific apps can prove to be incredibly useful tools. While it is true that apps easily promote individualistic practice, the odds are heavily against most American Buddhists finding actual communities with which to practice. Dharma centers are relatively sparse in America, and are often limited to larger metropolitan areas; within this already small field of possibilities, finding a specific tradition may be even harder, and finding a specific school within that tradition nearly impossible. In addition, we must consider at the most practical level that many Dharma centers typically have schedules which do not easily fit with American Judeo-Christian-centric calendars, causing scheduled sittings and holidays to occur at times when the practitioner cannot easily attend.

For the practitioner unwilling or incapable of relocating and rescheduling significant portions of their lives, "individual practice" may not be a choice they have made, but rather an accurate circumstantial description. For these practitioners, apps may allow the practitioner to connect with their larger community in a spiritual sense when they are incapable of doing so physically. For example, the *Daily Buddhist Prayers* app sold by Thupten Nyima (2013) teaches English-speaking Tibetan Buddhists a litany of daily traditional prayers, presents them with their meaning, the Wylie transliteration, and recorded audio of a former monk chanting them. In this way, the app could help a solo practitioner overcome language barriers that could limit authentic connection with his or her tradition, and could even hamper personal connection within a physical sacred space and community. So individualism is encouraged by the technology, even as a particular app may also paradoxically introduce a welcome element of online community at the same time, especially in the American context.

We can see the personalization of encounter that apps invite in the design of many of those currently available for download. Meditation timers, such as iMindful (Seokhwan Cho, 2010) and Luna Stone (Cadin Batrack, 2011), help practitioners by prompting them when to begin and end meditation. My Prayer Wheel offers a digital prayer wheel that can be spun to generate good karma (Gottfried Chien, 2011). So, whereas the interactive digital prayer wheel is placed within a photograph of the Jokhang Temple in Lhasa, users can use it all by themselves without leaving home. Mantra Tracker (Phurba, 2011) allows individual users to keep track of meditation activities and back up the data for later review. iSatori (Dan Worley, 2010) offers a series of images of flowers, with the invitation to gaze upon them without judgment, as an aid to enlightenment. Other apps, such as Walking Meditation (i-Mobilize, 2010), offer individualized ritual guidance for how to practice meditation.

Because digital Dharma practice is so individualized in America, there are very few Buddhist social media apps at the iTunes store. One of the few Buddhist social media apps available is Practice Everywhere, designed for Buddhist author Cheri Huber. Practice Everywhere offers "push notifications" to alert you when to meditate, as well as bell tones for orientation while meditating. It also offers a "social networking" function that directly utilizes one's mobile device. Huber's (n.d.) website explains:

> Several times a day Cheri sends short awareness practice reminders by way of text messages, computer, *Facebook*, *Twitter*, and iPhones. We really like using text messages to receive *Practice Everywhere* reminders because our cell phones are always with us. Since *Practice Everywhere* will be sent out 4–6 times a day, we suggest you choose the technology (or technologies) that you have with you the most throughout your day.

Although Practice Everywhere does employ social media, it is important to note the functionality here: This app is not a form of virtual group practice or even shared support. Those who utilize Practice Everywhere are simply recipients of Dharma teachings streaming in one direction only: to the user from Cheri Huber. App-linked social media sites on Facebook and Twitter merely serve as digital mailboxes for the delivery of messages that practitioners then must consume alone.

Holmes observes that North American Buddhist practitioners, in comparison to Buddhists in other parts of the world, "are embedded in their sense that it is good and right to realize and express individual selfhood." American Buddhists "often use Buddhism to promote their individual health and welfare, to heighten awareness of their own feelings, and to allow for more successful individual engagement." For Holmes (2010), this personalized engagement invites critique, since "when seen from the holistic worldview of traditional Buddhism, such an approach ignores the tradition's rich interpersonal vision of individuality" (55). iPhones and the apps we use on them only serve to reinforce Holmes's assessment of American religiosity in all its forms. The Dharma, when accessed via apps on mobile devices, becomes one of many apps we run—on ourselves and on our devices—and is most likely consumed as a stream of words or speech delivered *to* us, as we exercise immense liberty in deciding what aspect *we* will consume, when, where, and how, with seemingly no need for interaction within a larger community of practitioners.

DHARMA FOR SALE

Another potential problem with delivery of Buddhist teachings via iPhone apps is that the creators of such apps must, by necessity, place their apps in an online store, and thus are encouraged—through the need to be noticed in the ever-increasing stream of apps available—to engage in some form of advertising. One of the most well-known producers of Buddhist apps is the aptly named "Buddhist Apps" programming company. They are a "small 'mobile' application development company" and claim they do not produce a profit. Instead, if they receive enough financial support through "sponsors," they will distribute apps for free. Some apps don't generate enough sponsors, and so the company charges a "download fee," with the claim that even these minimal fees will not "cover the development expenses." They encourage supporters to sponsor an app by providing funds to enable free distribution and suggest that such financial activity is "Dharma work." If enough financial support is offered that the apps can be downloaded for free, the Dharma will presumably "be available to thousands and thousands of people, from the global iTunes app store" (Buddhist Apps FAQs). Interestingly, these same users will now have been exposed to the Buddhist Apps company and may thus be more likely to buy another app after having gotten one they like for free.

The website explains the origins of the Buddhist App company and its eventual acquiescence to marketing:

> Buddhist Apps started with just one goal, to provide easy access to prayers and teachings to the Buddhist community: though we knew how important marketing the apps would be but we felt that our pure intentions would somehow float us through but we were wrong. With more than a million apps in the iTunes app store, it's extremely difficult for people to find apps unless we provide them with easy information.[6]

The website explains that a Paypal account will allow those who wish to support the app development to do so via easy donations. The problem, of course, is that now the spreading of the Dharma is implicated with the business practices and profit motivations of at least two more non-Buddhist companies—Apple and Paypal.

It is an accepted truth that modern-day Western Buddhism is undeniably commercialized to some degree—be it monasteries with gift and book shops, "Dharma supply" companies selling meditative wares, or even Dharma centers and monasteries charging admission to special teachings and retreats.

However, advertisements are limited to Buddhist venues, magazines, and publications, and the companies involved are typically run with the purpose of spreading and teaching Dharma. But with apps, even more companies are involved, as the creators place advertisements in a wider array of magazines and media, on websites, and with Google and Facebook. Furthermore, because of low barriers to entry, some app designers are novices, or worse, know very little about Buddhism at all. The use of digital marketing tools, then, makes it easier for teachings to be generated by those without the experience or training to make them successful. Just because someone is skilled with programming does not mean they know much about Buddhism, and this leads to a widely varying quality of Buddhist apps.

And yet, community, tradition, and authority do matter. As Sumi London Kim, editor of *Blue Jean Buddha: Voices of Young Buddhists,* puts it, "There is something appealing about the integrity of a tradition that has liturgy, cosmology, ethics and practices that have been developed over the centuries so that they work together to transform a person" ("The Future of Buddhism" 2008). On the other hand, it is important to point out that there are certainly real-life Buddhist centers that are also exceedingly individualistic in practice. As Kim reflects, "It's so lonely there." Rod Meade Sperry, manager of the pop Dharma website *The Worst Horse,* agrees: "You're quiet, you go in, you bow, you sit down, you hear a talk, and then everybody leaves" ("The Future of Buddhism" 2008). Apps exacerbate this tendency.

Kim also expresses concern for the increasing commodification of the Dharma, pointing out how young people may choose to attend free retreats rather than join centers that require payment. For young people, especially, "affordability is a key issue." Robin Barooah, creator of the Buddhist app *Equanimity*, recognizes the dangers of commercial Buddhist products, but explains, "commerce is the only way we (humans) have managed to organize ourselves to develop this level of technology so far. So there simply isn't an alternate choice at this time for doing this kind of thing." He registers concern "about the alignment of the various businesses involved—i.e., what human qualities they demonstrate, because I think these are communicated to us through their products." He does believe that "commerce and the way money is constructed are currently corrosive to human and spiritual values" but admits he doesn't think "they're going anywhere soon so I try to simply accept them and do what I can to make sure that cynical projects aren't all that exist."[7] Generally accepting of the fact that apps will cost money and be utilized through devices like the iPhone, Barooah sees this as—if not a necessary evil,–at least a necessary concession. The disagreement among the American Buddhist community itself about the commodification of practice, however, shows that this is hardly a settled issue. Furthermore, commodification cannot be divorced from the medium of the software device itself, which is sold and consumed, deeply dependent on the affordances included by programmers.

BUDDHIFY ME

Genre is a vessel. It defines what we can and what we cannot do. Bogost's claims about the "procedural rhetoric" that drives computational processes also applies to ritual processes, and suggests that both are behavior shapers. Accordingly, apps designed for Buddhist practice will be shaped not just by the internal programming, but also by what is possible and what is not possible to do on an iPhone or mobile device. This includes both the physical limitations of the device as well as consumer expectations of the format: that is, the genre of the app itself. The Buddhify app, recently released, is a good example of how apps are often shaped by hardware, by software possibilities, and by consumer expectation.[8]

The Buddhify app does not situate itself within any single Buddhist tradition, and in this respect reflects the American Buddhist tendency to synthesize elements of many different streams of Buddhist tradition. Buddhify is marketed as a form of "skillful means" to be utilized primarily in a contemporary urban context. The creator of the app, Rohan Gunatillake, becomes a shaper of a new mode of practice by translating commonly accepted ideals of meditation into a new digital environment that itself is shaped by user expectations for apps as a genre. As a coder, he becomes a ritual creator too. And the Dharma he shares is passed through, molded, and transformed by the digital options users expect in an app. Genre shapes content.

Buddhify is billed as "the urban meditation for modern life. Practical, playful and beautifully designed, Buddhify increases your well-being by teaching you mindfulness-based meditation on the go." Here we see the expectations of the iPhone shaping how Dharma is delivered. We can access meditation "on the go," so it doesn't interfere with our busy schedules. An app called Mindfulness Meditation (Mental Workout Inc.) makes a similar claim: "Always making excuses for not meditating? This is simply the best way to learn and enjoy mindfulness meditation—and it's always in your pocket for short breaks, trips, and outdoor practice!"

Whereas forms of meditation that invite focusing within the midst of everyday life are nothing new, what makes this kind of claim novel is the suggestion that mindfulness can only—or perhaps best—be achieved by streaming it through the iPhone and literally carrying it in your pocket. Delivery of Dharma becomes a commodity passed from device to ears, usually via personal headphones that wall off competing sounds from the world around us. In this way, the isolation the app invites via hardware, software, and equipment seems to push against the contextualization, connectedness, and plurality that Buddhist-informed communications theorists urge. Whereas Buddhism has room for many different modes of practice—individual and communal—here the device itself creates a physical barrier between the user and the world. Accordingly, the app and device can become a hindrance to the "tri-world" communication advocated by Ishii that invites us not to divide between things (in this case, us and others, or the world engaging us

via an iPhone and the world engaging us in our immediate environment),
but rather to engage in a form of unifying "communication" that helps us
realize our connection with everything. On the other hand, is it possible that
the device can help to close off our senses from the onslaught of information
in the outside world that has traditionally been thought of as an impediment
to progress on the path of meditation? A common image in Buddhism is of
the monk with his senses withdrawn, like a tortoise with its limbs pulled
safely into its shell (see for example, *Sutta Nipata* 35.199 *Kumma Sutta*).[9]
Can the cocoon of iPhone and earbud possibly help to achieve this effect?

   The Buddhify app also concedes a number of formal elements to user
expectations of apps, primarily in its insistence that choice is a desirable
feature. When you use the Buddhify app, you tell it where you are: at
home, commuting, walking around town, or working out at the gym. Then,
you choose one of four "flavors" of meditation, then one of two "sizes"
of meditation. The app promises "bonus features" that include the ability for "assessing how you're getting along." In our iPhone apps, we are
accustomed to customization, and recorded assessment of our progress as
a nearly universal expectation—and one of today's fastest-growing forms
of gamification (the cultural fascination with games as a cultural practice).
Practice, in this case, becomes shaped by pre-existing digital genres with elements like "features" and "assessments."

   Another way that genre expectations can affect Dharma teaching is if
they are transformed into games, a more extreme form of the codification of
digital experience. Very few Buddhist-themed apps involve games, but those
that do place Buddhist teachings within received frameworks of expectations and, thus, affect how we receive the content. The app iworship, for
example, enables users to "improve their lives" by integrating prayer with
a point system and leveled stages of development. Buddhism Trivia Quiz
offers the strange option of playing "Battleship" as you practice your expertise in the history and terminology of mainstream non-tradition-specific
Buddhism. Another game, the unfortunately named Buddha Balls (iTrivia
Games, 2010) comes complete with a fantasy-based backstory:

> A machine of unknown origin is unearthed in an archaeological dig on
> a planet in the Aldebaran System. The machine is transmitting energy
> waves which have been disrupting the "inner path" throughout the uni-
> verse. These energy waves are in effect responsible for all human con-
> flict and misery since the stone age. An elite team of Buddha Masters
> has gained control of one of the machines receptor ports [*sic*]. You as a
> Supreme Buddha Master must unlock a sequence of energy packets into
> the receptor in order to disable it.[10]

Is something lost when teachings are framed within another story, another
purpose, which has entertainment as well as didactic rationales? The answer
to this is not simple when we consider that framing teachings within a

larger, entertaining story has been a central—and apparently successful—tactic of Buddhism, since the earliest collections of *Jataka* tales that told of the Buddha's exploits during previous lives. Here, we find narratives in which the Buddha had exciting adventures as all manner of beings during the course of his cycle of rebirth, such as monkeys, elephants, and birds, during which villains are defeated, treasures are found, spells are cast, and lessons are learned. We might also ask whether meditation can be effectively enacted while one is concurrently driven to amass points and solve puzzles. In what way might the game itself distract from the centering that meditation invites in other non-gaming contexts? Can Dharma *be* a game? Again, there is precedent for "gamification" in the Buddhist tradition itself, where in Tibet we find an age-old practice of public debate where learned monks display their intellectual skills in often-raucous encounters that end in a winner and a loser, and often involve humor, laughter, and even ridicule.[11] Georges Dreyfus, who is one of the few Westerners to complete the full course of traditional Tibetan Buddhist higher learning, recounts that during one of his earlier debates, his opponents sensed that he was losing his way and "took great delight in playing with me like cats with a mouse" (Dreyfus 2003, 262).

Is there a point at which so much transformation has occurred via the medium that the Dharma is subsumed within another message entirely? Buddhist app designer Robin Barooah recognizes the dangers of poor app design in affecting one's ability to effectively access Dharma via digital programs:

In as much as meditation is distinct from other activities, I think meditation apps are different from other apps. I think that meditation is a special kind of activity, which can be very influenced by the mental setting you bring to it. Making meditation into a competitive game (for example) might well bring negative qualities into the meditation. Advanced meditators would simply avoid programs that had undesirable traits, but beginners could well be influenced negatively.

(Barooah, e-mail correspondence with the author, July 31, 2011)

BuddhaBelly might be the kind of "undesirable" app Barooah has in mind. Buddha Belly offers a gamified experience far removed from the meditative guides to enlightenment also available as apps of the sort that Barooah designs. The game offers these directions: "Rub Buddha's belly and get lucky! This ancient Asian tradition is the centerpiece of this game. This fast paced action game will enchant you with its unmistakable charm. Your path will lead through 5 different stages of enlightenment. Enjoy, and find out why everybody is rubbing their fingers so fast over their iPhone!"

Another app, not explicitly labeled a game but utilizing some of the same tropes, is the Karmamater (Bogdan Bolkhovetskyi, 2011), which "allows you to keep steady track of your good and bad actions and to observe the miraculous world of your karma." After you perform an action in the world, you click on images on the screen, which then reflect back for you the "size" of your karma. Another app, Wheel of Death, invites users to spin a roulette wheel every day, to meditate on a different possible means to die. This activity, the creator Valeria Clark proposes, will help you to "embrace mortality" and "appreciate the good fortune you enjoy today."[12]

Like all forms of gamification, the practices enacted in these apps are typically subsumed underneath the expected structure of digital games, with common tropes like point accumulation, leveling up, and "winning" or "losing" overwhelming the more traditional religious functions of Dharma practice, sometimes in favor of the hope of marketing success. This is a pitfall that all app designers must face, since the iTunes store is, after all, a store—with all the problematic associations that come with selling programs intended for spiritual enhancement.

CONCLUSION

This discussion is a preliminary attempt to make sense of the place of popular technology in contemporary Buddhist practice, inviting us to consider the collection of influences that affect how the Dharma is received and engaged via smartphone apps. We have demonstrated that there are multiple ways that meaning is impacted: through the original programming of the app and what is possible to do and what is not when using it; the genre expectations that determine how the app is programmed; the advertising that allows the app to be viewed and selected by potential buyers; the placement of the app on a single person's iPhone device; the use of the app by a practitioner in a variety of contexts; the association of the app with the iPhone device itself, inviting considerations of issues like portability; use of isolating headphones; integration into other life activities, such as working out at the gym or sitting on a commuter train; and the attitude of the person using the app, with all the affiliated particularities of life situation that affect its use and effectiveness. In all of these cases, however, we can be fairly certain that if it resides on an iPhone, the app will be accessed largely alone, and likely with the assistance of headphones, whereas in many, but certainly not all, traditional settings the Dharma will be accessed in a group, with the assistance of a supporting community. Thus, the heightened individualism of the digital experience, whatever else it may also be, must be acknowledged, even if it is too early to determine what the effects of this might ultimately be.

For Joonseong Lee, "practicing spirituality" is a mode of overcoming the dualism of online and offline, real life and cyberspace. "Practicing spirituality" is not about entry into or removal from a sacred or transcendent space; rather, it "habituates spiritual or religious practices such as prayer, meditation, chanting, or keeping a diary, timelessly and placelessly in a way to cultivate the self" (Lee 2009, 98). The point of spirituality, in this understanding, whether online or offline, whether using an iPhone or using nothing at all, is to cultivate an understanding of one's true nature and generate greater awareness. If the devices we use circumvent this purpose through the ritualized engagements that they necessarily promote using coded, scripted processes such as apps, then the Dharma may be disrupted, and thus the user's path to recognizing the connectedness of all things—both online and offline, both wired and unplugged, both digitally mediated and immediately experienced—may also be diminished. However, if the aspects of these apps that cohere well with the Dharma are highlighted, then they may prove to be a welcome and useful addition to the treasury of tools for the practice of Buddhism.

NOTES

1. See http://www.accesstoinsight.org/tipitaka/kn/snp/snp.1.03.than.html.
2. See http://en.dhammadana.org/sangha/dhutanga.htm.
3. We chose the term "Buddhism" as our keyword, as it is a likely search term that someone new to Buddhism would utilize, allowing the term to act as a "gateway" for the searcher.
4. A previous search from October 30, 2011, yielded slightly different results, the most notable shift being a sharp increase from 2011 to 2013 in Buddhism apps under the category of "lifestyle" (from 83 to 116) and a slight decrease in apps under the category of "books" (from 98 to 70). Indeed, the category of "lifestyle" is the site at which many religious apps are increasingly placed.
5. Interestingly, a mala could, in fact, be considered a "digital" technology, because when one chants and counts the chants by reference to the beads on the string, one is essentially dividing up an analog process of chanting into discrete quanta demarcated by each bead.
6. Since this quote was accessed on October 15, 2011, the company has moved from offering "in-house projects" to include "client projects," and in 2014 is no longer inviting donations (buddhistapps.com).
7. These quotes from Robin Barooah are taken from an e-mail exchange on July 31, 2011.
8. To see the Buddhify commercial, go to http://vimeo.com/30506593.
9. In the yoga tradition of Patañjali, the withdrawal of the senses from their engagement with the outside world is known as *pratyahara* (*Yoga Sūtras* 2.54). In both the Buddhist and yogic traditions, withdrawal of the senses is not a physical procedure, but rather a mental one, where the mind does not grasp at the sensations. It cannot be achieved by simply covering the eyes or ears. However, doing so should not harm and might help the aspirant along the way.
10. This description was taken from iTunes on November 2, 2011 (http://itunes.apple.com/app/buddha-balls/id389928125?mt=8). The app, however, is no longer available on iTunes.
11. For an excellent account of the techniques of Tibetan debating, see Dreyfus (2003) chapter 11, "Debate in the Curriculum." Note that the author ponders the pitfalls of this system as well, stating, "we must observe that the emphasis on debate is not without its problems, for it encourages students to put more

effort into performing spectacular debates than into pondering texts" (Dreyfus 2003, 245).

12. Taken from the iTunes description of the app, https://itunes.apple.com/us/app/wheel-of-death-free/id462238954?mt=8.

REFERENCES

Adhikary, Nirmala Mani. 2010. "*Sancharyoga*. Approaching Communication as *Vidya* in Hindu Orthodoxy." *China Media Research* 6(3): 76–84.

Bogost, Ian. 2007. *Persuasive Games: The Expressive Power of Videogames*. Cambridge, MA: MIT Press.

Dreyfus, Georges. 2003. *The Sound of Two Hands Clapping: The Education of a Tibetan Buddhist Monk*. Berkeley: University of California Press.

"The Future of Buddhism in a Post Baby Boomer World." 2008. Forum interview with: Sumi Loundon Kim, Rod Meade Sperry, Iris Brilliant, Zoketsu, and Norman Fischer. *Buddhadharma Magazine*. http://www.thebuddhadharma.com/web-archive/2008/12/1/forum-next-gen-buddhism.html. Accessed July 28, 2014.

Holmes, Cecil. 2010. "Buddhism." In *The Routledge Encyclopedia of Religion, Communication, and Media*, edited by D. A. Stout, 53–55. New York: Routledge.

Huber, Cheri. n.d. "Living Compassion." http://www.livingcompassion.org/about-practice-everywhere. Accessed June 23, 2014.

Ishii, Satoshi. 2001. "An Emerging Rationale for Triworld Communication Studies from Buddhist Perspectives." *Human Communication* 4(1): 1–10.

Lee, Joonseong. 2009. "Cultivating the Self in Cyberspace: The Use of Personal Blogs among Buddhist Priests." *Journal of Media and Religion* 8(2): 97–114.

Miike, Yoshitaka. 2010. "An Anatomy of Eurocentrism in Communication Scholarship." *China Media Research* 6(1): 1–12.

Wagner, Rachel. 2012. *Godwired: Religion, Ritual and Virtual Reality*. New York: Routledge.

Part IV
Case Studies

9 Virtual Tibet
From Media Spectacle to Co-Located Sacred Space

Christopher Helland

Recognizing the importance, significance, and potential of the Internet to support the Tibetan community in diaspora, in 1996 Tibetan Buddhist monks from the Namgyal Monastery used a variation of the Kalachakra Tantra (a sacred ritual) to bless the network and sanctify the newly created "cyberspace" for this purpose. To conduct the ritual, the monks used sacred chants while they visualized the interconnected network of computers that make up the Internet and the "space" created by these networks. An image of the Kalachakra Mandala (which had been created as a complex sand mandala earlier) was digitized and put up on a computer screen. This further helped with the visualization of the Internet as being part of a giant mandala that was now spiritually anchored within the virtual world. The event was timed to coincide with the "24 hours of Cyberspace" program conducted globally on February 8, 1996, to raise awareness of the positive impact the Internet could have on society and culture.

At first glance, it might seem paradoxical that an ancient religion would respond in this way to new media and the social spaces it affords. Yet, from the perspective of the monks, cyberspace was not simulated but a space that people were engaging in a very "real world" way, and while the Internet was a new media it was similar to pre-modern Tibetan forms of social and religious practices. In their view, there was no dichotomy between online and offline activity, rather the new online environment was viewed simply as a place where people could do things. As the monks put it, "We pray to reduce the negative things that may happen in cyberspace and to increase the positive things . . . The person using the Internet has the choice."[1]

Media practices, such as the Kalachakra Tantra, demonstrate that despite "geographical" Tibet being subsumed under the Chinese state, the Tibetan government in exile, official religious organizations, and politically and religiously motivated individuals actively engage the Internet to promote Tibetan sovereignty and maintain their religious and cultural identity. This chapter asks, "What role has digital media played in the diaspora?" It argues that, although digital media has had an important and significant role in communicating information about the Tibetan situation to the global community, online network activity within this group has shifted from "media spectacle" to an internal focus on community and identity maintenance. This chapter presents a detailed investigation and documentation of a "mediascape" that examines not only the flow of a diaspora religious tradition through these digital networks but also assesses the impact of this flow on the people that engage with it. In particular, this chapter analyses the modifications and transformations that occur in religious activities as they are "digitized" and engaged through Internet networks. Expanding on current theories and methods for examining the impact of Internet technology and social networking platforms on ritual engagement, liminal space, the concept of co-location and community perceptions of sacred space, this chapter will argue that Tibetan religion in the diaspora is being transformed from a media spectacle into a co-located sacred space as the tradition shapes new media to help meet its political, religious, and spiritual needs.

TIBET AS NETWORKED SOCIETY

As the World Wide Web developed, a number of websites were created to promote and support the "Tibetan situation," while Tibetan communities in diaspora began to develop comprehensive websites that provided information on everything from Tibetan restaurants and crafts, to localized political activities and international news (Prebish 2004). By 2004, Internet use within the diaspora had become so significant that Thubten Samphel, the Secretary of the Department of Information of the exile Tibetan Government, wrote:

> Tibetans in exile are embracing the Internet just as they did Buddhism more than 1,300 years ago. Like a new revelation, the power of the Internet to create virtual communities has fascinated Tibetans in exile. This fascination is intensified by the fact that the ability to create a cohesive community, across international borders, has been denied to Tibetans in Tibet by an Internet-shy China. And Tibetan exiles, scattered as they are across the globe, are converting this fascination into a rash of cyberspace activities that, because of their power to transmit information instantaneously, are profoundly changing the world of the Tibetan Diaspora and beyond. In the process, Tibetan exiles have created a virtual Tibet that is almost un-assailable, free, revelling in its freedom, and growing.

(Samphel 2004, 167)

Interestingly, Tibetan culture seems pre-adapted for the World Wide Web. Writing before the creation of the Internet and the Web, Beatrice Miller was interested in the strong social networks historically used by the Tibetan community to maintain identity. Consider as she writes, "to gain some understanding of the resilience and durability of Tibetan society it must be examined from the vantage point of the web of inter-connections" (Miller 1961, 197). She found that despite ongoing cultural contact through sophisticated trade networks, various political struggles, shifting national borders, and inter-sect rivalries between the major religious communities, "threads of a web" were spread far past political borders that united the diverse Tibetan communities and anchored them in their tradition and identity. The central strands of this web were the networks used to connect the monastic system.

With the main religious leaders leaving Tibet to live in exile (e.g., van Schaik 2011), they continued to develop and maintain a web of connectedness between themselves and their communities, which were living in a form of "stateless diaspora" abroad (Hess 2006; Misra 2003; Sheffer 2003), or still within the traditional territories that were now under the political control of the Chinese government. As new Internet communication tools became available, the Tibetan religious authorities began to explore, and then develop, these networks to communicate news and information about the Tibetan situation to both Tibetans and non-Tibetans, and to strengthen the communications between the monastic centers (religious authorities) and the Tibetan diaspora community. Originally relying on volunteers in Canada, the United States, and Britain, several bulletin boards and listserves were developed for this activity (Anand 2000; Bray 2000; Brinkerhoff 2012; Drissel 2008; Helland 2012b; McLagan 1996).

Diaspora communities in particular tend to place an emphasis on maintaining close ties with a homeland and often a place of religious origins (e.g., Berns McGowan 1999, Vertovec 2000, 2004). Despite the many definitions of diaspora, a key characteristic is the relationship between "globally dispersed yet collectively self-identified ethnic groups" and the countries of origin and settlement (Vertovec 1999, 2). Shortly after it was available to the public, the Internet was being utilized as a tool that provided diaspora populations with a new mechanism where they could develop and maintain social networks and connect with their community on a global scale (e.g., Cohen 1997; Helland 2008; Ignacio 2005; Mallapragada 2006; Wilbur 1997). As the Internet developed, many diasporic religious groups also began utilizing the medium to establish significant and continuous contact with their place of origin (see, e.g., Eickelmann and Anderson 1999; Miller and Slater 2000; Mitra 1997).

A primary example of this activity can be seen at the website called The Global Hindu Electronic Network (www.hindunet.org). The website was started in November 1996 and provided people with massive amounts of information concerning Hinduism and also other religions in India. The site also catered specifically to Hindus in the diaspora by providing information about temples in different countries and their locations, information about Indian food and lifestyle, news concerning human rights issues, and up-to-date news from India. Along with providing this information, the website also hosted a vibrant discussion area where people could talk about their religious beliefs and practices (Helland 2012b).

VIRTUAL TIBET: A FOURTH ESTATE

Thubten Samphel was the first person to use the term "Virtual Tibet" within the context of the Internet. His view concerning the new online activity was that it became woven into a fourth estate when combined with other forms of media that successfully challenged the Chinese government over issues of information and propaganda. Samphel's Virtual Tibet, which included websites, newspapers, magazines, and radio services (Voice of America and Radio Free Asia) had three successful functions. First, it changed international public opinion and halted the global advance of Chinese propaganda concerning the Tibetan territory and the traditional leadership of the Dalai Lama. Second, within Tibet, this new fourth estate was able to present information in the Tibetan language to Tibetans. This allowed the community still within the traditional territory to receive information and news that had not been censored by the Chinese government, including positive information about the Dalai Lama and his work. Samphel believed that this new activity was helping them to "shape the thinking" of the Tibetans within Tibet itself. And finally, the Tibetan Government in Exile was able to get information into China, broadcast in Chinese, to "penetrate borders and Chinese minds." An example of this activity can be seen in August 2000, when Tibet.net (the official website for the government in exile) was made available in Traditional Chinese (Han). Within the first week of its availability in Han, it received more than 10,000 unique visitors, mostly from within China itself (Samphel 2004).

As this online network for projecting and strengthening Tibetan identity inside and outside of China continued to develop and expand, Internet use within the diaspora community began changing based on the needs of the community. Referred to as the social shaping of technology and the "spiritualizing of the Internet" (Campbell 2005), the users shifted the emphasis from a fourth estate used for combating Chinese propaganda, to an online network that began to significantly strengthen the diaspora community. In many ways, this primary shift can be viewed as a change from using the Internet to help create a "media spectacle" to using the Internet for maintaining identity. One key factor in this development was the push by the diaspora community to develop Internet accessibility and connectivity within "Little Lhasa" or Dharamsala, which had now become the religious and political center for the Tibetans in exile. Although a major undertaking, Air Jaldi, a non-profit organization dedicated to creating wireless networks for the Tibetan community in diaspora, facilitated a meeting in 2006 where they built one of the largest WiFi networks in the world. Using a complex wireless mesh network, they linked more than 2,000 computers throughout the Himalayan region of Northern India. This allowed for the Tibetans in the Dharamsala area to be "wired" despite the poor quality of phone services and limited access to computers. In support of the developing network and the Air Jaldi conference, the Dalai Lama welcomed the delegates and volunteers building the mesh network and in a written message prayed, "that the fruits of your good work will be far reaching and long lasting."

Because the Web is a diverse environment that provides the ability for diaspora communities to be both consumers and producers of knowledge and representation (Sokefeld 2002), centralized, traditional, authorities have difficulty maintaining control over this network (e.g., Barker 2005: Campbell 2007, 2010; Helland 2000; Turner 2007). In fact, the new Internet networks "may represent the first time that diaspora members are able to consider aspects of their identity, question traditional interpretations of religion and culture, and choose for themselves what their identity 'truth' is" (Brinkerhoff 2012, 94). In an attempt to increase representation of the monastic centers and religious authority within this online environment, the Dalai Lama's official website (originally online in October 1999) was transformed in 2005–2006 to shift from being purely an information source that promoted the Dalai Lama, to a website that engaged with the diaspora community by providing news, teachings, rituals, messages, and speeches. Monastic centers that were being re-established in exile also created websites that increased their connectivity with the community.

Within a relatively short period of time, Virtual Tibet became something far greater than just a medium used to shape public opinion. It became a "third space" (Hoover and Echchaibi 2012) that allowed for online connectivity and online community, while it also strengthened the networks used for maintaining a globally dispersed group of Tibetans. This overlap between online and offline community identity is much more reflective of a "networked society" where the diaspora group is "culturing the technology . . . so that it can be incorporated into the community and provide opportunities for group or self-expression" (Campbell 2012, 64). Through actively engaging the Internet in a number of progressive ways, the Tibetan community in diaspora began socially shaping the technology to meet the community's unique political, religious, and spiritual needs. These shifts in online activity are particularly timely, as there is now a clear democratization process underway (e.g., Boyd 2004; Hess 2006; Sangay 2003), and a developing separation between political and religious leadership in the Tibetan diaspora (Ardley 2002). The most recent example being the relinquishing of political power by the Dalai Lama in 2012 and the democratic elections of a non-religious authority as the Sikyong (political leader). This is effectively altering authority (both charismatic and institutional) within the community, allowing for political activities, disagreements, and disputes to be removed from the religious sphere. In light of the difficulty in maintaining Tibetan cultural identity in diaspora (e.g., Dorjee and Giles 2005), these recent changes are seen as a larger transformation and modernization process that is part of a broad "cultural survival strategy in which the main actors must alter tradition in order to preserve it" (Whalen-Bridge 2011, 103).

VIRTUAL TIBET AS A MULTI-SITE NETWORK

Although there are digital divides (Selwyn 2004), this new form of networked society has become extremely significant to members of the Tibetan diaspora living in the West, for a number of different reasons. In the contemporary online environment, Virtual Tibet is best interpreted as a multisite network that is structured on five nodes or spheres of websites. Each node plays a pivotal role in maintaining Tibetan identity both online and off, in what can best be described as a multisite reality (Campbell 2012). In Campbell's examination of "networked religion," she argues:

> Connected to the idea of a multisite reality is that the online world is consciously and unconsciously imprinted by its users with the values, structures, and expectations of the offline world. Multisite reality means online practices are often informed by offline ways of being, as users integrate or seek to connect their online and offline patterns of life. It also means that there is often ideological overlap and interaction between online religious groups and forums and their corresponding offline religious institutions.
>
> (Campbell 2012, 82)

Religious belief and practice within the Tibetan culture have always been a key pillar of Tibetan identity. With the rise of "networked individualism" (Raine and Wellman 2012), members within the diaspora community are constantly challenged and influenced by "multiple modernities" (Whalen-Bridge 2011) and alternative and competing networks. This struggle of identity and community maintenance is a constant challenge in diaspora, particularly with second-generation members who may focus more on developing new ties, rather than on nourishing or rediscovering old social networks (Ardley 2002; Beyer 2006; Nowak 1984; Hiller and Franz 2004; Vertovec 2009). To connect the community in diaspora, multiple online networks help maintain community identity, common goals and beliefs, and leadership structures. As such, Virtual Tibet represents the new development of a technologically hybridizing community that is connecting deeply rooted traditional structures of power and authority with new social media. The five nodes making up the multisite network are (1) Tibetan Government in Exile websites, (2) Tibetan news websites, (3) Cybersanghas and comprehensive websites, (4) social networking sites, and (5) Tibetan monastic and religious websites.

1. The main website for the Tibetan Government in Exile is Tibet.net. First hosted on a website out of London, England, in December 1996 (Tibet.com), the website evolved into a dynamic platform used for providing every aspect of information related to the Tibet administration and the Tibetan government in diaspora. This website posts

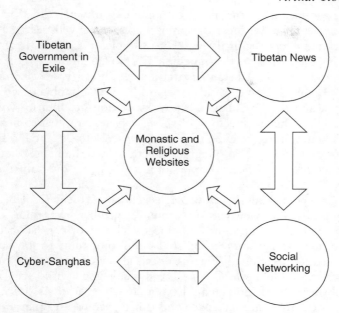

Figure 9.1   The five nodes of the multisite network. (Created by Chris Helland)

major announcements and provides continuous information regarding political activities and issues. Another prominent website for engaging political issues is the *Tibetan Political Review* (https://sites.google.com/site/tibetanpoliticalreview/). *Tibetan Political Review* is an online journal dedicated to advancing constructive discussions concerning the important political issues facing the Tibetan nation.

2. Tibetan news websites are the most frequently viewed sites by members of the Tibetan diaspora community. Of these websites, the most popular is Phayul.com. First online in July 2001, Phayul.com has been a primary source of news and information about the Tibetan situation for Tibetans and non-Tibetans alike. This website is often one of the first sources to report on breaking news within Tibet, and it has earned the reputation for being reliable and accurate. Phayul.com is presented online in English and is often used as a news source for the BBC and other major news outlets when it comes to obtaining information about activities within Tibet. Other news websites include Tibetsun.com, Tibettime.net, thetibetpost.com, and tibetreview.net.

3. "Cybersangha" was a term coined by Charles Prebish (2004) to describe the community-based Buddhist websites that were developing online to represent the *sangha*'s (community's) programs and emphasis. These websites are developed around the diaspora community's location and provide information for the community at a local and national level. Although in "cyberspace", cybersanghas

are geo-located in the major communities in which the Tibetan diaspora members are located. In most cases, these websites function at a national and a regional level. For example, in Canada there is Tibet. ca, which represents the Canadian Tibetan Committee. At the regional level, there is the Tibetan Association of Alberta (www.albertatibetan. com/), the Tibetan cultural Society of British Columbia (www.tcsofbc. org/), and the Canadian Tibetan association of Ontario (www.ctao. org/). The main objectives of these websites are "(1) to nurture the Tibetan culture, religion and traditions (2) teach and preserve the Tibetan language (3) integrate Tibetans in Canadian Society (4) to represent the Tibetan community at large" (www.albertatibetan. com/).

4. Social networking sites now play a significant role in the Tibetan diaspora. In an interview with a community member, I was told, "everyone has a Facebook account." Online social networking has become an extremely important mechanism for the community to stay connected while they are globally dispersed; this also includes staying connected with people living in China. The difficult issue with social network websites is that individuals have as much "voice" as officials. This is a strongly contested space and it has become a primary outlet for challenging authority over issues, including the role of women within the tradition, issues of equal rights and nepotism, and the debate over Tibetan independence or autonomy. Despite the possible online conflicts, charismatic figures within the Tibetan Buddhist tradition have significantly high social media measures (Twitter followers, re-tweets, Facebook "likes," website hits, etc.), and this high level of charismatic authority has transferred well into the social network. His Holiness the Dalai Lama, His Holiness the 17th Gyalwang Karmapa, and Pema Chodron are good examples, with millions of followers online. As of October 2013, the Dalai Lama has 6.5 million likes on Facebook and 8 million Twitter followers. Although there is only a small amount of information provided in "tweets" or Facebook postings, these social networking sites often act as portals that bring "followers" to official websites that provide more information and activities.

5. Tibetan monastic and religious websites play an important role within the diaspora community. As religion remains a key factor in issues of "Tibetanness," many of the diaspora community members now have limited access to monks and very limited opportunity to attend the sacred rituals conducted by the major lamas in India and for the lay Tibetans, the concern is not the absence of the monks, but how to properly proceed without them (Mullen 2006). As the monastic institutions and religious authorities have historically been key pillars in maintaining Tibetan identity, their availability "online" has now become an important method for connectedness. Monasteries that have been rebuilt within the diaspora have significant online

representations and continue to utilize cutting-edge Internet technology to develop meaningful and significant contact with their followers. The most dynamic example of this can be seen at the Dalai Lama's official website (www.dalailama.com), where they use the most current Internet technology (HD live webcasts, You Tube, "UStream" online television, Google+, etc.) to provide live broadcasts of teachings, messages, ritual activity, and news and information.

VIRTUAL TIBET: THREATS AND CHALLENGES

The Tibetan community in diaspora is aggrieved and persecuted. They are in a constant struggle with China over issues of territory, independence, autonomy, and authority. This struggle is evident in cyberspace and websites such as Phayul.com, Tibet.net, and Dalailama.com (to name but a few) have been the focus of concerted cyber-attacks and online surveillance. The Citizen Lab at the Munk School of Global Affairs (University of Toronto) recently identified a cyber-attack focused on the Tibetan diaspora community that compromised a network of more than 1,295 infected computers in 103 countries. Up to 30 percent of the infected computers were considered high-value targets and include computers located at ministries of foreign affairs, embassies, international organizations, news media, and nongovernmental organizations (Tracking Ghost Net 2009).

Mobile messaging software has also been infiltrated with malware to specifically target members of the Tibetan community in diaspora. In a sophisticated targeted attack, an email account of a high-profile Tibetan activist was compromised and used by attackers to send targeted malware to the activist's contact list. The attacks were sophisticated and presented an email about the recent World Uyghur Congress. People reading the e-mail were encouraged to download an app with information on the event. When they did, attackers collected data from infected devices, including contacts, call logs, SMS messages, geo-location, and phone data (Munk School for Global Affairs 2013). In the most recent case, the spyware being used was so sophisticated that it could not be detected by the major anti-virus and anti-malware software used by most members of the public.

It appears that the latest cyber attack against members of the Tibetan community in diaspora corresponds with a crackdown on cellular phone use within Tibet. One key reason is an attempt by the Chinese government to limit information about the dramatic increase in self-immolation deaths as protests against the current political situation within the Tibetan Autonomous Region (TAR). Since March 2011, within these territories, there have been more than 100 self-immolation deaths alone. Images, information, or any data concerning these events sent by cellphone is seen as a serious offense by the Chinese government, resulting in harsh prison sentences of as much as seven and a half years. With newly developed software, Chinese authorities are now scanning cellphones at various monasteries within the TAR to see if any information has been communicated outside of China. Even having pictures of these events on a cellphone camera can result in a prison term, a recent example being Ngawang Topden, a twenty-year-old student who was sentenced to two years for having a picture of a Tibetan flag and a self-immolation on his phone. The official charge was "encouraging other Tibetans to sabotage ethnic unity and misinforming about political issues" as reported in *Tibet Post International* and Phayul.com on February 2, 2013.

In a recent presentation at Emory University, Sherab Woeser, the editor-in-chief for Phayul.com, presented a talk titled "A Window into Tibet: Assessing the Flow of Information." In the discussion, he detailed other crackdowns limiting Internet use within TAR and surveillance measures that have significantly impacted how people within that country can receive information and also get information out to the Western world. In order to access the Internet, Tibetans must now have a second-generation "swipe card" that identifies them on the computer they are using and records all of their Internet surfing. All land phone lines are monitored and, if need be, the Chinese government can use cellphone and Internet-jamming devices that can literally shut off all communications within a thirty-mile radius.

VIRTUAL TIBET: VALUE BEYOND THE CHALLENGES

Despite the constant threats and challenges posed by the Internet, for a diaspora community, this new form of media has become an essential and vital component for maintaining identity. Within the Tibetan diaspora, there are three clear benefits derived from online activity. The first is that it allows for a networked identity within the community itself (Helland 2007). Through the Internet, Tibetans living throughout the world can connect in a deep and meaningful way with other members of the community who may not be living within the same nations or even continents. Non-diaspora people do this as a matter of choice, for the diaspora community it is done as a matter of survival.

The second significant benefit achieved by utilizing new media within the Tibetan diaspora is to connect monks and religious specialists with the community through websites and online activity. Websites such as www. rigpa.org or www.drikung.org allow Tibetans and non-Tibetans alike the opportunity to connect with important religious figures in a way that was not available in the past. For example, a member of the Tibetan community living in Calgary, Canada, can take distance learning with a lama, participate in online courses, and watch ritual events in real time, despite being thousands of miles away. In diaspora, there is also a developing divide between the lay community and the monastic community as the lamas are often affiliated with various Buddhist meditation centers that have an elite group of Western followers. These followers often pay large sums of money to attend workshops and teachings and present a high level of devotion to the teachers. The monks must rely on this livelihood for their survival but this often means that members of the Tibetan community only have the opportunity to connect with their monks during Losar or special festivals (Mullen 2006). With the power of the Internet, the diaspora community now has unlimited access in a new, albeit different, way to their religious specialists.

The third important benefit to the community builds on the second. This new form of connection with religious authorities has developed into a complex network of online ritual activities that co-locate the most sacred aspects of the Tibetan tradition in a very real and meaningful way with the members of the diaspora. New forms of online ritual activity have been developed and facilitated through websites such as www.dalailama.com to allow Tibetans in exile (and within Tibet, for that matter) the opportunity to have a close and powerful encounter with the most sacred component of the tradition. By placing ritual online, the Tibetan community can engage the very fabric of the religion: the teachings, ritual events, and sacred lamas, which are central to the identity and practices of Tibetan Buddhists.

VIRTUAL TIBET: CO-LOCATING THE SACRED

Ritual activities and charismatic authority do not always transfer well into the Internet medium (Helland 2012a). What is unique about the Tibetan situation is how well the charisma of the high lamas is perceived by the community to be accessible, tangible, and real, even if it is facilitated through computer networks. There are two key factors that may influence why online ritual seems to work so well for this community. The first can be explored with "ritual transfer theory" (see Miczek 2008; Radde-Antweiler 2006). Placing ritual online is a process that requires adaption and changes within any religious tradition and can be viewed as an ongoing activity that involves the three components of transformation, invention, and exclusion. Transformation is the process of shaping or reshaping a ritual that already exists, changing its content or structure in certain ways so it can be facilitated online. For this process to proceed, there may need to be innovation within the ritual based on the new media environment, and new aspects or components may have to be developed to allow for the ritual to work online. The final element is exclusion, since certain things inevitably have to be left out of the ritual activity in order for it to take place online. When these three forces act upon the ritual, the people participating are then left with a different ritual than they have previously participated in and they have to decide if the ritual works or if it has failed. For many people, the exclusion from physically presence is too much of a change and they will not participate, for others it might be the lack of nature, the taste of the wine, or the meal after the ceremony. In any case, the ritual transfer process will fail if these three forces somehow destabilize the ritual to the point that people will not recognize it as an authentic ritual activity. For other participants, the changes and transformations that occur to bring the ritual online will be seen as being within a margin of acceptability and they will view the ritual as still authentic (Helland 2012a).

Within the Tibetan Buddhist tradition, many ritual activities transfer well. At a basic level, most of the ritual activities facilitated online are teachings about sacred Buddhist texts. In this case, the online ritual is considered an aid for greater understanding and to gain awareness and spiritual awakening, resulting ultimately in liberation from the cycle of rebirth (Connelly 2012). However, because these teachings are conducted by the high lamas, their power and "sacredness" is perceived to also be transmitted online when people receive the teachings. In effect, by viewing the teachings, even if you do not understand all of the texts' complexities, one still gains merit just by being part of the transmission process of the teachings. Due to this perception, the lamas are not merely a visual sign or "summarizing symbol" for the Tibetan tradition and identity, but rather they are iconic representation of the divine. Within this tradition, the lama or *Rinpoche* ("Precious One") is sacred and holds spiritual or supernatural power that can be bestowed on their students. This occurs during formal and informal oral transmissions. Although in the past this was done face-to-face, through the Internet, it is also now perceived to be doable online. Technology such as Skype and real-time syncretic HD video feed allows for a new form of contact to occur between the teacher/ritual specialist and the person receiving the teachings and empowerment. As such, the Rinpoche has a powerful effect on those people who perceive his charisma in this way. David Morgan argues this would be an iconic form of representation of the sacred:

> Seeing icons is a visual practice of producing the Real as visible among a group of people who want it very badly. Seeing an icon means being seen by the one who looks through his or her image. This is presence, as close to the Real as one may come. The power of such images consists of their ability to show the Real, as if that were possible . . . To see them is to feel the arrival of the sacred one they herald. The aura of that elusive reality may be called spiritual, that is, the evocation of the Real within the web of connections.
>
> (Morgan 2011)

Beyond the ritual transfer theory, the second way that online ritual has such a significant impact on the Tibetan community in diaspora is that the lamas, and particularly the Dalai Lama, are already viewed by the community as being between worlds, both as spiritual beings (bodhisattvas) or incarnate deities and as human monks. This sacredness is conceived as a focus of transcendence, which can rupture normal time and space.

It transfers well online because the Internet itself disrupts normal time and space on a regular basis. What makes this online activity more than just a form of "long-distanced" ritual practice (which is very common within Hinduism) or virtual pilgrimage (which is very common within Christianity) is the "co-location" of the sacred through the Internet. Members of the Tibetan tradition in diaspora feel a genuine, authentic, and powerful encounter with the lamas when they engage in online ritual activity.

Co-location was first presented as a theory in relation to online ritual activity by Dan Pinchbeck and Brett Stevens (2006). They argued that virtual reality has a number of common features similar to ritual and that through the liminality of the online environment, people could feel like they were having an authentic experience when they were online. In this case, it was the perception of the participants that gave them a sense of "being there" or a sense of presence in cyberspace. The second use of the term "co-location" was developed by Connie Hill-Smith (2011), where she argued that through co-location, sacred pilgrimage sites could be authentically replicated online. In this situation, it was the sacred place that was co-located in cyberspace and people who went on "virtual pilgrimage" felt a true sense of connecting with the real place despite it being an online simulacrum of the authentic sacred site.

What makes the co-location that occurs in Virtual Tibet different than the other two cases is that first and foremost, the people engaging in the ritual are not in a virtual reality environment. They are in diaspora, which is a liminal space in its own right, but it is in the "real world" at a computer. For example, recently, an elderly member of the Tibetan diaspora community watched the Dalai Lama's teachings and ritual activity broadcast live from the Main Tibetan Temple in Dharamsala. The ritual conducted in "Little Lhasa" was a teaching on Tsongkhapa's "Three Principal Aspects of the Path" and included a very special ritual called the White Tara Permission. The Dalai Lama stated during the live online broadcast that this ritual was taken from the "Secret Visions of the Fifth Dalai Lama," which he received in Tibet from Tagdrag Rinpoche. To receive the White Tara Permission from the Dalai Lama, who had received it from a very important lama in Tibet, is a very fortunate and auspicious event for a Tibetan Buddhist. The fact that the person was participating online, in diaspora, rather than at the temple in India was not seen as a great loss. Rather, it was viewed as a great benefit and a valid connection between the practitioner and the Dalai Lama. The person participating in the online ritual and teaching lit incense, placed offerings and flowers in front of the computer, and intensely watched the high definition broadcast, listening to the teachings and reciting the proper mantras when instructed by the Dalai Lama.

The second feature that is different from the other two theories of co-location involves the question of place. With virtual pilgrimage, there is a feeling that the sacred place is authentically recreated in cyberspace in such a way that people genuinely feel they encounter the liminal, sacredness of the site; Lourdes, France, or the Western Wall in Jerusalem being good examples. Within the Tibetan diaspora, there is a deep sense of loss and frustration concerning the Tibetan territory. However, the online representations of Virtual Tibet are not focused as much on the traditional land (or trying to virtually recreate them) as they are focused on maintaining the tradition and Tibetan identity itself. In many ways, this is similar to the conception of a networked community that maintains its "place" through interconnectedness rather than just traditional territory and political borders. As Massey (1991) argues, "What gives a place its specificity is not some long internalized history but the fact that it is constructed out of a particular constellation of social relations, meeting and weaving together at a particular locus" (28). Within Virtual Tibet, the locus and center maintaining the network is the Dalai Lama.

In the case of Virtual Tibet, co-location occurs in a three-step process that begins online with a ritual activity that is perceived by the community to work. If the community accepts that the ritual can be facilitated online with a level of authenticity that is acceptable within the tradition, then the online ritual "space" creates a liminal environment that the participants can encounter. This liminal space is in-between worlds, and shrinks the real-world distance that separates them from the ritual activity. It may be that the person is in New York City, sitting at a desk looking into a computer screen. But due to the liminality of the online ritual event, that person is in the present, encountering the transcendent element of the tradition, even if the ritual is being conducted 3,000 miles away. What makes co-location different than just watching a ritual on television (which can be a powerful experience in its own right) is the networked community or the multisite network. Participants are engaged within a web of connectedness when they go online for the ritual. It may be that they are going online to the Dalai Lama's website, or a monastery website, and there they will encounter the network used by the community for maintaining their identity. The final aspect that makes co-location tangible to the participants is the icon and "sacred center" around which the ritual is structured.

Much like an icon within the Christian tradition, there will be members of the community who do not view the representation as something that is divine or spiritual. In many ways, this is a good indicator of insider and outsider relationships to the group. An iconoclast will not participate in the rituals associated with icon reverence or worship and they will feel no sense of the sacred in the object so revered by the icon-worshipping community. However, for the believer, it is an encounter with the divine.

For the Tibetan people, the Dalai Lama is "the single most important figure around which Tibetan identity circulates" (McMillin 2001, 173), and as a personification of the protector deity he is the primary symbol of Tibetan unity (Kolas 1996, 57). For the vast majority of community members, the Dalai Lama has an "aura of sacredness" and a level of charismatic authority that is both institutionalized within the structure of the monastic tradition and sanctified by the community itself (e.g., Smith 1998; Weber 1978). Any opportunity to have an intimate or close encounter with the Dalai Lama is seen as being a profound and significant event. Through these new digital networks, the monastic orders are socially shaping Internet technology to provide their community in diaspora with the opportunity to experience the ritual activity and charisma (or sacredness) of their leadership in a new and dynamic way. This is reaffirming, maintaining, and strengthening the bonds between the monastic centers and the community, wherever they are located.

CONCLUSION

This chapter has argued that the development of the Internet has created a new form of connectedness within the Tibetan diaspora. Although there are digital divides and issues of Internet access, the diaspora community has gone to great lengths to create a complex system of interconnected online environments that help support and maintain their identity. Through the social shaping of technology, it is clear that the Tibetan community has developed and now maintains new forms of social networks that are linking them with each other, their religious specialists and religious leaders, and a Tibet that is not limited to a geographical territory.

Through the use of this new technology, the Tibetan tradition has also shown that religious ritual is adaptable, dynamic, and engaged with a culture that is wired and now almost constantly online. With the development of smartphones, Wi-Fi, high-speed Internet, and inexpensive computers, the world as we know it is changing. Religion and religious practices are not disappearing due to these technological advances; rather these practices are thriving online and transforming praxis in myriad dynamic ways. Within the Tibetan Buddhist tradition, the lamas and the sacred powers that are engaged through the rituals travel just as well through the online world as they do through the everyday world. As Thubten Samphel recognized very early on, the online multisite network of a Virtual Tibet is a powerful tool for promoting the Tibetan situation to the Western world and for challenging Chinese authorities and powers for the "hearts and minds" of Tibetans. For the diaspora community, the Internet has become a vital tool for communicating information, challenging ideological and political powers, and promoting "Tibetanness." However, it has also allowed for voices within the Tibetan community to likewise challenge tradition and authority and question their identity in a global world where they are living in a form of stateless diaspora. It is transformative. Yet by developing a strong online religious presence, the tradition itself is changing and allowing for change, while at the same time it is recreating and re-establishing ancient networks that have maintained a community from the top of the world and the Tibetan Plateau to wherever Tibetans have become located.

NOTE

1. See www.namgyal.org/blessings/cyberspace.cfm.

REFERENCES

Anand, Dibyesh. 2000. "(Re) Imagining Nationalism: Identity and Representation in the Tibetan Diaspora of South Asia." *Contemporary South Asia* 9(2): 271–287.

Ardley, Jane. 2002. *Tibetan Independence Movement: Political, Religious, and Gandhian Perspectives*. New York: Routledge.

Barker, Eileen. 2005. "Crossing the Boundary: New Challenges to Religious Authority and Control as a Consequence of Access to the Internet." In *Religion and Cyberspace*, edited by Morten Hojsgaard and Margit Warburg, 67–86. London: Routledge.

Berns McGowan, Rima. 1999. *Muslims in the Diaspora*. Toronto, Canada: University of Toronto Press.

Beyer, Peter. 2006. *Religions in Global Society*. New York: Routledge.

Boyd, Helen. 2004. *The Future of Tibet: The Government-in-Exile Meets the Challenge of Democratization*. New York: Peter Lang.

Bray, John. 2000. "Tibet, Democracy and the Internet Bazaar." *Democratization* 7(1): 157–173.

Brinkerhoff, Jennifer. 2012. "Digital Diasporas' Challenge to Traditional Power: The Case of TibetBoard." *Review of International Studies* 38(1): 77–95.

Campbell, Heidi. 2005. "Spiritualising the Internet: Uncovering Discourse and Narrative of Religious Internet Usage." *Online: Heidelberg Journal of Religion on the Internet* 1(1). http://www.ub.uni-heidelberg.de/archiv/5824. Accessed June 25, 2014.

———. 2007. "Who's Got the Power? Religious Authority and the Internet." *Journal of Computer-Mediated Communication* 12(3): 1043–1062.

———. 2010. "Bloggers and Religious Authority Online." *Journal of Computer-Mediated Communication* 15(2): 251–276.

———. 2012. "Understanding the Relationship between Religion Online and Offline in a Networked Society." *Journal of the American Academy of Religion* 80(1): 64–93.

Cohen, Robin. 1997. *Global Diasporas: An Introduction*. Seattle: University of Washington Press.

Connelly, Louise. 2012. "Virtual Buddhism: Buddhist Ritual in Second Life." In *Digital Religion: Understanding Religious Practice in New Media Worlds*, edited by Heidi Campbell, 128–135. New York: Routledge.

Dorjee, Tenzin, and Howard Giles. 2005. "Cultural Identity in Tibetan Diasporas." *Journal of Multilingual and Multicultural Development* 26(2): 138–157.

Drissel, David. 2008. "Digitizing Dharma: Computer-Mediated Mobilizations of Tibetan Buddhist Youth." *International Journal of Diversity in Organisations, Communities and Nations* 8(5): 79–91.

Eickelmann, D., and J. Anderson. 1999. *New Media in the Muslim World: The Emerging Public Sphere*. Bloomington: Indiana University Press.

Helland, C. 2000. "Online Religion/Religion Online and Virtual Communitas." In *Religion on the Internet: Research Prospects and Promises*, edited by J. Hadden and D. Cowan, 205–224. New York: JAI Press.

———. 2007. "Diaspora on the Electronic Frontier: Developing Virtual Connections with Sacred Homelands." *Journal of Computer-Mediated Communication* 12(3): 956–976.

———. 2008. "Canadian Religious Diversity Online: A Network of Possibilities." In *Religion and Diversity in Canada*, edited by P. Beyer and L. Beaman, 127–148. Boston, MA: Brill Academic Publishers.

———. 2012a. "Ritual." In *Digital Religion: Understanding Religious Practice in New Media Worlds*, edited by Heidi Campbell, 25–40. New York: Routledge.

———. 2012b. "Online Religion in Canada: From Hype to Hyperlink." In *Religion and Canadian Society: Traditions, Transitions, and Innovations*, edited by L. Beaman, 375–390. Toronto: Canadian Scholar's Press.

Hess, J. M. 2006. "Statelessness and the State: Tibetans, Citizenship, and National Activism in a Transnational World." *International Migration* 44(1): 79–130.

Hill-Smith, Connie. 2011. "Cyberpilgrimage: The (Virtual) Reality of Online Pilgrimage Experience." *Religion Compass* 5(6): 236–246.

Hiller, H., and T. Franz. 2004. "New Ties, Old Ties and Lost Ties: The Use of the Internet in Diaspora." *New Media and Society* 6(6): 731–752.

Hoover, S., and N. Echchaibi. 2012. "The 'Third Space' of Digital Religion." A discussion paper for The Center for Media, Religion, and Culture. Boulder: University of Colorado, Boulder.Ignacio, E. 2005. *Building Diaspora: Filipino Community Formation on the Internet*. New Brunswick, NJ: Rutgers University Press.

Kolas, A. 1996. "Tibetan Nationalism: The Politics of Religion." *Journal of Peace Research* 33(1): 51–66.

Mallapragada, M. 2006. "Home, Homeland, Homepage: Belonging and the Indian American Web." *New Media and Society* 8(2): 207–227.

Massey, Doreen. 1991. "A Global Sense of Place." *Marxism Today* 35(6): 24–29.

McLagan, M. 1996. "Computing for Tibet: Virtual Politics in the Post-Cold-War Era." In *Connected: Engagements with Media*, edited by G. E. Marcus, 159–194. London: University of Chicago.

McMillin, L. 2001. *English in Tibet, Tibet in English: Self-presentation in Tibet and the Diaspora*. New York: Palgrave.

Miczek, N. 2008. "Online Rituals in Virtual Worlds: Christian Online Services between Dynamics and Stability." *Heidelberg Journal of Religions on the Internet* 3(1). http://www.ub.uni-heidelberg.de/archiv/8293. Accessed June 25, 2014.

Miller, B. 1961. "The Web of Tibetan Monasticism." *Journal of Asian Studies* 20(2): 197–203.

Miller, D., and D. Slater. 2000. *The Internet: An Ethnographic Approach*. Oxford: Berg.

Misra, A. 2003. "A Nation in Exile: Tibetan Diaspora and the Dynamics of Long Distanced Nationalism." *Asian Ethnicity* 4(2): 189–206.

Mitra, A. 1997. "Virtual Commonality: Looking for India on the Internet." In *Virtual Culture: Identity and Communication in Cybersociety*, edited by S. Jones, 55–79. London: Sage.

Morgan, David. 2011. "Aura and Effect: The Media of Religions," paper presentation sponsored by the IFK (International Research Center for Cultural Studies), Vienna, Austria, June 16.

Mullen, E. 2006. "Tibetan Religious Expression and Identity: Transformations in Exile." In *Materialising Religion: Expressions, Performance, and Ritual,* edited by E. Arweck and W. Keenan, 175–189. Burlington, VT: Ashgate Publishing.

Munk School for Global Affairs. 2013. Permission to Spy: An Analysis of Android Malware Targeting Tibetans. https://citizenlab.org/2013/04/permission-to-spy-an-analysis-of-android-malware-targeting-tibetans/ Accessed June 25, 2014.

Nowak, M. 1984. *Tibetan Refugees: Youth and the Generation of Meaning*. New Brunswick, NJ: Rutgers University Press.

Pinchbeck, Dan, and Brett Stevens. 2006. *Ritual Co-location: Play, Consciousness and Reality in Artificial Environments*. http://citeseerx.ist.psu.edu/viewdoc/download?doi=10.1.1.105.8448&rep=rep1&type=pdf. Accessed June 25, 2014.

Prebish, C. 2004. "The Cybersangha: Buddhism on the Internet." In *Religion Online: Finding Faith on the Internet,* edited by D. Cowan and L. Dawson, 135–150. New York: Routledge.

Radde-Antweiler, K. 2006. "Rituals Online: Transferring and Designing Rituals." *Heidelberg Journal of Religions on the Internet* 2(1). http://www.ub.uni-heidel berg.de/archiv/6957. Accessed June 25, 2014.

Raine, L., and B. Wellman. 2012. *Networked: The New Social Operating System.* Cambridge, MA: MIT Press.

Samphel, T. 2004. "Virtual Tibet: The Media." In *Exile as Challenge: The Tibetan Diaspora,* edited by D. Bernstorff and H. von Welck, 167–185. New Delhi, India: Orient Longman.

Sangay, L. 2003. "Tibet: Exiles' Journey." *The Journal of Democracy* 14(3): 119–130.

Selwyn, N. 2004. "Reconsidering Political and Popular Understandings of the Digital Divide." *New Media and Society* 6(3): 341–62.

Sheffer, G. 2003. *Diaspora Politics: At Home Abroad.* New York: Cambridge University Press.

Smith, D.N. 1998. "Faith, Reason, and Charisma: Rudolf Sohm, Max Weber, and the Theology of Grace." *Sociological Inquiry* 68(1): 32–60.

Sokefeld, Martin. 2002. "Alevism Online: Re-imagining a Community in Virtual Space." *Diaspora* 11(1): 85–124.

Turner, B. 2007. "Religious Authority and the New Media." *Theory, Culture and Society* 24(2): 117–134.

van Schaik, S. 2011. *Tibet: A History.* New Haven, CT: Yale University Press.

Vertovec, S. 1999. "Conceiving and Researching Transnationalism." *Ethnic and Racial Studies* 22(2): 1–11.

———. 2000. "Religion and Diaspora." Working paper, Institute of Social and Cultural Anthropology, University of Oxford (WPTC-01–01).

———. 2004. "Religion and Diaspora." In *New Approaches to the Study of Religion,* edited by P. Antes, A. Geertz, and R. Werne, 275–304. Berlin: Verlag de Gruyter.

———. 2009. *Transnationalism.* London: Routledge.

Weber, M. 1978. *Economy and Society.* Berkeley: University of California Press.

Whalen-Bridge, J. 2011. "Multiple Modernities and the Tibetan Diaspora." *South Asian Diaspora* 3(1): 103–115.

Wilbur, S. 1997. "An Archaeology of Cyberspaces: Virtuality, Community, Identity." In *Internet Culture,* edited by D. Porter, 5–22. New York: Routledge.

10 Our Virtual Materials
The Substance of Buddhist Holy Objects in a Virtual World

Jessica Falcone

One morning in the fall of 2011, in the virtual world of Second Life (SL), my avatar sits on a green meditation cushion. A virtual world is an online environment in which avatars or simulations of operators can move through a crafted landscape in cyber space.[1] Second Life is a particular virtual environment in which the content is largely created by its in-world denizens,[2] who themselves establish virtual spaces, relationships, and economies. Therefore, in Second Life, the Buddhist landscapes, monasteries ,and stupas have been created, crafted, and "offered" by the Second Life citizens themselves. I did my research in Second Life primarily in a site called the Buddha Center, which is a non-denominational Buddhist simulation that specializes in meditation sessions and dharma talks (lessons about Buddhist religious texts and practices).

In front of my avatar in SL, there is a virtual Buddha statue, surrounded by around a half-dozen other pixilated persons all waiting for our scheduled meditation session to begin. The Buddha statue, which was radiating "oms," was the focal point at the center of the room. Just before 11 a.m. SLT (Second Life Time), our meditation facilitator, Gaia Tryx, arrived in the main chapel of the Buddha Center. Her avatar was dressed in a sari blouse and petticoat (sans sari), and wearing a Buddhist mala (rosary). Presumably in actual life (AL) our facilitator put her cursor on the glowing orb close to the entrance and clicked it,[3] since we viewed her avatar doing three prostrations in quick succession in front of the Buddha statue. She seated her avatar at the front of the room, looking out at the fewer-than-half-dozen avatars on cushions before her—the Buddha statue situated just to her left. Gaia then typed: "Good morning and welcome, sangha. This morning we will begin with the Green Tara mantra." Then she sent us each a digital note card with the mantra, which we could open in order to follow along. The preparation for meditation continued with quick recitations of the Four Noble Truths, the Eightfold Path, and the Seven Factors of Enlightenment. After sending each of us "Calm Abiding" instructions to guide our meditation, she rang the gong. As it rang audibly three times, each noise was visualized by a vibrating yellow stream of spheres moving between the gong and Gaia Tryx. We all sat in silent meditation until Gaia Tryx enabled a single gong at 11:29 SLT. She did an optional recitation of bodhisattva vows for those who have taken them. We all thanked her via text chat as she rose to leave. She acknowledged our thanks, but she did not immediately sign out or teleport to another region. First, she prostrated to the Buddha in the temple three times, as she had on entering. Then she walked outside of the temple, and prostrated again in front of a statue located there. Only then did Gaia Tryx finally wink offline.

How do we understand virtual Buddhist objects both anthropologically and Buddhologically? In this chapter, I examine what motivates people to build holy objects in Second Life and make offerings to them. Virtual materiality poses challenges within all Second Life subcultures, but anyone specifically investigating Buddhist groups online must work to understand how they frame their interactions with sacred objects: what are we to make of a virtual avatar in Second Life chiming a gong at the end of a meditation session, and then going to bow before two Buddha statues before flashing out of Second Life altogether? What was she bowing to and why? In some ways, this meditation session was eerily similar to Buddhist meditation sessions that I had participated in offline at the Root Institute in Bodh Gaya, India, for example. The actual statues in Bodh Gaya had been consecrated and they were considered by "devotees" to be space in which the Buddha exists, and I found myself wondering if my informants in Second Life believed the same thing of their Buddha statues.

Following several ethnographies of the virtual human in the social world of Second Life,[4] I engaged in a multiyear study of Buddhist practices of meditation, merit-making, and materiality in the virtual world of Second Life.[5] I base my observations on two years of fieldwork on Buddhist holy objects in actual life from 2005–2007, which has been supplemented with participant observation in Second Life with community members in a handful of Buddhist spaces from 2010–2012.[6] Methodologically, I am in accordance with the co-authors of "Ethnography and Virtual Worlds," when they note that ethnography presupposes long-term sustained participant observation, which is just as possible (and important) in virtual spaces as actual ones (Boellstorff, Nardi, Pearce, and Taylor 2012).[7]

My contribution to this volume illustrates the practices of Buddhist materiality in Second Life, and the extent to which Buddhist concepts such as "holy objects," "merit-making," "guru devotion," and "sacred space" have been refracted and re-imagined in this virtual world. Within all Asian Buddhist traditions, holy objects have particular spiritual valences that transcend their value as mere aesthetic or art objects (Schopen 1997; Strong 2004; Trainor 1997). This understanding of holy objects has been imported to various degrees by most new or hybrid Western Buddhisms, although not all new Buddhists embrace this particular aspect of the religion. Buddhist holy objects are understood to be special, especially if they are consecrated within the purview of the particular tradition. In certain circumstances, the Buddha or a bodhisattva is thought to inhabit a consecrated sacred object.

Does the virtuality of these objects alter our conversations in either material culture studies or Buddhist studies? It may seem counterintuitive to study materiality in virtual worlds, but I would argue that doing so is a key piece of the larger puzzle in comprehending digital Buddhist life. Horst and Miller (2012), as well as Boellstorff (2008), have already argued that materiality in virtual worlds is an important topic of study. In fact, Boellstorff (2008) emphasized the central importance of making objects and building things in his study of Second Life, noting that, "building could act as a craft—a form of techne—by which the virtual became actual" (101).

This chapter demonstrates that because virtual objects and actual objects point toward a practitioner's intentionality, the Buddhist objects are perceived as having merit. Understanding the merit of virtual objects is significant, because it demonstrates that the Buddhist objects that people make in SL simultaneously make SL Buddhists who and what they are. For instance, in her ethnographic work on the Uru, a community that spanned several virtual worlds (including Second Life), Celia Pearce observed that some of the aspects that knitted the virtual Uru community together were the artifacts (architecture, places and objects) that they built in digital spaces (Pearce and Artemsia 2009). Pearce demonstrated that it was the shared knowledge of deeper meaning that built affiliation with the community. Buddhist materiality does similar cultural work in both SL and AL. To build my case, I will begin with attention to the Buddhological perspective on actual, offline holy objects, and then shift to how virtual Buddhist objects are understood by Buddhist practitioners in SL. I will then expand on these themes through discussions of several ethnographic engagements with Buddhist materiality in the Buddha Center "sim" (as virtual spaces are known in Second Life).

SACRED MATERIALS IN ACTUAL LIFE

In order to even begin the conversation about virtual Buddhist sacred materials, one must understand the significance and variations in how these objects are understood in the physical world. Holy objects in actual Buddhist milieus include statues, relics, thangkas (Tibetan Buddhist paintings of deities, gurus, and other religious icons), precious malas (Buddhist rosaries), and so on. While the emptiness of all things is a cornerstone of Buddhist belief,[8] most Buddhists do not consider emptiness of objects to be at odds with the sacralization and worship of holy objects.[9]

In contemporary Buddhist life, images often take center-stage in religious spaces, either as paintings or statues of the Buddhas, bodhisattvas, and learned teachers, since the veneration of sacred objects is thought to have many karmic benefits to the makers and worshippers of the object.[10] Steven Collins, social and cultural historian of Buddhism, makes a keen observation that Nirvana is just one of the many rewards and "felicities" desired and sought by practicing Buddhists, and this is illustrated precisely by the literature that outlines in detail the many benefits of making various holy objects (Collins 1998). For example, Lama Zopa Rinpoche, a contemporary Tibetan Buddhist teacher with a sizable transnational flock,[11] has written and talked extensively about the notion that making and worshipping stupas and statues has extensive benefits toward purification and merit-making (Courtin and Zopa 2003).

While trying to understand the complexity of Buddhist sacred objects in virtual life, it is necessary to see that complexity, ambiguity, and variation begin in actual life understandings of sacred Buddhist things. For example, in AL, Buddhist statues and other sacred objects are usually thought to be most efficacious when they themselves hold relics,[12] although only the image itself is visible, while the relics are usually hidden. While not all statues or stupas contain cherished relics of powerful Buddhists from the past, almost all holy objects undergo a rite of recognition, consecration, or "sacralization" (Kopytoff 1986). Even many smaller statues in the Tibetan Buddhist tradition are filled and consecrated with mantras. I will discuss the extent to which this consecration ritual is replicated or ignored by Buddhists in Second Life later, but, regardless, it should be understood that the significance of consecration in making a holy object important is not universal or absolute. For example, Kirti Rinpoche, a prominent Tibetan Buddhist lama teaching in Dharamsala during my fieldwork period in India, told me during an interview that consecration is just a formality when the donor is sincere:

> When someone makes a statue or stupa, the Buddha or Bodhisattva of the site will come if the person who has done this does so with great motivation. They [the Buddhas and Bodhisattvas] have clairvoyance, so they know when to come and they will be in the statue. This is because of the sincere motivation of the maker.

Thus, in actual life, a holy object is already a stand-in for something else, metaphorically, but also quite literally. As Kirti Rinpoche told me:

> They are inside the statue even before the consecration. We consecrate for the ordinary beings, for the ordinary people who have doubts. So the ceremony of consecration is done so it helps the people to feel assured that the Buddhas are now blessing the statues. Before the ceremony, there is no doubt that the Buddha is there, but also afterwards.

To understand the presence of the Buddha in the holy object as it is understood in Tibetan Buddhism, he drew on a digital example to illustrate the presence of the Buddha in the actual object. He said:

> These days we have a computer; when you want information it has to be shown on the screen, but the information is already there. But even as the statue is being built the Buddha is there, and after the consecration

then the blessing in the statue is like the information appearing on the screen.

As we work toward an understanding of the ways in which the sacredness of objects is understood in virtual settings, Kirti Rinpoche's interview with me was telling, given his recognition of the existence of Buddha as permeating everything, and just becoming more recognizable with the aid of a physical marker. If we extend this analogy toward Second Life, then how different could SL holy objects be from AL ones? In the next section, we will see how my informants have tackled the complex question of virtual materiality.

SECOND LIFE BUDDHIST SELVES, OBJECT, AND MERIT

I sit on a meditation cushion in the Deer Park area of the Buddha Center (see Figure 10.1).[13] In front of me, a large statue of the Buddha sits in a small pool, with the ocean spreading out in the distance behind him. Animated deer graze nearby; it is a peaceful, serene landscape. I have been here many times before, as there are often teachings and meditations here, so I am struck by the new addition to the virtual-scape: burning candles have been placed in front of the statue. These are no normal offerings to the Buddha statue—they have been placed here by Second Life Buddhists who are praying for the health of a teacher who is very sick in actual life, perhaps on his deathbed. The offerings are thought by most of my informants here to be efficacious in some way, but what precisely is the nature of the effects that they seek to cause with their orientation towards Buddhist virtual objects?

Figure 10.1 Second Life Buddhist Selves, Object, and Merit. (Second Life snapshot by Jessica Falcone)

My research indicates that the virtual selves of Second Life are not an alienating notion to the practicing Buddhists who have thought through or experimented with the phenomenon. The concept of *anatman* (no-self) extends itself neatly into the virtual Buddhist world. Robert Geraci, a religious studies scholar working on cyber-theology, makes some rather sweeping claims about Second Life Residents, saying that they find SL preferable to AL: "Fundamentally, Second Life residents revel in virtual reality because they find it superior to current reality" (Geraci 2010, 77). I have not found that statement to be accurate, as most of my informants saw their Buddhist practices in SL as fairly practical and instrumentalist; most found it to be a convenient and creative space for worship and religious exploration, and they often had Buddhist experiences outside of SL, as well. That is, my informants seemed to see their SL and AL personas and places as much more intertwined than Geraci's dualistic assertion would imply. For instance, Gregory Grieve, American scholar of religion and digital media, has written that from a Buddhist perspective, an avatar is an extension of the self, not a copy. "Theoretically, and thinking back to the concept of anatman, residents can be understood as cyborg, fluid selves, whose bodies are multiple and distributed across a number of 'windows'" (Grieve 2010, 44).

When I began work in Second Life in 2010, I wondered whether people believed that avatars had separate opportunities for merit-making. I asked informants whether an avatar could make merit, and they always said "no," as merit can only accrue to the AL operator of the avatar. SL avatars are mediated extensions of AL persons, so they cannot make merit themselves; if and when merit is being made (for not all SL Buddhists believe in "merit"), then it is accruing to the people operating the avatars. As Grieve says, the SL self is cyborg, but I hasten to add, the AL self is cyborg, too.

Louise Connelly's interview with SL Buddha Center's co-founder Zino reveals that he believes that merit can be earned by the person if the avatar's actions are done with the "same intention" as in actual life (Connelly 2010, 17–18). If Zino was saying the same amount of merit would be accrued from SL actions as AL actions, well, then this is not uncommon at all, but there are those who complicate this perspective. Lama Thutop, for example, who teaches at the Buddha Center, argues that while merit can be accrued to actors in SL who make or touch a prayer wheel, it is not necessarily the same amount of merit that would be earned by someone who made or spun a prayer wheel in AL. I would suggest that the difference in their perspectives primarily hinges on their status and commitment to actual gurus—in fact, this difference separates their views on the efficacy and power of AL sacred objects, as well.

In working on holy objects in Tibetan traditions in actual life (both in Tibetan and non-Tibetan communities), I found that some people take holy objects as literally sacred objects inhabited by the presence of an enlightened or elevated being, while others see the presence as a figurative one. As I did research in AL on how new transnational non-heritage Buddhist practitioners dealt with the challenges of embracing faith in holy objects, I began to sort my informants into fuzzy sets: "students" and "devotees."[14] I would like to suggest that in looking at non-heritage Buddhists, one might establish a continuum of belief and commitment: "searchers," "students," and "devotees." *Searchers* are often very new to Buddhism, and may be dabbling, testing it out informally, or casually trying it on for size. *Students* are more actively committed to learning about Buddhism and trying to put it into practice in their lives; students are often willing to question the authorities and experts in their practice, and they are more likely to be forging their own personal path. Finally, *devotees* have made a strong commitment to a Buddhist guru or teacher, and are wont to be committed to following a path as laid out by that authority figure. The distinction is non-essential, as some people go back and forth in different points in their life. The students are simply more comfortable picking and choosing how to practice Buddhism, whereas the devotees have made a commitment to a teacher or teachers that entail some level of faith and commitment in that teacher's vision over his or her own.

In AL and SL, searchers and students were much more likely to see holy objects as symbols. On the other hand, devotees were much more likely to either believe, or be working very hard to believe, what their guru told them about the inherent spiritual efficacy of actual life holy objects, and, therefore, they are less likely to equate their significance. This is an imprecise division, but the key is really whether a Buddhist is committed to trying to imbibe a holistic teaching and doctrine from a guru (or several) in whom s/he has put her faith. The doctrine of guru devotion in Tibetan Buddhism makes this a very important intention, but even in other Buddhist practices making a commitment to a guru is serious business. Even where students have connections with teachers, they are still exploring, and still taking teachings as a means to advance their own eclectic and developing practices and beliefs. Students may have some faith, but first and foremost they trust in their own ability to organize their disparate paths.

Based on all of my research with Buddhist groups in SL so far, I would argue that most of the people actively practicing Buddhism in SL are students, as opposed to devotees.[15] In AL, Buddhist students (as I've identified them) tend to view sacred objects as symbols that point to positive attributes and potentialities, rather than seeing them as inherently powerful in and of themselves. The students that I have interviewed based on their involvement in SL all see the holy objects in SL as equivalent to those in AL; both actual and virtual materials are symbols of mental and spiritual achievement and should be respected as such. All the students said that Buddhist objects are symbolically important in both Actual Life and Second Life, but that in neither environment are sacred objects powerful from their own side.

I have met only a few informants in SL that I would categorize as devotees, and their views about virtual materials are more complex. One of my informants, a student called Moosewood Max, made an observation that I very much agree with—many practitioners who have given themselves over to faith in an AL teacher's perspective do not come to SL, at least not to practice Buddhism. When they do come, they are often teachers, hoping to spread the word of their own gurus, and provide people with the opportunity to learn more about the Dharma. However, those who do see themselves as devotees (whether they use that word or not) definitely do have a strong tendency to agree with the mores of their heritage Buddhist gurus who invariably see holy objects as having a power and efficacy of their own.

VIRTUAL MATERIALS AT THE BUDDHA CENTER

While there are always Buddhist statues and thangka paintings in the main Buddhist chapel of the Buddha Center, these spaces, much like AL spaces, do change slowly and occasionally over time: sometimes there are multiple statues, sometimes just one; images and paintings get switched out; the floor is redesigned, sometimes with a pool in the middle, sometimes not; plants and cushions change shape and/or color, and so on. There are many Buddha statues and sacred landscapes laid out throughout the Buddha Center sim. My very favorite Buddha statue in the Buddha Center was on a cliff face backed by three waterfalls that pool around the statue and continue down the hill as a single stream of water (see Figure 10.2). This waterfall Buddha statue had a few stones in front of it that were coded to enable avatars to sit in peaceful meditation. Although it was just my SL avatar sitting in that

Figure 10.2   Virtual materials at the Buddha Center. (Second Life snapshot by Jessica Falcone)

utopian cyberspace, the beauty of the landscape appealed acutely to my AL self; it was my AL self that relaxed, exhaled, and enjoyed the solitude and peaceful quality of the landscape.

I would like to note that while the builds and sacred landscapes at the Buddha Center are somewhat fanciful and fantastic, they are meant to feel familiar. They are supposed to be loose replications of familiar natural and sacred spaces. The main teaching temple features a centrally placed statue and an arrangement of meditation cushions that feels familiar to practitioners with actual life experience. Since the Buddha Center is non-denominational, one can find holy objects in various regional and aesthetic styles, such as Tibetan thangka, a Japanese tea house meditation space, and a Chan Buddha statue. The Buddha Center's builds are creatively designed landscapes dotted with familiar SL copies of holy objects. There is an effort to be whimsical, but serious, and that means that no one has taken liberties to change the gender, face, or fashion of the Buddha. Although SL's platform gives one the freedom to remake Buddhist objects in whatever way one can imagine, in my fieldwork in SL, I never saw a Buddhist object that had been really *transformed*, instead they were being meticulously re-created.

Lama Thutop is a teacher at the Buddha Center, and a Buddhist devotee. He believes that the holy objects in AL are receptacles of Buddhas and bodhisattvas, and he is open to their efficacy in SL, although he does not see them as equivalent. Lama Thutop is a white man of European heritage, and studied in person with his ethnically Tibetan Nyingmapa gurus before finally taking vows and beginning to teach himself. Lama Thutop recognized that it was somewhat easier for certain other types of Buddhism to thrive in SL, whereas the nature of guru devotional practices and empowerments requires actual life presence. He said, "Well, for a relationship to exist between teacher and student in [Tibetan] Buddhism, you need physical presence. Basically, you need to hang out with the teacher, if you're a student, and as a teacher, the most effective transmission happens when both teacher and student are present. Some instructions cannot be given through the medium of SL, and should not be given." Lama Thutop talked about the importance of touch and presence in making significant connection with a teacher, especially for empowerments. He recommends to his SL students that they seek AL teachers as well in order to move their practice to the next level.

At first, Lama Thutop suggested to me that since all objects are ultimately empty there is little fundamental difference between SL and AL objects, but his caveats about the importance of AL embodiment for advanced practices extended to certain merit-making practices. For example, he noted that a pilgrimage to a sacred space in AL requires much more effort and therefore would make more merit than a visit to a copy of that sacred space in SL. He also noted that prostrations to statues in SL are meritorious, but not as much as AL prostrations.

I feel that with prostrations there's very much the physical action that is a factor. The prostrating itself, you don't have that in SL, so I would never accept students who did part of their Ngondro in SL. I would still request 100K [real life] prostrations. However, if someone is very ill, I think I would try to make SL prostrations work for that person. Or if someone is disabled. Then the experience of prostrations may still create imprints someone can carry over into a next birth.

Lama Thutop went on to explain that he sees small Buddhist objects in SL like "images in a textbook," and does not bless them the way he would bless a mala before giving it to a student. When I asked him if he ever consecrates Buddhist spaces and things in SL, he told me that he does "bless gompas or whole sims," if it is requested of him, since he acknowledges the difference in the expenditure of effort and complexity of the build. "Gompas take many people many hours to complete, they have to call in resources, it usually is a community effort," he told me as he explained why he would bless an SL temple, but not an SL thangka. Lama Thutop noted that there are times that a community organizes ritual blessings. For example, he told me that a defunct Buddhist sim had ritually disbanded: "I know for instance that when Bodhi SL stopped functioning, its members collected all prims in one object, a vase like you use when you dissolve a sand Mandala, and then [they] deleted that." The replication of AL ritual in the erasure of a lovingly built Buddhist sim demonstrates that some SL Buddhists do see holy objects in SL as having a special significance. Even so, devotees such as Lama Thutop are quick to point out that AL holy objects have an even more profound, embodied sacredness than their SL copies.

Another teacher at the Buddha Center, Phra Paisan, a non-heritage Thai monk, was very much more on the aniconic side of Buddhist thinking than the typical heritage Buddhist Thai. He sees SL avatars/persons and objects as "pointers" that calm our "monkey minds." He views sacred objects in actual and virtual spaces as placeholders for memory and reverence. He noted in an interview in 2010 that all personhood and materiality in actual life is predicated on illusion:

There is no difference between the illusion of me sitting on my chair at home, and the illusion of me as an avatar on this mat. There is a difference in terms of physical sensation. But the visual and audio is the same. I don't feel the cold in SL. The light touching the eyes is a difference. The physical difference isn't a major difference. What SL gives us is just a lesser audio and visual experience. Buddhism doesn't have a problem there . . . In Buddhism we are dealing with what is going on inside. The reality is our experience.

I ask him if he has heard of blessing and consecrations happening in SL, and he has, but he does not support the practice. "To me it's pushing it to consecrate virtual objects. It is like buying into the illusion. Consecrating in AL, maybe. But virtual—I don't know. I look at SL as a more utilitarian way." Phra Paisan reveals here that he is himself a builder in SL, and while he doesn't see these Buddhist objects as sites in which the Buddha is actually present, he sees Buddhist objects as symbolically and culturally efficacious.

Moosewood Max, who practices most often at the Buddha Center, eschews the Buddhist label, but says he actively seeks Buddhist teaching in AL and SL when he can get them. He would fit into my definition of "student," and he actually self-defined himself as a student, as well. Moosewood Max has a special teacher–student relationship with Lama Thutop, but still Moosewood Max picks and chooses what he is willing to believe—that is, he takes some of Lama Thutop's teachings and leaves others. His perspective on holy objects does deviate from his primary teacher's, as he is a perfect example of someone who finds the holy objects of SL to be exactly as symbolically meaningful as AL holy objects—no more or less. He makes the point that they serve to build community by replicating the Buddhist landscape of AL. When I asked him if he has an altar in AL, he said,

> I don't have a traditional Buddhist altar. A grouping of plants and whatever pleases me at the time. It is a space to meditate. I don't go in a lot for the symbolic stuff over meditation. I care about the daily ongoing practice of compassion. Keeping that in mind as a way of life. An altar can help.

Given that he seemed to devalue the significance of Buddhist objects in AL in contrast to his guru, I asked him to discuss the role Buddhist objects play in SL. He said, "It's important here in SL. Community practice in SL here—the main temple proves a focus point. The big Buddha with the meditation cushion. It's a place to go, a symbol that you are looking at while meditating with others. Spaces like that here give us a focus for meditating as a community." So, he argues that in both spaces, the altar or ritual space can help people focus on the meditation at hand. I pressed him to consider whether there is a difference between virtual and actual objects.

> MOOSEWOOD: To me they have the same things in [real life]. They are there. I may not venerate them, but the rituals the symbols the gongs. They help us focus. They become entry points to particular practices.
>
> FALCONE: Would you say that they are sacred? In either SL or [actual life]?
>
> MOOSEWOOD: Sacred? Yes, but I was brought up in a Protestant background, so I've not held statues or other things as sacred. They are sacred with the ideas that we imbue them with; they aren't sacred in and of themselves. We give them meaning, and everyone gives them a different meaning. This

is especially true in SL . . . Ritual to me is a form that guides us. They are sacred in the sense that we take it into our hearts and we allow it to become sacred to us, to further our practice as a community. I want to divorce the concept of the sacred from worship. I don't think that a statue is ever a power object in and of itself . . . the people that I know and have talked with like [Lhundrup Llama and Margery Apple], they see it in much the same way as I do. In the discussion with [Lama Thutop] we get things going. Some people in [real life] focus more on ritual than how to follow the eightfold path. Here people are following it more—

FALCONE: So you think that the kind of people who believe in holy objects and associated rituals are less likely to come into SL?

MOOSEWOOD: Yeah, ritual goers won't come into SL. More philosophical people—like me—we are searching for the deeper meaning. Not just seeking a ritual to follow to make them feel better . . . Worshipping in front of a statue seems wrong to me—I am looking for focus, compassion. Compassion builds on itself.

In effect, Moosewood represents the consummate student perspective on holy objects: they are useful, but not actually powerful in and of themselves; we give them sacredness, but they are not inherently sacred. I found it particularly significant that Moosewood, though vocally dubious about the inherent importance of holy objects, was himself a Buddhist builder in SL. He builds not for larger SL communities like the Buddha Center, but rather he builds altars and private Buddhist spaces in SL for members of his SL sangha.

FALCONE: You told me that you build Buddhist places in SL. What do you build?

MOOSEWOOD: In SL, I build altars, but not big things. Simple altars. I can build a house, not the furniture inside them. I have been building points to focus on.

FALCONE: Can you tell me more?

MOOSEWOOD: A Buddhist friend of mine, well, her father had passed away in [real life], and some of us, we wanted to create a space of peace. We wanted to create a space for her. We built a small temple.

FALCONE: What did you put inside?

MOOSEWOOD: A Buddha statue. And I purchased a wall hanging of a laughing Buddha. We put a blue Buddha in a wall alcove. I built the altar. It was a simple design. It is a home for singing bell and candle and an incense holder. I didn't make the things themselves; I just built the house and altar.

FALCONE: So it was a memorial for the deceased?

MOOSEWOOD: Not a memorial, but a place for her to find peace.

Although Moosewood Max does not believe in the literal power of altars and holy objects, he is very keen to use them as spaces that have significant social and personal meaning. In effect, he is building Buddhist spaces and sanghas at the same time. He is community "build"-ing.

Moosewood Max is not alone in being ambivalent about the sacred properties of SL Buddhist objects, and yet unabashedly embracing them in practice. I opened the previous section of this chapter with a description of the candles that had been offered to the Buddha statue in Deer Park of the Buddha Center sim in order to seek blessings for an ill teacher, Lama Thutop. I asked several informants about these offerings, and whether they indicated a belief in the magical efficacy of offerings to statues in SL. Not one of the students I asked felt that the offerings would have actual effects on his health, and neither were they convinced of karmic benefit (either for themselves or the lama). "I didn't make an offering for karma. I made it as a gesture to show Lama Thutop that we care about him. It's a symbolic gesture, but one that shows my emotional attachment to him as one of my teachers," said one of my female informants, in retrospect. On the other hand, a devotee, one of the organizers and teachers, said that she was "willing to believe" that the offerings would be karmically efficacious, and could have actual benefits to Lama Thutop's health, just as her actual life offerings could. The episode with the candles is just one of many such examples that show that the distinction in belief about the magical/sacred properties of holy objects in SL has more to do with one's views about holy objects in general, and much less to do with the mediated platform of SL itself.

CONCLUDING THOUGHTS ON BUDDHIST MATERIALITY IN A VIRTUAL WORLD

None of my informants argued that holy objects had no place in SL, and all of them saw some degree of virtue in their presence. In this chapter, I have shown that for students, AL and SL Buddhist objects share a rough equivalence as symbolic pointers toward a particular intention and promise. On the other hand, devotees believe (or assert that they believe) that while SL holy objects are significant, they are not as powerful as holy objects in AL. This argument counters the conventional wisdom that virtual things are just unreal, pixilated non-objects that are unable to do actual religious work. In fact, actual objects are always already more virtual than we thought, and virtual objects are more actual than we might expect. The lack of physicality does not erase the fact that both kinds of objects are made by people, and serve to make people. I agree with Horst and Miller (2012), important theorists of Material Culture Studies, who articulated this point beautifully when they wrote, "the digital, as all material culture, is more than a sub-strate; it is becoming a constitutive part of what makes us human" (4). Buddhist objects do this work. Although they are thought to be inherently empty, they are full of cultural significance.

It is only insofar as specific cultural worlds must wrestle with their own ontologies that we are called on to trace the differences in meaning between AL and SL objects. For devotees who believe that the Buddhas and bodhisattvas have been invited through consecration to inhabit AL holy objects, there is a tendency to view holy objects in SL as lesser-than their AL originals. These phenomenological Buddhist views on their virtual materials show that either way SL Buddhist objects and spaces serve to create and "build" community. Buddhist builds mediate people's experiences and replicate an environment that signals an intentionality shared by the people and groups who create them. In general terms, actual and virtual objects both have their own "social life" and their own special kind of cultural agency. The objects in SL are not unfamiliar—they seem modeled on AL statues and paintings; there is creativity in building (and especially in landscape design), but not *creative* building. For example, despite the fact that some of my non-heritage student informants in both actual and virtual Buddhist spaces noted that the next Buddha could be a woman, there was nowhere in SL Buddhist spaces a female Maitreya Buddha. Buddha statues in SL look like Buddha statues in AL.

ALL OF OUR MATERIALS ARE VIRTUAL

I turn now to what virtual holy objects can teach us about material culture more generally. I first want to point out that actual life objects were once quite a bit more solid than they are today. Once upon a time, an anthropologist sought to define what an arrowhead or sculpture meant or how it was used. Nowadays, for a scholar to speak of "the purpose" or "the sole meaning" of an object is too firm and too atemporal; today, we talk more about the "social life" (Appadurai 1986) or "cultural biography" (Kopytoff 1986) of an object, since that allows for a more complex and diachronic view of an object's lifespan. Objects are no longer just tools, but, like people, they are simultaneously shaped by, and shaping, the societies around them (Appadurai 1986). Daniel Miller, a key theorist in Material Culture Studies, also seeks to destabilize our conventional view of objects, writing, "In short, we need to show how the things that people make, make people" (Miller 2005, 38). Upon reflection, the solidity of all things melts into a kind of culturally mediated ooze—things are given their shape, their backbone, by culture. Attention to virtual objects can serve to remind us that our "actual" objects were always already mediated.

The actual and imputed effects of holy objects give them a special place in the discussion of the agency of objects. Alfred Gell (1998) has written of the "secondary" agency of objects in which the objects that humans create have the ability to affect human lives (20). His discussion of idols, such as statues or paintings of a goddess in Hinduism, shows that the eye contact between image and devotee creates an interdependent pathway of agency, a mirroring effect as the devotee implicitly sees the statue seeing her (120). This is not entirely different from the way that a Tibetan Buddhist might experience taking a blessing from a statue, such as the Jowo statue enshrined in the Jokhang Temple in Lhasa. Some of the transnational devotees I interviewed in India in 2005–2007 reported experiences with certain stupas, relics, and statues that constituted feelings of mutual recognition. For holy objects that are thought to embody Buddhas and bodhisattvas, the agency imputed to actual life objects by believers is thought to be "primary" not "secondary." Holy objects seen in this light are extensions of the holy persons, and are often thought to be able to bless or grant favors, at least from the perspective of devotees. It is in this light that relics, statues, and altars must be seen, as objects that blur the boundaries between "primary" and "secondary" agency, if indeed the boundary exists at all. As I've noted, the SL Buddhists, as converted students, generally do not grant any AL or SL Buddhist object either primary or secondary agency. On the other hand, a devotee, someone like Lama Thutop, is likely to grant a SL holy object "secondary" agency, while seeing consecrated AL holy objects as having more "primary" agency.

If the lack of physicality (pixels instead of atoms) of virtual objects makes it seem disingenuous to assert that they are as material as any AL object, then I take comfort in the fact that I am not alone in this view. Horst and Miller (2012) have also concluded that virtual objects are materially substantive in the ways that matter most to the human experience: "Our final principle acknowledges the materiality of digital worlds, which are neither more nor less material than the worlds that preceded them" (4). Anthropologically, both SL and AL objects have a material quality that makes them substantially significant aspects of cultural practice. My Buddhist informants have made it abundantly clear that the material culture of SL is not a background concern—Buddhist objects make Buddhist space and they make Buddhists, in virtual and actual environments.

NOTES

1. Boellstorff and company (2012, 7) define a virtual world as a more embodied place than some other networked environments. As they define it, a virtual world has the following characteristics: (1) they are "places" that establish a distinct sense of "worldness"; (2) they are multi-user, and avatars can interact with one another; (3) they are "persistent" in that they do not wink off when an avatar does—while some avatars may log off, other avatars occupy the world and can make changes to it; and (4) they allow users to embody themselves so that they can participate in the world (often as visual avatars, or sometimes as "textual avatars").

2. Most of the content is user generated, but the platform rules regulated and delimit user control in some ways. The platform itself is run by a corporation, Linden Lab. For a detailed discussion of the creation and crafting of the platform, see Malaby's (2009) ethnography of Linden Lab and the "Lindens."
3. Upon reflection, I have chosen to follow directly in Boellstorff's footsteps and use the term "actual," rather than "real," to signal physical, offline experience (Boellstorff 2008, 2012). While most of my informants tended to use the notion "real life," and it pains me to adjust their terminology, there are many SL denizens who feel that the term denigrates virtual environments as lesser-than. Plus, to contrast "virtual" in opposition to "real" worlds would undermine one of the main conclusions of this study: virtual world phenomena *are* real. This recognition is also bolstered by the work of Neil Whitehead and Michael Wesch, who wrote, "the Internet and other new form of social media forms increasingly integrate with even the most mundane aspects of everyday life in even the most remote regions of the world, and the 'virtual' blurs with and ultimately becomes the 'real'" (Whitehead and Wesch 2012).
4. For example, see *Coming of Age in Second Life* (Boellstorff 2008), *Making Virtual Worlds* (Malaby 2009), and *Communities of Play* (Pearce and Artemesia 2009), as well as other research being done on the cultures (Horst and Miller 2012; Schroeder 1996; Smith and Kollock 1999; Sunden 2003) and religions (Connelly 2010; Geraci 2010; Grieve 2010; Schroeder, Heather, and Lee 1998; Wertheim 1999) of virtual spaces.
5. I would like to acknowledge and thank my informants for their time and willingness to answer my nonstop questions. In addition, I would also like to thank Caitlin Reynolds, a graduate student at Kansas State University, who logged dozens of hours in Second Life serving as a research assistant for this fieldwork.
6. I spent 90 percent of my time in Second Life doing participant observation at the Buddha Center, but I also attended meditations, listened to teachings, and conducted interviews in Kannonji and Druk Yul. Druk Yul is located in the Play as Being region of Second Life, which is not itself a region dedicated to Buddhist spaces.
7. I agree with Boellstorff et al. (2012) about a number of virtual ethnographic conventions outlined in their methods handbook on fieldwork in Second Life. For example, in order to protect their confidentiality, I have changed both the legal AL names and the SL avatar names of my informants (Boellstorff et al. 2012, 137), unless they are already public figures. In keeping with the terms of my IRB proposal, I have always identified myself to informants as an anthropologist engaged in a study (both in my profile and in conversation with other avatars), and before doing formal or informal interviews with informants, I obtained their informed consent and promised anonymity. Like Boellstorff and company, I attempted to retain some of the character of the avatar name without revealing the identities of my informants In terms of the interplay and complexity of AL and SL identities, I have deigned to respect the details my informants provided about their actual life identities and genders without actually myself verifying these details in actual life; that is, I only worked to triangulate and verify claims being made about virtual socio-cultural practices. Boellstorff and company write, "The best policy is to follow the social conventions set down by the participants. If two avatars of the same person are treated as a single person, we should follow suit" (100). While their handbook was not published until after I finished the bulk of my fieldwork, I feel that their methodological writing is sound, and their compelling arguments should allow the rest of us the breathing room to focus on the content of our findings rather than constantly defending the method of our finding it.

8. The notion of emptiness is not akin to nihilism, but rather, it is most generally understood through the recognition that things are interdependent and do not exist independently of their parts.

9. Although there have been periods and philosophies that promoted an aniconic view in Buddhism (Swearer 2004), Buddhist image worship is ubiquitous throughout Asia. Swearer notes, for instance, that the Zen koan, "if you meet the Buddha, kill him!" represents a lingering aniconic view that is held by some Buddhists, including some notable contemporary Thai Buddhist figures (Swearer 2004, 248). However, holy objects have a long history within Buddhism in general. While the aniconic view persists, it has been largely subsumed in many Buddhist traditions by fierce dedication to images. While no object is actual in the ultimate sense, holy objects are considered efficacious.

10. Karma, in very general terms, is phenomenon that links causes from the past (sometimes from past lives) with effects in the future (sometimes into future lives).

11. Lama Zopa Rinpoche is a co-founder of the Tibetan Buddhist organization the Foundation for the Preservation of the Mahayana Tradition, which currently has more than 150 centers around the world.

12. For example, "corporeal relics" (Trainor 1997). Relics are the material remnants of famous Buddhist personages, which serve to embody, emanate, and echo the presence of the deceased (Schopen 1997; Strong 2004; Trainor 1997).

13. I tend not to separate my avatar, Aamrani Violet, from my actual, offline identity. My avatar would have had my legal name if that had been permitted when I first logged on. This runs in opposition to some scholars of digital worlds, who see their avatars as more separate entities. For example, Celia Pearce actually "co-authored" with her avatar, Artemesia. While I find Pearce's choice fascinating, I worry that it overstates the bifurcation between digital and actual personhood.

14. The distinction I'm making between students and devotees is especially applicable to non-heritage Buddhists. In SL, every single person I've interviewed is a non-heritage Buddhist of non-Asian ethnic descent. I know that there are a few Asians involved in the Buddha Center and other communities, but they are a very small minority, and I have not yet interviewed any of them. I have chosen not to use Jan Nattier's distinction between "elite" and "ethnic" Buddhists, since it presupposed that the one is economically elite and that there is a category of somehow non-ethnic people (Nattier 1998). I have also chosen to eschew the use of the word "convert," since there are second-generation non-heritage Buddhists whose parents converted to Buddhism.

15. Buddhist groups in SL do get their fair share of searchers who casually sit in from time to time. They do make up a small portion of the attendance at events, but by definition they are not active practitioners or community members, since that would elevate them outside the category.

REFERENCES

Appadurai, Arjun, ed. 1986. *The Social Life of Things: Commodities in Cultural Perspective.* Cambridge: Cambridge University Press.

Boellstorff, Tom. 2008. *Coming of Age in Second Life: An Anthropologist Explores the Virtually Human.* Princeton, NJ: Princeton University Press.

———. 2012. "Rethinking Digital Ethnography." In *Digital Anthropology*, edited by Heather Horst and Daniel Miller, 39–60. London: Berg Press.

————, Bonnie Nardi, Celia Pearce, and T.L. Taylor. 2012. *Ethnography and Virtual Worlds: A Handbook of Method*. Princeton, NJ: Princeton University Press.

Collins, Steven. 1998. *Nirvana and Other Buddhist Felicities: Utopias of the Pali Imaginaire*. Cambridge: Cambridge University Press.

Connelly, Louise. 2010. "Virtual Buddhism: An Analysis of Aesthetics in Relation to Religious Practice within Second Life." *Heidelberg Journal of Religions on the Internet* 4(1).doi: http://archiv.ub.uni-heidelberg.de. Accessed July 7, 2013.

Courtin, Robina, and Tenzin Zopa. 2003. *The Thousand Buddha Relic Stupa: Commemorating the Great Mahasdiddha Geshe Lama Konchok*. Nepal: Tenzin Zopa.

Gell, Alfred. 1998. *Art and Agency: An Anthropological Theory*. New York: Oxford University Press.

Geraci, Robert. 2010. *Apocalyptic AI: Visions of Heaven in Robotics, Artificial Intelligence, and Virtual Reality*. New York: Oxford University Press.

Grieve, Gregory. 2010. "Virtually Embodying the Field: Silent Online Meditation, Immersion, and the Cardean Ethnographic Method." *Heidelberg Journal of Religions on the Internet* 4(1). doi: http://archiv.ub.uni-heidelberg.de. Accessed July 7, 2013.

Horst, Heather, and Daniel Miller. 2012. "The Digital and the Human: A Prospectus for Digital Anthropology." In *Digital Anthropology*, edited by Heather Horst and Daniel Miller, 3–35. London: Berg Press.

Kopytoff, Igor. 1986. "The Cultural Biography of Things: Commoditization as Process." In *The Social Life of Things: Commodities in Cultural Perspective*, edited by Arjun Appadurai, 64–94. Cambridge: Cambridge University Press.

Malaby, Thomas M. 2009. *Making Virtual Worlds: Linden Lab and Second Life*. Ithaca, NY: Cornell University Press.

Miller, Daniel, ed. 2005. *Materiality*. Durham, NC: Duke University Press.

Nattier, Jan. 1998. "Who Is a Buddhist? Charting the Landscape of Buddhist America." In *The Faces of Buddhism in America*, edited by C.S. Prebish and K.K. Tanaka, 183–195. Berkeley: University of California Press.

Pearce, Celia, and Artemesia. 2009. *Community of Play: Emergent Cultures in Multiplayer Games and Virtual Worlds*. Cambridge, MA: The MIT Press.

Schopen, Gregory. 1997. *Bones, Stones and Buddhist Monks*. Honolulu: University of Hawai'i Press.

Schroeder, Ralph. 1996. *Possible Worlds: The Social Dynamic of Virtual Reality Technology*. Boulder, CO: Westview Press.

————, Noel Heather, and Raymond M. Lee. 1998. "The Sacred and the Virtual: Religion in a Multiple-User Virtual Reality." *Journal of Computer Mediated Communication* 4(2). doi: 10.1111/j.1083-6101.1998.tb00092.x. Accessed October 20, 2013.

Smith, Marc A., and Peter Kollock. 1999. *Communities in Cyberspace*. London: Routledge.

Strong, John. 2004. *Relics of the Buddha*. Princeton, NJ: Princeton University Press.

Sunden, Jenny. 2003. *Material Virtualities: Approaching Online Textual Embodiment*. New York: Peter Lang.Swearer, Donald. K. 2004. *Becoming the Buddha: The Ritual of Image Consecration in Thailand*. Princeton, NJ: Princeton University Press.

Trainor, Kevin. 1997. *Relics, Ritual, and Representation in Buddhism*. Cambridge: Cambridge University Press.

Wertheim, M. 1999. *The Pearly Gates of Cyberspace*. New York: Doubleday.

Whitehead, Neil L., and Michael Wesch, eds. 2012. *Human No More: Digital Subjectivities, Unhuman Subjects and the End of Anthropology*. Boulder: University of Colorado Press.

11 American Cybersangha
Building a Community or Providing a Buddhist Bulletin Board?

Allison Ostrowski

During a rare excursion outside of my bungalow, I was bombarded with images of the Lord Buddha. Movie posters featuring Chow Yun Fat as a Tibetan monk littered the theater walls, a small incense-laden shop on the corner was selling a stack of pillowcases with the Buddha's face, and finally Walmart was displaying a cherry-scented Buddha head candle right next to an "authentic" monastery bell. No, this did not occur in Buddhist-rich Taiwan or Japan but in a small city in upstate New York. Buddhist iconography and paraphernalia is increasingly seen in American pop culture and new media. The Buddhist presence online is growing at a rapid rate, providing users with access to information about the religion, means to contact other adherents, and ways to shop for Buddhist-related items. But how does the increased presence of Buddhist resources online influence the interpretation and continued development of American Buddhism? How are adherents harnessing the interactive features of social media to build virtual communities? This chapter will explore Buddhism online, determining who the users are and why they choose to interact with religious information in an online context, and what American Buddhist expression and community looks like as it is developed in an online medium.

Buddhism arrived in the United States during the World Parliament of Religions, part of the Chicago World's Fair in 1893 (Coleman 2001). Since that time, the tradition has expanded to become the third largest religion practiced in America (Pew Forum on Religion and Public Life 2013). Although the numbers are frequently contested, there are an estimated six million Buddhists in the United States currently, and all three major strains of Buddhism (Theravada, Mahayana, and Vajrayana) are represented (Buddhists in the World 2013). The numbers of North American meditation centers in 1997 included 152 Theravada, 423 Mahayana, 352 Vajrayana, and 135 Buddhayana, and out of these 22 percent were located in California (Morreale 1998). Buddhayana is an informal term used for mixed and non-sectarian Buddhist centers and organizations. Though Morreale has not provided recent numbers, in 2004, The Pluralism Project reports that there were 2,039 Buddhist centers in the United States (Pluralism Project 2013). Despite this seemingly large number of adherents, American

Buddhists comprises only 3.6 percent of the 1.5 billion total Buddhist population worldwide (Buddhists in the World 2013).

There is not a definitive type of a Buddhist practitioner in America, but scholars tend to agree on a few broad categories, namely white Americans who have embraced the teachings of the Buddha, immigrant and refugees who continue to practice their tradition from their mother country, and also Asian Americans who were raised in the United States as Buddhists (Seager 1999). However, much of this debate regarding who can be considered a Buddhist stems from the individual's identity. "For our purposes as scholars, Buddhists are those who say they are" (Tweed 2002, 24). This could include the "Night Stand Buddhists" from Prebish and Baumann's (2002) categorization of Buddhist self-identification. Night Stand Buddhists are not necessarily involved in the ritualistic aspects of Buddhism but are enamored with some of the philosophical tenets through exposure to popular culture and self-help books. Instead of meditating or working with a Buddhist teacher, the Night Stand Buddhist would work alone to apply relevant concepts to their daily lives. What is interesting about using self-disclosure as a means for identification is the fact the Buddhist label often elucidates particular aspects of the cultural and social sphere of the practitioner.

Stark and Bainbridge (1985) offer a very different means of classifying Buddhists in America, and their categorizations include those who attend formal teachings and participate in other group endeavors, those who have a relationship with a teacher of Buddhism, and those who have an interest in Buddhism and choose to label themselves as a Buddhist. Further, Coleman (2001) asserts that one area that is likely to unite American Buddhists is the practice of meditation. He conducted a survey based on student and teacher interviews from seven Buddhist centers in North America and concluded that American Buddhists tended to be middle or upper-middle class, white, from a former Christian background, equally male and female, and highly educated.

Despite the religious aspirations of these converts, an aspect of the tradition remains, making it difficult for Buddhists practicing in America. There is also an ethnic component to the acceptability of American Buddhists in American social culture. For example, an individual with an Asian physical appearance is more likely to be legitimated, as Buddhism is an accepted aspect of Asian culture. However, for Caucasian Buddhists, their identification as Buddhists is sometimes viewed as a rejection of American mainstream religious values (Tsomo 2002). Further, Tanaka argues that the ethnic Buddhist temples also serve cultural needs beyond spiritual ones, and these are especially important for recent immigrant communities (Tanaka 1998). The presence of these centers, while helpful to some Buddhist communities, do tend to emphasize the perceived link between Buddhism and ethnicity and is likely to add to the difficulty of the practice of non-Asian Buddhists being interpreted as authentic.

Another tension in American Buddhism is the sense of illegitimacy expressed by some Asian-born Buddhists. There is sometimes a feeling of resentment on the part of South/Southeast Asianists with respect to Americans converting to a traditionally Eastern religion. For instance, writer Pankaj Mishra suggests that Westerners who come to India for enlightenment are "indulging their privilege—the unique license offered to them by the power and wealth of their countries—to be whatever they wished to be: Buddhists, Hindus, Missionaries, Communists" (Lattin 2005). In a similar vein, it has been argued whether a religious tradition developed in an Eastern cultural realm can effectively be translated into Western thought and practice. Do certain cultural differences prevent the religion from being observed as it was in the country of origin and do concessions responding to societal requirements need to be incorporated? American Buddhism has widened the boundaries in two areas of the Buddhist tradition, namely egalitarianism in worship and the inclusive role of women.

In a general sense, Buddhism in Asia functioned as a structured system of hierarchical knowledge, with a few elder monks overseeing the monastic community (sangha) (Kornfield 1988). Students trusted in the knowledge and experience of their teachers and were not expected to question their instruction. Translating Buddhism in America required the adaptation of this hierarchical tradition in a collectivist society to a free-market system in an individualistic nation (Hofstede 2001). Another distinction lies in the separation between the monastics and the laity in traditional Buddhist countries. In Asian nations, the monks are clearly separate from laity and are revered by Buddhist practitioners who provide alms in exchange for spiritual merit. In American Buddhism, however, the distinction between a monk and a lay Buddhist is not as definitive (Coleman 2001).

One of the greatest changes that has occurred to Buddhism as it has developed in the United States is a greater democratization of the tradition, both in the creation of a more egalitarian structure of the faith but also the promotion of inclusive ideology for such groups as women and gays and lesbians (Tanaka 1998). Women have had an extremely influential impact on the evolution of Buddhism in American society, and are possibly some of the most serious converts (Seager 1999). In a sense, the structure of Buddhism does not discriminate between sexual orientations, only sexuality in general, asking celibacy regardless of gender (Coleman 2001).

Perhaps prompted by the sense of openness to spiritual forces or perhaps due to the egalitarian nature of the translation of Buddhism into American culture, people are converting to Buddhism. In the melting pot culture of America, there are very few finite lines between tradition, belief, and practice, and people often select aspects of other traditions they might believe in, some that they practice, and others yet that they choose to define themselves by (Tweed 1999). For instance, it would not be unusual to meet an American who describes themselves as Methodist but also attends a Passover Seder with Jewish friends and tends to subscribe to some of the beliefs of Buddhism, such as karma and issues of rebirth. "Religious identity also can be complex for converts. Conversion involves a more or less (often less) complete shift of beliefs and practices. The old tradition never fades completely; the new one never shapes exclusively" (Tweed 1999, 73). It is for this reason that religious self-identification is difficult to measure, particularly in situations concerning religious conversion. The question then is whether the association between Buddhism in America and a wealthier and more educated group of practitioners has any effect on whether someone chooses to identify themselves as a Buddhist or chooses to proceed with a formal conversion to the Buddhist tradition.

This issue is also related to access to Buddhist resources and the community of which a person is able to become a part. Not everyone has equal access to information, and this is particularly an issue with respect to online information access. Buddhist communities, or "cybersanghas," exist in cyberspace and are comprised of Buddhist teachers, students, practitioners, and others interested in the tradition. "Cybersangha" refers to the online Buddhist community and was first used by Gary Ray in 1991 (Prebish 1999). However, Buddhism did not make its online appearance as a chat room, but began with textual resources of Buddhism information, some discussion forums, and many databases of Dharmic and teaching material. In the late 90s, as the Internet evolved into a greater two-way communicative forum and less of a library resource, Buddhist forums and chat rooms also increased in prominence (Prebish 1999).

Prebish (1999) discusses three primary categories of Buddhist presence on the Internet; websites created by American Buddhists as a means of communication with others, virtual temples created by traditional Buddhist sanghas, and cybersanghas that have no physical home and exist solely in an online environment. While some question whether the Buddha would sanction monastics and lay Buddhists participating in an online Buddhist gathering, others see the cybersangha as a means of truly uniting Buddhists worldwide (Prebish 1999).

In some respects, cyberspace brings some challenges closer to the Buddhist practitioner than their general practice might provide. For instance, while a Buddhist temple generally can restrict access to members only or approved visitors, in general, cyberspace is open with free access. And while chat rooms and other Buddhist online communities can opt for a password entry, this seems to negate the teachings of detachment and maintaining practice even in the face of adversity. In a project exploring online Buddhism in Korea, Kim (2005) suggested that the features of the Internet can provide a particularly welcoming venue for the development of a cybersangha. For example, the Internet offers a wide range of religious information and space quickly, provides space for conversing without influence of religious authorities, and allows for interactivity and discussion of private and focused topics in a relatively free environment.

Since there are relatively few projects that have explored online Buddhist communities, Laney's (2005) exploration into Christian webspaces provides an interesting building block for investigation. Based on uses and gratifications theory, Laney's work explored the motivations of users to access online Christian resources. Through an online survey with Likert-scale measures administered to self-selected church website visitors, this project found that people use the Internet to satisfy a desire for knowledge, but this was not the only reason. Respondents indicated that they used media to overcome loneliness, to escape from daily life, and for relaxation. People also indicated that sometimes they used media to create a divide between themselves and other people. Since there is relatively little literature available concerning online Buddhist communities, assumptions about use from Laney's study could not be simply transferred and allowing participants the space to define their own motivation and spectrum of uses is necessary.

Further, Hayes (1999) was one of the few to begin asking these questions and probed the discussions on Buddhist newsgroups and electronic discussion lists. His conclusions are multifarious and have interesting implications for the understanding of the practice of Buddhism in America. Hayes asserted that the Internet provided a forum for American Buddhists to discuss issues and aspects of the religion with other practitioners that may not be as simple or comfortable to discuss with a formal religious teacher. "The use of electronic mail and news groups enables people to express their more shadowy thoughts and doubts—ideas to which they might hesitate to give free expression in the presence of a *lama* or a Zen master" (Hayes 1999, 168). Some of the most prominent recurring discussions centered on whether American Buddhists believed that having a formal teacher was necessary to properly practice the religion, the notion of rebirth and how literally the textual teachings should be interpreted, and the correct manner of practicing the Buddhist religion in America (Hayes 1999).

The issue of identity is not one that is lost in the electronic forum and remains ever-present for American Buddhists. Hayes illustrated that many of the email discussion groups do delve into issues of religious identity and defining as individuals as well as for the community what precisely it means to be American and an adherent of a religion developed in Asia (Hayes 1999). All of these discussions, questions, and concerns indicate that Buddhism is still a fresh entity in America and practitioners are still working to find their place and the place of the tradition in society. And, the Internet is an excellent venue for participants to work out these issues of identity, observance, and belief. It is in this direction that this study has been conducted; to understand *how* American Buddhists and those interested in the tradition are using the Internet to access Buddhist resources and the effect this is having on the development of the religious tradition in America. To assess these issues, the following research questions and hypotheses were derived.

Based on a dearth of theory on Buddhist communities online, the research questions were exploratory in nature and sought to determine who the individual users were and why they were accessing Buddhist resources. It is possible that those of a specific Buddhist lineage might be looking for different information than "general" Buddhists or those users who are of another religious tradition. Therefore, the final question was constructed to determine the relationship between currently practiced religious tradition and the ways individuals of different traditions might use online Buddhist resources.

RQ1: Who are the people accessing online Buddhist resources?
RQ2: For what purposes are online Buddhist resources used?
RQ3: What relationship does the current religious tradition have on the use of online Buddhist resources?

Research on American Buddhism does indicate that there is a difference in practice and worship between Caucasian Buddhists and Asian Buddhists in the United States (Hayes 1999). Therefore, this project asserts that Caucasian Buddhists who are displaced because of the small number of practicing Buddhists in the nation will be more likely to use the Internet for access to an online Buddhist community, whereas Asian Buddhists in the United States will likely have a stronger face-to-face faith community from which they may draw support from.

H1: Caucasian Buddhists use the Internet for Buddhist community purposes more than non-white Buddhists in the United States.

The second hypothesis suggests that those who are older and utilizing online Buddhist resources will also be more likely to visit Buddhist chat rooms. Older people could potentially have a more difficult time in locating other practicing Buddhists of their own age and therefore utilize the cyber-sangha for community support, whereas younger people might have greater access to practitioners of their own age, or at least have more mobility in order to physically locate other Buddhists for community building.

H2: The older a respondent is, the more likely they will be to visit Buddhist chat rooms.

METHODS

This project implemented a mixed methods approach to explore these questions, with a survey and interviews of Buddhist website users. A sample of websites concerning Buddhism was collected and an online general survey was administered through advertisement on these sites. Some of those respondents were further selected for interviews to obtain more nuanced understandings of Internet use and religious affinity. Questions were asked concerning the type of resources respondents consumed online and for what purpose, suggestions for improving their online religious experience, how their online religious experience related to their offline religious lives, and their attitudes toward the presence of an online Buddhist community. Further, demographic questions were asked regarding gender, ethnicity, age, location, and religious affiliation.

SAMPLE AND PROCEDURE

For this study, the first ten results were collected from the search engines Google, Yahoo, and AOL for the word "Buddhism." This yielded thirty sites and while not all were necessarily located in the United States, they were all in English and were the most frequently accessed online Buddhist resources in America. Fifteen of these sites were duplicates and were therefore only listed once; one site was not applicable, as it was just a directory to more Yahoo Buddhist sites, leaving fourteen Buddhist websites as the sample frame. Next, all of the site managers from the websites listed in these results were asked if they would allow a link to the survey to be posted on their site. Six responded to the requests and eventually two complied and allowed the survey link to be posted: Buddhism.about.com and www.ship.edu/~cgboeree/buddhaintro.html. Respondents took the survey online via a Web-based survey provider and subsequent interviews were conducted as email exchanges.

Results

R1: Who are the people accessing online Buddhist resources?

Based on this study, the profile of those using the Internet to access information on Buddhism was white (72 percent), and evenly distributed between twenty-three and forty years old and in locations throughout the United States. Gender of respondents was equally divided between male and female and the education attained was predominantly above the college level. This is not that dissimilar from the average American Internet user, who is also most likely to be white, aged eighteen through forty, and have a college education (Pew Research Internet Project 2014).

Those who accessed Buddhist resources also tended to be raised as Catholics (27.2 percent) or Protestants (26.1 percent) and were *not* members of a Buddhist temple or meditation center (74.5 percent). Further, participants indicated a wide range of current religious traditions, but tended to affiliate with no religion (21.2 percent), Buddhism of an unspecified sect (19.0 percent), a sense of spirituality (11.4 percent) or were still searching for a religious tradition (11.4 percent).

RQ2: For what purposes are online Buddhist resources used?

In general, respondents provided varied reasons for using Buddhist resources on the Internet. Most indicated that they lived in an area of the country where Buddhist temples or teachers were not easily accessible (32.6 percent), but this was not the only reason. One respondent said, "Being totally disabled, I am somewhat confined to my PC. And this site [Buddhism.about.com] has brought a wealth of information and hopefully I have gleaned something from it." In fact, 20.1 percent of people surveyed indicated that the convenience of the Internet was the main reason they accessed online sources; this includes convenience of obtaining large amounts of information and having access to resources without the requirement of traveling a physical distance.

Respondents also searched for a full spectrum of Buddhist resources available on the Internet. The majority, 52 percent, sought Dharma teachings online, while others tended to use Internet resources on Buddhist teachers, temples, culture, and other practitioners (see Table 11.1). Survey respondents also valued being able to contact other Buddhists and hear different perspectives on the tradition. "It's nice to know that I am not the only American that practices Buddhism. At first, I was very reluctant to let anyone know. I was afraid others would think I was a 'crackpot.' Knowing that other Buddhists are out there has given me the ability to be proud of my choice and to not hide how I feel about issues regarding my religion." Not all respondents sought those with similar perspectives and instead utilized the Internet to develop a broader understanding of the religious tradition. "I use Internet resources to get a different perspective, particularly perspectives from outside my own tradition. I use it for new ideas."

Despite the fact that 16.3 percent of those surveyed indicated they used the Internet to look for Buddhists in America, the majority of respondents said that they had not participated in Buddhist-oriented chat rooms (81 percent), whereas 11.4 percent admitted to frequenting the rooms only a few times. Further, of those who had frequented a Buddhist chat room at least once, 33 percent indicated that they felt a sense of a Buddhist community online, while 14 percent said they sometimes felt a sense of community, and

Table 11.1   Internet Resources Used

Type of Website Information	Percentage
Dharma teachings	52.7
Asian culture	18.5
Buddhist culture	22.3
Temples	23.9
American Buddhists	16.3
Buddhists worldwide	23.4
Buddhist teachers	26.1

Created by Allison Ostrowski.

28 percent indicated that they did not feel community at all. Those who did partake in Buddhist chats and felt part of the cybersangha suggested that community affiliation and being able to share ideas with like-minded people were the reasons they continued to frequent Buddhist chat rooms. "There is a sense that the Internet can help connect people to a loose world-wide sangha. I can ask spiritual questions to a Buddhist Internet group and someone always responds and even if an answer is not readily available I am wished support in my quest for answers."

One respondent also suggested a theological rationale for online interaction and suggested that by doing so her practice as a Buddhist was enhanced.

> It is easy for me to develop some arrogance ("I understand this and teacher agrees") or "my meditation seems superior to the other students here"; fortunately, when I go online (because there are so many wonderful and experienced people), the arrogance is shaken and I realize how much more diligent my practice must be.

Other respondents indicated that online Buddhist resources were important for self-verification and also to harness the medium to spread the word of the Buddha and encourage others to consider mindfulness.

Not everyone agreed that Buddhism online offered a spiritual connection to others. One respondent said that they only felt community online as they would with the rest of the world and that the Internet was for information and not communion. Another respondent said, "I feel a sense of community when I look into one's eyes." It appears as if there is a growing interest in participating in online Buddhist communities, but this aspect of online interaction does not appeal to everyone and, despite the bridging of distances that the Internet offers, this does not replace the in-person contact of communal discussion and worship that some seek.

RQ3: What relationship does the current religious tradition have with the use of online Buddhist resources?

Current religious tradition and its relationship to the use of online Buddhist resources only yielded marginal significance, and only among the Buddhist respondents. Those who identified themselves as current practitioners of the Buddhist religion tended to use Buddhist chat rooms, access online resources on Asian and Buddhist culture, temples, other American Buddhists, Buddhists worldwide, and Buddhist teachers more often than do current adherents to other religious traditions (refer to Table 11.2). This is not necessarily surprising, as they are searching for information about the particular religious tradition that they affiliate themselves with, but it is nonetheless interesting to note that for those who do not identify themselves as being practicing Buddhists, the respondents who were online were searching for different information.

Table 11.2   Current Religion and Information Accessed

Online Resources$_a$	M	SD	r	sig
Chat Rooms	3.78	0.64	0.31**	.000
Asian Culture	2.12	0.69	0.23**	.003
Buddhist Culture	2.08	0.72	0.26**	.000
Temples	2.07	0.74	0.22**	.005
American Buddhists	2.14	0.67	0.22**	.005
Buddhists Worldwide	2.07	0.73	0.24**	.002
Buddhist Teachers	2.04	0.75	0.26**	.001

**$p < 0.01$.

Variables coded by frequency of use: 1 (often) to 5 (never).
  M refers to the mean average on each response; SD indicates
  the standard deviation or how dispersed responses were
  around the mean; r refers to the strength of the correlative
  relationship found between current tradition and each use
  variable; sig indicates the percentage that this relationship
  occurred due to chance.

Created by Allison Ostrowski.

When exploring responses by specific denomination, one correlation was found between tradition and the use of online Buddhist resources. Those who identified themselves as practitioners of a specified sect of Buddhism, that is, Mahayana, Theravada, Zen, or Tibetan, were more likely to use online resources to obtain information about Buddhist temples, r (48) = .35, $p < .05$. It is apparent that the location of the subject in processing the religious tradition is indeed related to the way they use Buddhist resources online. This indicates that those who were born Buddhist or have chosen to become Buddhist have become involved into a particular sect, while those who are interested in or are new to the religion tend to identify themselves as Buddhists only and do not affirm any particular sect within the religion. Essentially, those Buddhists who declare themselves a part of a Buddhist sect as opposed to Buddhism in general were more likely to seek a specific temple or teaching lineage, likely because they knew specifically what type of temple, doctrine, and teachings to search for.

H1: Caucasian Buddhists use the Internet for Buddhist community purposes more than non-Caucasian Buddhists.

Based on assumed differences in the communities of Caucasian Buddhists versus Asian Buddhists in American society, it was hypothesized that the two groups would utilize online Buddhist resources in a different manner. However, this assertion received only partial support. There was a correlation between ethnicity and the frequency of Buddhist chat room use, asserting that Caucasians were more likely to visit Buddhist chat rooms than Buddhists of other ethnicities, r (163) = .22, p < .01. Though in general, there was not much visitation of Buddhist chats found across all the ethnicities.

Despite the fact that Caucasian Buddhists were more likely to frequent the chat rooms, they were not more likely to express a feeling of community for Buddhists online. It is interesting to note that respondents overwhelmingly expressed the lack of Buddhist community online, regardless of the theoretical discussions concerning the development of a cybersangha. Buddhists using the Internet in general expressed a sense of disconnection from community and instead used the technology to locate specific resources for their practice, such as the email address of a teacher, location of a temple, or webpages that give the necessary overview of the tenets of the tradition. No correlation was found between ethnicity and the types of information accessed by the respondents.

> H2: The older a respondent is the more likely they will be to visit Buddhist chat rooms.

Eighty-one percent of the respondents never visited a chat room, while 11.4 percent visited a few times, only 3.3 percent visited often, and 2.2 percent visited daily. However, a correlation between age and other Internet use was established. Older respondents tended to seek contact information for other Buddhists, whereas younger users were looking for general information about the Buddhist tradition, r (184) = .26, p < .01. This is intuitive, in the sense that older practitioners would most likely already be familiar with the basic tenets of the religion than would younger users. Further, older respondents were also more likely to be using the Internet to locate a teacher of Buddhism, r (128) = .23, p < .01. While the hypothesis was unsupported, related correlations indicate that age is a factor in the ways in which users access the Internet for Buddhist resources.

DISCUSSION

The results of this project portray a complex picture of Internet users seeking information about a minority religion in the United States. In general, the survey respondents were typical of American Internet users; white, educated, raised Christian, and with economic resources to obtain Internet access (Pew Research Internet Project, 2014). In other ways, though, this survey population was unique. Some users were more inclined to use the Internet to locate other believers, whereas others were seeking information about the basic tenets of the religion.

This is interesting, considering the minority status of the Buddhist religion in America. It could be presumed that those adherents might use a technology that specifically offers communication across distances to bridge the gap between the practitioners, yet only the older respondents tended to use online resources in that way. Overall, respondents accessed Buddhist resources for information about various aspects of the religion and emphasized the wealth of information immediately available in a convenient manner as their motivation.

However, not all users seemed pleased with the online Buddhist information and indicated a few changes in the presentation that would facilitate their location of desired information. One respondent said, "What would be wonderful, and what exists to some extent, is a single clearinghouse of all Buddhism sites." Many reiterated this sentiment and felt that while there is a diversity of resources available, at times it is cumbersome to locate all of the necessary information in a centralized location. Further, there was a definite distinction that many respondents delineated between Buddhism as a religious tradition and Buddhist-style New Age spirituality. "Truly Buddhist sites need to be identified and differentiated from 'new age' touchy-feely sites that are a mish-mash of trendy ideas." This differentiation between "traditional Buddhism" and perceived New Age expression of Buddhist ideas is indeed a tension found in American Buddhism, and it continues into the discussion of online resources. However, it is precisely this widening of the boundaries of what may be considered Buddhism that makes the tradition's adoption and practice in the United States so interesting.

This study is not without its limitations. While the participants were visitors to Buddhist webspaces, many were very new to Buddhism on the Internet and therefore could not comment at length about chat rooms and online Buddhist community. Also, as Buddhism as practiced in the American context develops further, more nuanced differences between Internet use and sect could be explored. Interesting questions could include whether Tibetan Buddhists in the United States utilize the Internet for Tibetan advocacy, whereas American Theravada or Mahayana Buddhists might contain their social engagement to activities within the United States.

As more traditionally Buddhist nations cross the digital divide and become active participants in the cybersphere, online Buddhism very well might change. As more practitioners and resources outside of the United States provide information about Buddhism it is possible that this tension between Caucasian and Asian Buddhists will grow, or perhaps through this growth, the notion of a cybersangha will develop into a strong online community force and ethnic and cultural differences will dissipate. These issues cannot be known, however, until more work is done exploring the representations of Buddhist community in an online context.

NOTE

A version of this chapter was previously published in 2006. Ally Ostrowski, "Buddha Browsing: American Buddhism and the Internet," *Contemporary Buddhism* 7(1): 91–103.

REFERENCES

Buddhists in the World. 2013. http://www.dhammawiki.com/index.php?title=Buddhists_in_the_world. Accessed September 2, 2013.

Coleman, James W. 2001. *The New Buddhism: The Western Transformation of an Ancient Tradition*. Oxford: Oxford University Press.

Hayes, Richard P. 1999. "The Internet as a Window onto American Buddhism." In *American Buddhism: Methods and Findings in Recent Scholarship*, edited by Duncan R. Williams and Christopher S. Queen, 168–180. Surrey, UK: Curzon Press.

Hofstede, Geert. 2001. *Culture's Consequences: Comparing Values, Behaviors, Institutions and Organizations Across Nations*. Thousand Oaks, CA: Sage.

Kim, Mun-Cho. 2005. "Online Buddhist Community: An Alternative Religious Organization in the Information Age." In *Religion and Cyberspace*, edited by Morten T. Hojsgaard and Margit Warburg, 138–148. London: Routledge.

Kornfield, Jack. 1988. "Is Buddhism Changing in North America?" In *Buddhist America: Centers, Retreats, Practices*, edited by Don Morreale, xi–xxviii. Santa Fe, NM: John Muir Publications.

Laney, Michael J. 2005. "Christian Web Usage: Motives and Desires." In *Religion and Cyberspace*, edited by Morten T. Hojsgaard and Margit Warburg, 166–179. London: Routledge.

Lattin, Don. 2005. "Bridging Eastern and Western Buddhism." *San Francisco Chronicle*, January 23. http://www.sfgate.com/books/article/Bridging-Eastern-and-Western-Buddhism-2703339.php. Accessed September 10, 2013.

Morreale, Don. 1998. "Everything Has Changed in Buddhist America." In *The Complete Guide to Buddhist America*, edited by Don Morreale, xv–xviii. Boston: Shambhala.

The Pew Forum on Religion and Public Life. 2013. http://religions.pewforum.org/reports. Accessed September 2, 2013.

Pew Research Internet Project. 2014. "Internet User Demographics." http://www.pewinternet.org/data-trend/internet-use/latest-stats/Data Trend. Accessed February 20, 2014.

The Pluralism Project. 2013. http://www.pluralism.org/resources/statistics/buddhism_distribution.gif. Accessed August 10, 2013.

Prebish, Charles S. 1999. *Luminous Passage: The Practice and Study of Buddhism in America*. Berkeley: University of California Press.

———, and Martin Baumann. 2002. *Westward Dharma: Buddhism Beyond Asia*. Berkeley: University of California Press.

Seager, Richard H. 1999. *Buddhism in America*. New York: Columbia University Press.

Stark, Rodney, and William S. Bainbridge. 1985. *The Future of Religion*. Berkeley, CA: University of California Press.

Tanaka, Kenneth K. 1998. "Epilogue: The Colors and Contours of American Buddhism." In *The Faces of Buddhism in America*, edited by Charles S. Prebish and Kenneth K. Tanaka, 287–298. Berkeley: University of California Press.

Tsomo, Karma Lekshe. 2002. "Buddhist Nuns: Changes and Challenges." In *Westward Dharma: Buddhism Beyond Asia*, edited by Charles S. Prebish and Martin Baumann, 255–274. Berkeley: University of California Press.

Tweed, Thomas A. 1999. "Night-Stand Buddhists and Other Creatures: Sympathizers, Adherents, and the Study of Religion." In *American Buddhism: Methods and Findings in Recent Scholarship*, edited by Duncan R. Williams and Christopher S. Queen, 71–90. Surrey, UK: Curzon Press.

———. 2002. "'Who Is a Buddhist? Night-Stand Buddhists and Other Creatures." In *Westward Dharma: Buddhism Beyond Asia*, edited by Charles S. Prebish and Martin Baumann, 17–33. Berkeley: University of California Press.

12 The Way of the Blogisattva
Buddhist Blogs on the Web

Beverley Foulks McGuire

At first glance, Nate DeMontigny's blog Precious Metal might seem atypical for a Buddhist blog (see Figure 12.1). Its logo shows a man with a shaved head and multiple tattoos, wearing a black t-shirt with a *dharma-chakra* on it, with two arms in a meditative gesture and two others making the "sign of the horn" or the "rock hand sign" while also holding Buddhist prayer beads and a *vajra*. The blog header reads: "The Road to Nirvana Is Paved with Samsara." While the interweaving of Buddhist symbols and ritual objects with heavy metal and punk motifs might seem anomalous, in fact the merging of Buddhism with other markers of identity is quite common in Buddhist blogs.

Blogs—short for "weblogs"—are online journals whose entries are composed by a single author and updated frequently. Their autobiographical nature makes them an ideal venue for expressing one's sense of identity. DeMontigny acknowledges this in the first post of Precious Metal from April 2, 2007, when he writes: "We all have the right to express ourselves, and this is my way of expressing the things I hold dear. Whether that means my spirituality, the politics of suffering (what we know of in the U.S. as Democracy) and just about everything else under the sun." The aim of his blog is to give voice to that which he finds precious, which includes—but is not limited to—his practice of Buddhism. Precious Metal is one of hundreds of Buddhist blogs written in English on the Internet that represent a subgroup of the larger Buddhist cybersangha, alongside webpages, virtual temples, and more cyber-religious groups located solely online (Prebish 2004, 145).

To date, there have only been two scholarly studies of Buddhist blogs, both of which concentrate on close readings (Connelly 2012; Lee 2009).[1] This chapter complements such in-depth analyses of Buddhist blogs by considering a broader scope for analyzing Buddhist blogs and showing some of the contours and possibilities available to future scholars of Buddhist blogs. As a preliminary study of Buddhist blogs written in English, it seeks to address the lacuna of scholarship on Buddhist blogs; however, it is only the first step in a much larger research project about Buddhist blogs, in which I eventually hope to identify and measure Buddhist blogging on the Internet, study some of the key substantive concerns in the Buddhist blogosphere, analyze the motivations of Buddhist bloggers and whether they consider it

Figure 12.1 Image from the blog Precious Metal. (Used with permission of Nate DeMontigny)

a religious practice, and explore theoretically and empirically how Buddhist blogging impacts Buddhist religiosity offline.

Here I address a fundamental question for future scholarship on Buddhist blogs, namely: What constitutes a "Buddhist blog"? How does one determine the extent to which a blog is—or is not—Buddhist? Does the blog have to mention Buddhism (or a particular Buddhist tradition) in its posts? If bloggers are Buddhist, are their blogs necessarily so? The tendency to assume that a "Buddhist blog" is a blog written by a Buddhist is problematic, for several reasons. First, while one might easily identify Buddhist monks or nuns as "Buddhist," such categorizations become more difficult when applied to Buddhist lay people—especially those in Western contexts, as has been pointed out by scholars of American Buddhism (Bielefeldt 2001; Nattier 1998; Prebish and Tanaka 1998; Tweed 1999; Wilson 2009). Second, some bloggers, taking full advantage of the anonymity provided by blogs, do not explicitly identify themselves as Buddhist, yet their blog may allude to Buddhist concepts in its content or include Buddhist iconography in its design. A final, subtle issue with this approach is that, by focusing on the identity of the blogger it overlooks the possibilities afforded by the blog as a medium: viewing it as merely a conduit for the blogger's ideas, it fails to address the particular characteristics of blogs that allow for unique expressions of Buddhist identity.

This chapter advocates a different approach to determining what makes a blog Buddhist—one that focuses on the opportunities and challenges presented by the form of the blog. It focuses especially on two Buddhist blogs—Nate DeMontigny's Precious Metal and Kyle Lovett's The Reformed Buddhist—to demonstrate the advantages of a scholarly approach focusing on the blog rather than the blogger. Instead of attempting to categorize Buddhist bloggers—a difficult, if not impossible, task—it examines the complex identities created in blogs that underscore the Buddhist idea of the self as constructed and lacking inherent existence. It shows how one can address issues of identity—a topic that has received a fair amount of scholarly attention in studies of other types of computer-mediated communication (Hoover 2006; Lövheim 2004; Lövheim 2013; Lövheim and Linderman 2005; Slevin 2000)—without having to categorize the blogger as a particular type of Buddhist. Occasionally, it refers to other blogs to demonstrate that these two blogs are far from atypical in the Buddhist blogosphere: one finds Buddhist lay teachers, monks, nuns, and practitioners strictly affiliated with particular traditions similarly taking advantage of the possibilities afforded by the blog as a medium.

"BUDDHIST BLOGS": A DEFINITION

What makes a blog Buddhist? To understand this, we first need to define blogs, which have two expectations that distinguish them from other types of online communication: first, that they have a single author, and second, that this author update his or her blog frequently. They have been described as online journals insofar as they are focused on personal content and composed of individual entries whose contents are intended for a public audience (Campbell 2010, 253; Herring, Scheidt, Bonus, and Wright 2004; Nardi, Schiano, Gumbrecht, and Swartz 2004, 41–46). The present-day format of blogs first appeared in 1996 and the term "weblog" made its debut in 1997 (Herring et al. 2004). Although it is difficult to estimate the number of blogs because many search engines do not share such information, and those that do may include dead blogs or those temporarily dormant, in 2009 Technorati indexed 133 million blogs, and Universal McCann estimated that approximately 77 percent of Internet users read blogs (Singer 2009). BlogPulse identified more than 182 million blogs as of January 2012 (Hurst 2012).

Although there are group blogs in which several authors rotate the responsibility for posting individual entries, the vast majority of blogs are singly authored and maintained. Prominent bloggers identify the personal voice as the single-most-defining feature of blogs (Reynolds 2003; Winer 2003), and scholars concur that blogs are expected to "express deeply felt emotions"(Nardi et al. 2004, 43) that can often be quite vitriolic in the case of "flaming" (Aycock 1995). Because of their personal voice and chronological entries, blogs resemble offline antecedents, such as handwritten diaries. While we might consider the two distinct because the former anticipate a readership, scholars have noted that not all manuscript diaries were meant for private consumption; in fact, many were either shared with or written for an audience (O'Sullivan 2005, 68). Amardeep Singh notes that two conventions of diaristic writing—the centrality of sincerity and immediacy—are especially emphasized in contemporary blogging culture, and he argues that a strong ethical association between writing and authorial signature operates in blog culture, such that even bloggers who publish pseudonymously are expected to uphold an authenticity of self-representation (Singh 2008, 25).

Just as the Internet blurs the boundaries between private and public by enabling people to participate in its public space from the privacy of their own homes, blogs similarly allow people to share personal thoughts and experiences in a public venue. Blogs are considered attractive because this "intermediate" quality allows authors to experience social interaction while giving them control over the communicative space (Herring et al. 2004, 11). Authors manage their own blog, deciding whether or not to allow comments, to include a blogroll, or to link to other blogs. For example, they might disable comments on their own blog while making copious comments on others' blogs. They can determine the extent to which they interact with other bloggers, and the degree to which other bloggers can relate to them.

In addition to personal voice, the second distinguishing feature of blogs is that they be frequently updated, which can become quite taxing for bloggers. Although there are certainly other structural features to blogs, such as its blogroll, its software used, its ability to post comments, its calendar, its archives, and its badges (icons that signal an affiliation with a product or group), blogs are considered dead or dormant unless they are updated on a frequent basis. This demand is not shared by websites, for example, that may have several webmasters responsible for such updates or only update occasionally. We cannot assume that the platform alone—Blogger and WordPress being the most popular—signals a blog, for sometimes they consist of static websites that are not updated.

Having considered what constitutes a blog, we can now address the difficult question of what makes a blog "Buddhist." We can begin by examining a directory of more than 300 English-language Buddhist blogs posted on the website for the Blogisattva Awards. The website recognizes achievement in Buddhism-inspired blogging by *blogisattvas*—those who have attained "excellence within the Buddho-blogosphere" (Blogisattva Awards 2011) (see Figure 12.2). Blogisattva Awards were first given in 2006 until 2008, when they were discontinued until bloggers Nate DeMontigny and Kyle

Figure 12.2   Image of the Blogisattva. (Used with permission of Anoki Casey)

Lovett resurrected the awards in 2010. Meant to recognize bloggers and foster a better sense of an online Buddhist community, the awards encompass not only the best blog or best post of the year, but also "Best Achievement in Kind and Compassionate Blogging," "Best Buddhist Practice Blog" and "Best Achievement with Humor in a Blog Post."

The image of the blogisattva from their website alludes to the multi-armed bodhisattva of compassion, Avalokitesvara, but in the blogisattva's hands are an emoticon, an arrow key, a WiFi symbol, a magnifying glass, an attachment sign, and an @ sign. The blogisattva's gaze peers down at the laptop computer where the OM symbol glows instead of an Apple. Comparing certain bloggers to bodhisattvas, the image implies that computer and Internet technology might serve as expedient means of liberation.

Unlike the awards, which are determined by a panel of judges including a scholar–practitioner, a journalist for *Tricycle Magazine*, and longtime Buddhist bloggers, anyone can add a blog to the directory: there is no vetting process for inclusion. As a result, the directory includes a diverse range of what it calls "Buddhism-inspired" blogs, which it divides into categories of "academic/scholarly," "group practice blogs," "monastic blogs," "ordained/ lay teacher blogs," and "personal practitioner blogs." Immediately, one notices that the category "personal practitioner blogs" constitutes two-thirds of the total blogs, significantly outweighing other categories.[2] In fact, the category of "personal practitioner" is a catch-all category: it includes an incredibly broad range of blogs and fails to capture their distinctive features.

This highlights one of the shortcomings of an approach that categorizes Buddhist blogs according to the blogger instead of the blog, which we will explore in greater detail later. Given such deficiencies, I would propose that "Buddhist blogs" instead be defined as online journals updated frequently by a single author that reflect an interest in—or identification with— Buddhist traditions, people, concepts, or practices in their content and/ or form. This definition has the advantage of being capacious enough to accommodate those who may not formally affiliate with a Buddhist tradi-tion but whose blog engages with Buddhism, as well as those who identify as Buddhist but consider it one part of their multifaceted identity.

THE CONSTRAINTS OF CATEGORIES

Much scholarly ink has been spilled on how one might categorize Buddhists, and it could easily be spilt in the task of trying to categorize Buddhist blog-gers. One could try to distinguish between blogs written by monastics, lay teachers, lay practitioners, or scholar-practitioners, as does the Blogisattva Awards directory. One could try to determine what tradition the blogger affiliates with, such as Zen, Pure Land, Dzogchen, and so on. One could seek to identify the blogger's gender, race, or ethnicity. One could differ-entiate between bloggers based on their geographical location. One could make a distinction between blogs authored by individual Buddhists, by indi-viduals on behalf of Buddhist sanghas, by individuals on behalf of Buddhist organizations, or by groups of Buddhists.

However, the attempt to categorize Buddhist blogs based on the iden-tity of the blogger is problematic. While one might easily identify Buddhist monks or nuns as "Buddhist," such categorizations become more difficult when applied to Buddhist lay people—especially those in Western contexts. Scholars have long debated how one might categorize the variety of Ameri-can Buddhists. One approach distinguishes between "two Buddhisms"— one practiced by Asian immigrants to the United States, the other by Euro-Americans who convert to Buddhism (Prebish 1993, 187). As noted by Charles Prebish, who originally coined the term "two Buddhisms," the bifurcation between "heritage" and "convert" Buddhists makes the issue of identity and membership a "murky problem" (Prebish and Tanaka 1998, 7). While some view the typology as useful for reminding scholars of real inequi-ties in the American racial landscape, others have criticized it as reinforcing racial boundaries and portraying Asian Americans and European Americans in stereotypical terms (Wilson 2009, 840). Alternately, Jan Nattier proposed a typology based on three different styles of transmission, distinguishing between "import" or "demand-driven" transmission in which an individual actively seeks out Buddhism, which she calls "Elite Buddhism" because it requires money and time; "export" transmission of actively proselytizing groups such as Soka Gakkai, which she calls "Evangelical Buddhism"; and "baggage" transmission of those who immigrated to America for non-religious reasons, which she terms "Ethnic Buddhism" because they are defined primarily because of their ethnicity (Nattier 1998, 189–190). Her approach has been criticized for not accounting for groups with multi-ethnic constituencies and for overlooking the role of Asian missionaries in the importation of Buddhism to the United States (Hickey 2010).

Both approaches have their shortcomings, as demonstrated by scholars who have identified outliers to such typologies of American Buddhists. Thomas Tweed suggests that there are "Buddhist sympathizers" or "Night Stand Buddhists"—those who have sympathy for Buddhism but do not embrace it exclusively or fully—that do not fall within such categorizations (Tweed 1999, 74). They may practice meditation, subscribe to a Buddhist magazine such as *Tricycle*, or keep a Buddhist book on their night table, but when asked they would not identify themselves as Buddhist. One study suggests that these sympathizers may outnumber those who formally identify with Buddhism: Robert Wuthnow and Wendy Cadge found that 12 percent of Americans said Buddhist teachings or practices had an important influence on their thinking about religion or spirituality (Wuthnow and Cadge 2004, 371). Other scholars have proposed adding subcategories within the "Buddhist sympathizer" category, such as "freelance Buddhists" who identify themselves as Buddhist but do not belong to any Buddhist organization, and "client Buddhists" who make use of Buddhist organizations without belonging to them (Bielfeldt 2001).

While there are certainly bloggers who identify as Buddhist and affiliate with a particular Buddhist organization or tradition, many others would fall into the categories of "Buddhist sympathizers," "freelance Buddhists," or "client Buddhists"—especially those who first encountered Buddhism online. For example, when narrating his entry into Buddhism, DeMontigny describes moving to Knoxville, Tennessee, with his wife and son and how he found a Buddhist Web forum while surfing the Internet after his son was in bed. It was then that he started reading posts and websites, and afterwards he purchased Thubten Chodron's *Buddhism for Beginners*. He said the online forum was especially helpful, since he lived more than two hours away from a Buddhist temple or center (DeMontigny 2013). He openly admitted being new to Buddhism, lacking ties to particular Buddhist institutions or organizations, and having encountered Buddhism via online forums and websites. His experience with Buddhism was computer mediated, unregulated, and unsupervised—characteristic of what Christopher Helland has called "online religion" as opposed to "religion online," in which established religions present information in a top-down fashion online (Helland 2000, 207). Simply categorizing blogs such as that of DeMontigny as those of "personal practitioners" fails to acknowledge the range of religious identification and participation found on the Internet.

In addition, some bloggers vocally object to being pigeonholed into categories such as that of "heritage" or "convert" Buddhist. This was illustrated by the reaction of Buddhist bloggers to a post by a twenty-three-year-old Sinhalese woman named Tassja living in Minnesota, who vented against convert Buddhists in America. Recounting the difficulty of identifying herself as Buddhist in a place where Christianity dominates, and how Buddhism is inseparable from her culture, she shared her frustration at what she perceived as "imperialist, disrespectful, and mostly racist" white appropriation of Buddhism, asking:

> How can you claim something as part of your identity, on par with people who grew up living and breathing that culture everyday? How can you claim to own something you've never had to defend, or fight for? And please, spare me the details of how your white Lutheran parents disapproved of your visits to the meditation center . . . I don't go to a meditation center, I don't know what "lovingkindness" is supposed to mean, I don't conceive of myself as a serene speck of unruffled dust floating along the karmic Universe; in short, I have no part in the individualistic, elite, consumer-oriented, pseudo-hippie global tourist bullfeces that Whiteness tries to pass off as practicing Buddhism.
>
> (Tassja 2011)

Her post generated a great deal of commentary in the Buddhist blogosphere: some said white American Buddhists should listen closely to her remarks, whereas others pointed to exceptions in their own racially and ethnically diverse Buddhist communities. Kyle Lovett, whose online identity was predicated on poking fun at Buddhists who took themselves too seriously, adopted a more scathing tone in his response to Tassja's post. Not only did he object to her claiming ownership over Buddhism, her insinuating that convert Buddhists don't have to defend themselves—discussing his own experience of being a closet Buddhist with a Christian Evangelical boss in the South—and her portrayal of all convert Buddhists as elite, consumer-oriented, pseudo-hippie global tourists, but he then criticized Sinhalese Buddhism as not embodying the values of social justice that Tassja appeals to in her post, referencing the violence committed against Tamil Hindus in the Sri Lankan civil war. He ends, "It is very sad that she calls white Buddhists racist, when she doesn't even see her own stereotyping and racist attitudes towards white people."

While debates about American Buddhist identity are by no means restricted to cyberspace, the blogosphere provides a unique forum for addressing such issues. As a medium of communication, blogs have certain strengths and weaknesses. On the one hand, unlike *Tricycle, Shambhala Sun,* or other American Buddhist magazines that appeal to particular constituencies, the blogosphere cuts across a variety of groups and traditions, bringing together a diverse population of Buddhists as well as those who may not consider themselves Buddhist. So-called "convert" Buddhists can encounter "heritage" Buddhists on the Internet that they might not otherwise meet offline, a rare opportunity, since, as Rick Fields notes, instances of fellowship and communication among the two groups remain more the exception than the rule (Fields 1998, 203). In addition, as Charles Prebish observes, such inclusivity is not characteristic of the cybersangha as a whole (Prebish 1999, 231). On the other hand, one could argue that such diversity is mitigated by the fact that bloggers and blog readers have a certain degree of socioeconomic privilege, insofar as they have access to the Internet and enough leisure time to spend reading or posting on the Internet, and they mostly comprise white men. Moreover, while back-and-forth comments on blogs can result in productive dialogues among diverse groups of Buddhists, exchanges can frequently become quite vitriolic, as evidenced by the tone of both Lovett and Tassja's blog posts.

FLUID IDENTITY AND ANONYMITY

Not only do categorizations fail to capture the range of identities that one finds online, but they also imply that a blogger's religious identity is static or transparent, when most bloggers take advantage of—and occasionally, pleasure in—the possibility of adapting their identity or being anonymous online. Admittedly, there are those for whom gender, race, ethnicity, geography, and monastic or lay status are important markers of their online identity—so much so that they use them in their blog names: for example, Angry Asian Buddhist, Angry Tibetan Girl, Bayou City Buddhist, Buddhist in Nebraska, High Plains Buddhist, or Toledo Buddhist. However, more often, one finds blog names that include general Buddhist terms or traditions (especially Zen), or that reflect a combination of Buddhism and other interests or identity markers, such as Buddhist Geeks for technophiles, Dharma Loss for those concerned about weight loss or healthy living, Buddha Mama Sans Drama or Cheerio Road for parents, My Buddha Is Pink for the gay and queer community, Tattoozen for tattoo artists and clients, Run with Mu for runners, The Meditative Gardener for gardeners, The Punk Rock Buddhist for punk rockers, Metal Buddha and Precious Metal for heavy metal musicians and fans, and Scott Mitchell's former blog The Buddha Is My DJ for those interested in popular culture. One also finds bloggers changing their blog name following shifts in offline identities: for example, the blogger Damchoe initially entitled her blog Reflections of Reflections but after becoming ordained adopted a name that plays on her new monastic status: Damchoe's Nun Sense.

Scholars of online religion have emphasized the complexity underlying the social construction of personal identity on the Internet (Aycock 1995), and this is particularly true in the case of Buddhist blogs. Oftentimes, bloggers acknowledge this complexity in their "About Me" pages. For example, as Katherine Rand notes on her blog It's All Dhamma: "I have a complex religious identity and, in this context, am happy to leave it at that. People don't tend to like the in-between, the multiple, the ambiguous, but the reality is that's where many of us are in this pluralistic world." Indeed, even bloggers who seem to easily fit categories defy such assumptions: in her blog 如(thus)是, Seon Joon Sunim writes, "Ordained Buddhist monastic. / Incorrigible bibliophile. / Novice shutterbug. / Aspiring practitioner. / Coffee-lover." Simply categorizing her blog as a "monastic blog" overlooks the fact that she also identifies herself as a practitioner, as well as a photographer and a lover of books. While her monastic status constitutes one aspect of her identity, it is arguably not the most prominent.

Similarly, Lovett's objection to Tassja's portrayal of convert Buddhists stems from the fact that it failed to capture his own sense of identity. Instead, Lovett described himself as a "troll," which is Internet slang for someone who posts inflammatory or off-topic messages in an online community in an attempt to provoke an emotional response. In his final blog post on August 4, 2011—less than two months after responding to Tassja on June 23— Lovett posted a "trollface" and complained that too many eBuddhists took themselves too seriously. He wrote, "It was a fun 5 years of being an attention whore and a general pain in the ass to everyone. I wouldn't take it back for the world." Indeed, Lovett's blog reveled in lowbrow humor that poked fun at various Buddhist practices and people, and he often assumed the role of trickster. DeMontigny embraced another type of online identity that combined his identification as a death-metal rocker and Buddhist. Admitting that some might find his violent songs dissonant with his Buddhist affiliation, he insisted that his songs about death and pain concurred with Buddhist teachings about impermanence.

The online identities of Lovett and DeMontigny share features identified by scholars of identity construction with those forged in open-ended institutional environments like the Internet. As James Slevin has pointed out, people online participate in "a skillful splicing together of differential interactional situations" (Slevin 2000, 113). The Internet forces one to negotiate mediated experience and make it relevant to oneself, it increases one's ability to intervene in events not normally "within reach," its diversity can shatter one's parochialism, and it can expose one to conflicting dispositions and a broader social world. This certainly applies to the case of Lovett and DeMontigny, as each tries to negotiate between Buddhism and their identity as trickster and rocker, as their Internet use allows them access to Buddhist groups and resources not "within reach" in Virginia and Tennessee, and as they encounter dissenting perspectives and expectations online. In the case of DeMontigny, he explains in a post from July 24, 2011, that despite his good intentions when he started blogging, once he started reviewing Buddhist books and DVDs, as well as vegetarian/vegan food products, he found himself caught up in promoting and marketing Buddhist products instead of sustaining his own practice. In their analysis of Christian blogs, Cheong, Halvais, and Kwon argue that they provide "an integrative experience for the faithful" and fulfill the need for transmission of values, entertainment and escapism, and integration and interaction (Cheong, Halavais, and Kwon 2008, 107, 122). As we have seen in the case of Lovett and DeMontigny, Buddhist blogs can fulfill similar needs, but they provide not only integrative but disintegrative experiences. These are the risks associated with online religion, or computer-mediated religiosity.

FOCUSING ON THE BLOG AS A MEDIUM

We have explored some of the drawbacks of an approach that defines Buddhist blogs based on the identity of their bloggers: first, the categories fail to capture the range and diversity of online identities, and second, they overlook the fact that bloggers rarely offer specific details about themselves, and when they do, they often defy such facile categorizations. A third shortcoming is that such an approach overlooks the possibilities afforded by the medium of the blog itself. We have seen how certain features of blogs—including blog names, "About Me" posts, and graphics or images—allow for novel and unique constructions of Buddhist identities online. Similarly, blogrolls, tag clouds, and badges also enable people to create multifaceted and complex portraits of their online identities.

Blogrolls are lists of hyperlinks to other blogs (and websites) that typically appear on the right or left sidebars of blogs. Sometimes, they are divided into categories, such as 108zenbooks' "Dharma Brothers" and "Dharma Sisters," or Precious Metal's "Blogs I Read and Enjoy" and "Dharma for Kids." In the latter case, the links reflect DeMontigny's identity as a heavy-metal musician, as a father, and as someone living in the South: the links connect his blog to others with these same interests and markers of identity. Not only is such clustering—around particular Buddhist traditions, philosophical approaches to Buddhism, geographic locations, or interests (such as recovery, heavy-metal music, punk rock, parenting, minimalist lifestyles, weight loss)—quite common in blogrolls, but also one frequently finds multiple clusters within a single blogroll. This underscores an important characteristic of the blogosphere, namely that it allows bloggers the flexibility to form multiple, diverse connections and explore various facets of their identity online. Finally, it is important to note that it is not uncommon for a single person to maintain multiple blogs, which further amplifies the ability of the blogger to become a *bricoleur* able to construct and deconstruct many different identities online. For example, the scholar–practitioner blogger Justin Whitaker has founded multiple blogs, not only his popular American

Buddhist Perspective, but also American Buddhist in England, A Foot in the Stream, Hodgkin House, Buddhist Ethics, and Progressive Buddhism.

The image of the blogisattva is one of many "badges" or "widgets" that might appear on a Buddhist blog's sidebar. The most common badges are those of Facebook and Twitter, though one occasionally sees widgets that display the number of current online visitors to the blog or a map of where they are from. "Donate" buttons appear in quite a few Buddhist blogs, which invite readers to make a single donation or a monthly donation to the blogger via Paypal. In the case of Precious Metal, DeMontigny's badges connect him to the Blogisattva Awards and several websites maintained by Anoki Casey, who designed the blogisattva character as well as the Precious Metal character, including his nonprofit charity website entitled BuddhaBadges, his website Altar-Bot, where individuals can upload pictures of their home altars, and his website Dharma Dots that filters and directs readers to postings on Buddhist blogs and websites. In this way, badges and widgets can signal affiliations with certain online communities or connections with particular individuals.

While blogrolls and badges indicate connections with other bloggers or websites, "tag clouds" visually illustrate particular topics of concern to the blogger. Tags are simple keywords that bloggers can use to categorize content of blog posts, so that they can group related posts together; "tag clouds" visually represent such tags, typically indicating the importance of tags by their font size. For example, Smiling Buddha Cabaret includes the tag cloud in Figure 12.3.

Buddhism clearly occupies the bulk of her blog posts, however ethics, politics, and ego are also frequently discussed topics, followed by social activism, commercialization, and Zen. Her tag cloud not only suggests issues that occupy her thoughts, but also interests and identity markers, such as travel and vegetarianism. In this way, tag clouds convey a sense of a blogger's identity that is more multifaceted than identifying a blogger according to their gender, race, ethnicity, or affiliation with a particular Buddhist tradition.

8 Fold Path Anger Books **Buddhism** Christianity Commercialization Compassion Death Desire Drugs Ego Enlightenment Ethics Fear Festivals & Holidays Hinduism History Home Leaving Humor Islam Karma Koan Language Martial Arts Media Medicine Meditation Music New Age Politics PTSD Reviews Science Sects Sex Social Activism Spiritual Tourism Sufi Terrorism Tibetan Transcripts Travel Vegetarianism War Zen

Figure 12.3 Smiling Buddha Cabaret tag cloud. (Used with permission of Marnie Froberg)

CONCLUSION

When we focus on the medium of the blog—including its blog name, "About Me," graphics, blogrolls, badges, and tag clouds—we can better appreciate the range and diversity of Buddhist blogs on the Web. Moreover, we also get a better sense of bloggers' complex online identities, which are often eclipsed when one tries to categorize bloggers according to their ethnicity or their affiliation with a particular Buddhist tradition. As we have seen, such categorizations can become caricatures and stereotypes that bloggers find constraining or offensive. They fail to capture the fluid, multifaceted, and creative possibilities of blogs, which is particularly appealing to people who acknowledge the complexity of their religious and personal identity.

While blogs have the tremendous capacity to allow for such identity construction, they also have the disadvantage of requiring frequent updates. Occasionally, this becomes a formidable challenge for bloggers. In the case of Nate DeMontigny and Kyle Lovett, within a year of resurrecting the Blogisattva Awards in an effort to uplift the Buddhist blogging community (Breeder 2010), both decided to take a break from their Buddhist blogs. Describing the choice to discontinue his Buddhist blog, in a post from August 4, 2011, Kyle Lovett wrote, "Frankly I got a whole lot of nothing to say on the subject anymore." In a post on September 19, 2011, DeMontigny explained his decision to "unplug" as stemming from the fact that excessive computer use was harming his health and damaging his personal relationships. Later he posted that physical exercise had improved his seated meditation, but ultimately he decided to discontinue his blog. Although scholars identify the disembodied quality of online religion as a fundamental distinction between it and offline religion (Cowan 2007, 370), DeMontigny's remarks highlight the fact that online religion does have a bodily dimension—namely a sedentary quality—that can adversely affect one's health, relationships, and meditation practice. Their decision to discontinue their blogs raises the question of whether the temporal and physical demands of a blog impede Buddhists from their practice rather than help them sustain it.

Another topic for further consideration is whether Facebook and Twitter might herald the death of Buddhist blogs altogether.[3] One finds many examples of blogs that were discontinued because their authors turned to other social media outlets (Ground Peace Zero, Open Buddha, My Itchy Third Eye). One blogger wrote, "Blogger feels kind of old and rickety and so much like yesterday's news. And all the action these days is on Facebook anyway and with their timeline, it's really more blog like these days" (YogaDawg 2012). Tweets and Facebook status updates allow for a kind of "microblogging" that some prefer to blogs themselves. If they do bring about the end of blogs, perhaps it is fitting: it shows how Buddhist blogs—like all conditioned things—are subject to impermanence.

NOTES

1. In his article "Cultivating the Self in Cyberspace: The Use of Personal Blogs among Buddhist Priests," Joonseong Lee actually analyzes a social networking site in Korea entitled Cyworld that is analogous to Facebook—a "micro-blog" that allows users to broadcast short messages ("microposts") in continuous streams. In her dissertation entitled "Aspects of the Self: An Analysis of Self-Reflection, Self Presentation, and the Experiential Self within Selected Buddhist Blogs," Louise Connelly explores the experiential aspect of human existence online through an ethnographic study of three Buddhist blogs: The Buddhist Blog, The American Buddhist, and ThinkBuddha.org.
2. The directory's 321 blogs include 7 academic blogs, 20 group practice blogs, 20 monastic blogs, 50 ordained/lay teacher blogs, 204 personal practitioner blogs, and 19 "miscellaneous" blogs.
3. Potential evidence of the shift from blogs to such social media is the shutting down of BlogPulse, the full blog search engine, in January 2012. It was replaced by NM Incite, which focuses more on mobile applications and social media including Facebook, Twitter, and Pinterest (Hurst 2012).

REFERENCES

Aycock, Alan. 1995. "'Technologies of the Self': Foucault and Internet Discourse." *Journal of Computer-Mediated Communication* 1(2). DOI:10.1111/j.1083–6101. 1995.tb00328.x. Accessed August 15, 2013.

Bielefeldt, Carl. 2001. "Comments on Tensions in American Buddhism." *Religion and Ethics Newsweekly,* July 6. http://www.pbs.org/wnet/religionandethics/2001/07/06/july-6-2001-comments-on-tensions-in-american-buddhism/15941/. Accessed August 15, 2013.

Blogisattva Awards. 2011. "Awards Guidelines." http://blogisattva.blogspot.com/p/award-guidlines.html. Accessed August 21, 2013.

Breeder, Emily. 2010. "The Blogisattvas: Recognizing Excellence in Buddhist Blogging." *Examiner.com*, October 24. http://www.examiner.com/buddhism-in-national/the-blogisattvas-recognizing-excellence-buddhist-blogging. Accessed August 21, 2013.

Campbell, Heidi A. 2010. "Religious Authority and the Blogosphere." *Journal of Computer-Mediated Communication* 15: 251–276.

Cheong, Pauline Hope, Alexander Halavais, and Kyounghee Kwon. 2008. "The Chronicles of Me: Understanding Blogging as a Religious Practice." *Journal of Media and Religion* 7: 107–131.

Connelly, Louise. 2012. "Aspects of the Self: An Analysis of Self Reflection, Self Presentation, and the Experiential Self within Selected Buddhist Blogs." PhD diss., Edinburgh, Scotland, University of Edinburgh.

Cowan, Douglas E. 2007. "Religion on the Internet." In *The SAGE Handbook of the Sociology of Religion,* edited by James A. Beckford and N. J. Demerath III, 357–377. Los Angeles, CA: Sage.

DeMontigny, Nate. 2013. "Precious Metal." *The Worst Horse.* http://theworst horse.com/nated/nated-1.html. Accessed August 21, 2013.

Fields, Rick. 1998. "Divided Dharma: White Buddhists, Ethnic Buddhists, and Racism." In *The Faces of Buddhism in America*, edited by Charles Prebish and Kenneth Tanaka, 196–206. Berkeley: University of California Press.

Helland, Christopher. 2000. "Online-Religion / Religion Online and Virtual Communitas." In *Religion on the Internet: Research Prospects and Promises*, edited by Jeffrey K. Hadden and Douglas E. Cowan, 205–223. New York: JAI.

Herring, Susan C., Lois Ann Scheidt, Sabrina Bonus, and Elijah Wright. 2004. "Bridging the Gap: A Genre Analysis of Weblogs, Proceedings of the 37th Annual Hawaii International Conference on System Sciences (HICSS'04)." http://www.computer.org/portal/web/csdl/abs/proceedings/hicss/2004/2056/04/205640101babs.htm. Accessed October 6, 2011.

Hickey, Wakoh Shannon. 2010. "Two Buddhisms, Three Buddhisms, and Racism." *Journal of Global Buddhism* 11. http://www.globalbuddhism.org/11/hickey10.html. Accessed August 28, 2013.

Hoover, Stewart M. 2006. *Religion in the Media Age*. New York: Routledge.

Hurst, Matthew. 2012. "Farewell to BlogPulse." *SmartData Collective*, January 14. http://smartdatacollective.com/node/44748. Accessed April 14, 2013.

Lee, Jeoonseong. 2009. "Cultivating the Self in Cyberspace: The Use of Personal Blogs among Buddhist Priests." *Journal of Media and Religion* 8(2): 97–114.

Lövheim, Mia. 2004. "Young People, Religious Identity, and the Internet." In *Religion Online: Finding Faith on the Internet*, edited by Lorne L. Dawson and Douglas E. Cowan, 59–74. New York: Routledge.

———. 2013. "Identity." In *Digital Religion: Understanding Religious Practice in New Media Worlds*, edited by Heidi A. Campbell, 41–56. New York: Routledge.

———, and Alf G. Linderman. 2005. "Constructing Religious Identity on the Internet." In *Religion and Cyberspace*, edited by Morten T. Hojsgaard and Margit Warburg, 121–137. New York: Routledge.

Nardi, Bonnie A., Diane J. Schiano, Michelle Gumbrecht, and Luke Swartz. 2004. "Why We Blog." *Communications of the ACM* 47(12): 41–46.

Nattier, Jan. 1998. "Who Is a Buddhist? Charting the Landscape of Buddhist America." In *The Faces of Buddhism in America*, edited by Charles S. Prebish and Kenneth K. Tanaka, 183–195. Berkeley: University of California Press.

O'Sullivan, Catherine. 2005. "Diaries, On-Line Diaries, and the Future Loss to Archives; or, Blogs and the Blogging Bloggers Who Blog Them." *The American Archivist* 68(1): 53–73.

Prebish, Charles. 1993. "Two Buddhisms Reconsidered." *Buddhist Studies Review* 10(2): 187–206.

———. 1999. *Luminous Passage: The Practice and Study of Buddhism in America*. Berkeley: University of California Press.

———. 2004. "The Cybersangha: Buddhism on the Internet." In *Religion Online: Finding Faith on the Internet*, edited by L. L. Dawson and D.E. Cowan, 135–147. New York: Routledge.

———, and Kanneth K. Tanaka, eds. 1998. *The Faces of Buddhism in America*. Berkeley: University of California Press.

Reynolds, Glenn Harlan. 2003. "The Good, the Bad, and the Blogly." *The Blog Herald*, June 18. http://www.blogherald.com/2003/06/18/the-good-the-bad-and-the-blogly/. Accessed August 15, 2013.

Singer, Adam. 2009. "70 Usable Stats from the 2009 State of the Blogosphere." *The Future Buzz*, December 10. http://thefuturebuzz.com/2009/12/10/blogging-stats-facts-data/. Accessed October 20, 2011.

Singh, Amardeep. 2008. "Anonymity, Authorship, and Blogger Ethics." *symploke* 16(1–2): 21–35.

Slevin, James. 2000. *The Internet and Society*. Malden, MA: Blackwell Publishers.

Tassja. 2011. "The Unbearable Whiteness of Being, Part III: A Brown Buddhist and a Handful of Mustard Seeds." *Womanist Musings*, June 22. http://www.womanist-musings.com/2011/06/unbearable-whiteness-of-being-part-iii.html. Accessed October 20, 2011.

Tweed, Thomas. 1999. "Night-Stand Buddhists and Other Creatures: Sympathizers, Adherents, and the Study of Religion." In *American Buddhism: Methods and*

Findings in Recent Scholarship, edited by Duncan Ryuken Williams and Christopher Queen, 71–90. Surrey, UK: Curzon Press.

Wilson, Jeff. 2009. "Mapping the American Buddhist Terrain: Paths Taken and Possible Itineraries." *Religion Compass* 3(5): 836–846.

Winer, Dave. 2003. "What Makes a Weblog a Weblog?" *Weblogs at Harvard Law,* May 23. http://blogs.law.harvard.edu/whatmakesaweblogaweblog.html. Accessed August 15, 2013.

Wuthnow, Robert, and Wendy Cadge. 2004. "Buddhists and Buddhism in the United States: The Scope of Influence." *Journal for the Scientific Study of Religion* 43(3): 363–380.

YogaDawg. 2012. "Bye Bye Bloggie—Join Me on Facebook." *My Itchy Third Eye,* September 9. http://yogadawg.blogspot.com/. Accessed August 29, 2013.

Contributors

Christopher Accardo is an Ithaca College graduate and a practicing Tibetan Buddhist currently working as an outdoor professional in Ithaca, NY. While attending Ithaca College, he founded and led the multi-denominational Ithaca College Buddhist Community, was a founding member and leader of the first Ithaca College Interfaith Council, and acted as a representative for his religion at many community and interfaith events at Ithaca College. Chris is interested in the development of the American Buddhist identity, as well as interfaith and intrafaith influences in Buddhism, and plans to attend graduate school in the near future.

Louise Connelly is Head of Digital Education at the Institute for Academic Development, University of Edinburgh, where she provides pedagogical advice to academic teams for the development of online postgraduate provision as well as the development of massive open online courses (MOOCs). She received her PhD from the University of Edinburgh in 2012, with her dissertation titled "Aspects of the Self: An Analysis of Self Reflection, Self Presentation and the Experiential Self in Selected Buddhist Blogs." Her current research interests include Buddhist ritual and identity in the online world of Second Life, how social presence manifests online, social media and research ethics, and how social media and virtual worlds can be used in educational contexts. Her recent publications include "Virtual Buddhism: An Analysis of Aesthetics in Relation to Religious Practice within Second Life" (2010), *Heidelberg Journal of Religions on the Internet*; "Virtual Buddhism: Buddhist Ritual in Second Life" (2013), in H. Campbell (ed.), *Digital Religion: Understanding Religious Practice in New Media Worlds*; and "Virtual Buddhism: Online Communities, Sacred Places and Objects" (forthcoming), in S. Brunn (ed.), *The Changing World Religion Map*.

Jessica Falcone is Assistant Professor of Anthropology at Kansas State University, where she teaches courses on expressive culture, futurity, South Asian culture, and ethnographic methods. She graduated with a PhD in Sociocultural Anthropology from Cornell University in 2010. Her dissertation project, "Waiting for Maitreya: Of Gifting Statues, Hopeful Presents and the Future Tense in FPMT's Transnational Tibetan Buddhism," was a cultural biography of a 500-foot statue of the Future Buddha that is currently being planned as a gift to India by a community of international converts to Tibetan Buddhism.

Beverley Foulks McGuire is Assistant Professor of East Asian Religions in the Philosophy and Religion Department at the University of North Carolina, Wilmington. She received her PhD in East Asian Languages and Civilizations from Harvard University in 2009 and her MDiv from Harvard Divinity School in 2003. Her academic areas of interest include Chinese Religions, Buddhism, Comparative Religious Ethics, and Religion and Media—especially the Buddhist blogosphere.

Gregory Price Grieve is Associate Professor in Religious Studies at the University of North Carolina, Greensboro; Director of MERGE: a Network for Collaborative Interdisciplinary Scholarship in UNCG's College of Arts and Sciences; and co-chair of the American Academy of Religion's section on Religion and Popular Culture. A leader in the field of digital religion, and a pioneer in the emerging field of religion in digital games, he is the author of *Retheorizing Religion in Nepal* (2007), and co-editor of *Historicizing Tradition in the Study of Religion* (2005).

Christopher Helland is Associate Professor of Sociology of Religion at Dalhousie University, Canada. His research examines the role of new media in relation to issues of religious authority and power, religious information-seeking behavior, ritual practices, and changing belief systems. His current research is investigating the effects of computer-mediated communications on diaspora religious traditions.

Laura Osburn is a Doctoral Candidate in the Department of Communication at the University of Washington. During her time at university, Laura has conducted research on religious communities, religious authority, and religiously motivated political activism on the Web. Her dissertation research analyzes the relationship between narratives and hyperlink networks on Tibet Movement websites and Tibet-focused Chinese propaganda websites. Prior to her studies in Communication, Laura received her MA in Comparative Religion (2006) at the University of Washington's Jackson School for International Studies. There, she studied Buddhism, East Asian indigenous traditions, and new religious movements.

Allison Ostrowski is an adjunct instructor for the Annenberg School for Communication and Journalism at the University of Southern California. She earned a PhD in Communication from the University of Colorado and an MS in Communication from Cornell University. Her research interests involve micro-social media effects, mediated religion and culture, and quantitative research and statistical methodology. She currently teaches courses on research methods, global marketing, and media effects for the Communication Management graduate program at USC Annenberg. She is also the Associate Director of Institutional Research at Excelsior College and is spending her spare time putting the finishing touches on her first book. Currently under contract, this work explores the media framing of the Catholic clergy sexual abuse scandals and investigates an alternative methodology for media-framing research.

Charles S. Prebish is Professor Emeritus at both the Pennsylvania State University and Utah State University (where he held the Charles Redd Endowed Chair in Religious Studies). His books *Buddhist Monastic Discipline* (1975) and *Luminous Passage: The Practice and Study of Buddhism in America* (1999) are considered classic volumes in Buddhist Studies. In 1993, he held the Visiting Numata Chair in Buddhist Studies at the University of Calgary. He has been an officer in the International Association of Buddhist Studies. In 2005, he was honored with a "Festschrift" volume by his colleagues, titled *Buddhist Studies from India to America: Essays in Honor of Charles S. Prebish*.

Daniel Veidlinger is Associate Professor in Comparative Religion and Humanities at California State University, Chico, and is the author of *Spreading the Dhamma: Writing, Orality, and Textual Transmission in Buddhist Northern Thailand* (2006). He is on the editorial board of Oxford Bibliographies Online: Buddhism, and his chapter "When Friend Becomes a Verb" was an early study of religion and social media.

Rachel Wagner is Associate Professor of Religion at Ithaca College in upstate New York. She has published a number of chapters and articles relating to the study of religion and popular culture, especially religion and videogames. Her book, *Godwired: Religion, Ritual and Virtual Reality* (Routledge, 2012), places religious studies theory in conversation with gamer theory to reveal the key concerns of wired culture as it engages with human-created, idealized, digitally crafted worlds. She is co-chair of the American Academy of Religion's Religion, Film, and Visual Culture Group.

Index

Page numbers in *italics* indicate tables, figures, and images.

RECEIVED

FEB 1 0 2015

GUELPH HUMBER LIBRARY
205 Humber College Blvd
Toronto, ON   M9W 5L7